13.50

D0856957

Cambridge studies in medieval life and thought

Edited by WALTER ULLMANN, LITT.D., F.B.A.
*Professor of Medieval Ecclesiastical History
in the University of Cambridge*

Third series vol. 3

THE CHURCH AND THE TWO NATIONS IN MEDIEVAL IRELAND

CAMBRIDGE STUDIES IN MEDIEVAL LIFE AND THOUGHT

THIRD SERIES

THE CHURCH AND THE
TWO NATIONS IN
MEDIEVAL IRELAND

J. A. WATT

Senior Lecturer in History
University of Hull

CAMBRIDGE
AT THE UNIVERSITY PRESS
1970

Published by the Syndics of the Cambridge University Press
Bentley House, 200 Euston Road, London N.W.1
American Branch: 32 East 57th Street, New York, N.Y.10022

© Cambridge University Press 1970

Library of Congress Catalogue Card Number: 72-120196

Standard Book Number: 521 07738 9

Printed in Great Britain
by Alden & Mowbray Ltd at the Alden Press, Oxford

CONTENTS

Contents

MAPS

FOREWORD

'Into Ireland', wrote Maitland of the age of Bracton, 'Englishmen
have carried their own law. A smaller England has been created
across the Channel, with chancery, exchequer, "benches", council,
sheriff, coroners, all reproduced upon a diminished scale. Statutes and
ordinances and the "register of original writs" were sent from
England into Ireland: the king's English court claimed a supremacy
over his Irish tribunals and multitudinous petitions from Ireland
came before the English council at its parliaments.' Into Ireland then,
Englishmen carried their own view of the relationship between the
Church and the civil power. This 'smaller England' knew, too, the
stresses and strains to which the evolving principles and practices of
the common law subjected that relationship. This book attempts to
tell something of the story of how Crown, clergy and papacy
conducted themselves towards each other in the English colony in
Ireland, in the first two centuries or so of its history. In a word, it
treats of what men of a later age than the medieval will call the
problem of Church and State.

In part it is a story which closely parallels the experience of the
Church in England of which, to an extent, it was an extension. But in
another part, and that its most fundamental, it is very different from
any English experience. When Henry II entered Ireland in 1171 it was
to encounter an Irish hierarchy of primate, three other archbishops
and some thirty-five bishops, a Church of venerable tradition but at
that time in process of vigorous reform and change. The *ecclesia hibernicana* was now to be forced to come to terms with the invader. The
anglicization of the Irish Church was destined to be a painful process.
In trying to sketch its course, the historian is seeking to understand the
specifically ecclesiastical dimension of the situation which dominated
the whole history of medieval Ireland after 1171: the conflict of the two
naciones or *lingue* (to use medieval terminology), Irish and English.

Shortage of source material, limitations of its type and its textual quality make the reconstruction of any episode of medieval life far from easy. This is particularly true for the history of the medieval Irish Church. For the period with which this study is concerned, there are no extant episcopal registers and for the majority of dioceses no documents of cathedral chapters have survived. The extant legislation of the provinces and dioceses in this period is very restricted in compass. Few religious orders or individual religious houses within Ireland have left documentation. The attempt to found a university in Ireland was a total failure. Scarcely a contemporary history, Latin or Irish, is worthy to be called a chronicle; almost all are merely annals. In short, source material from ecclesiastical sources within Ireland is very limited indeed.

For the most part, the life of the Irish Church has to be glimpsed as it is reflected, dimly and distortedly, in the records of governments. Primarily, these are the records of the colonial administration based on Dublin (but the bulk of these were casualties of war in 1922), those of the home government and those of the papacy. There are some scattered materials from the ruling bodies of some religious orders, most notably of the Cistercians. Together, these classes of source material allow a good deal to be known about the policies and attitudes of officialdom. There is comparably much less direct evidence concerning the practical implementation of governmental decisions and the effectuality of central governments in a country characterized by a considerable degree of particularism.

The greatest obstacle of all, however, to true historical perspective, is that while the historian can learn much of the mind of English administrators about the Irish, he is compelled, much of the time, to obtain his knowledge of Irish reactions from the records of those same administrators. Rarely does he have chance to read of an Irish opinion at first hand. The great dearth of source material from native Irish prelates and religious, as well as from Irish temporal rulers, is the severest handicap with which the historian of the medieval Irish Church must contend.

A word must be said about nomenclature in the context of medieval Ireland. It is important to realize, as has been so emphatically stated by Mr Richardson and Professor Sayles, that the 'kings of England who became lords of Ireland were not even Normans:

they were as French as Frenchmen could be'. It has long been the practice of historians to speak of the Anglo-Norman Invasion of Ireland, of the Anglo-Norman settlement, of the Anglo-Norman government and society. I have ventured to depart from this practice and to substitute the term Anglo-French. But when, relatively early in the thirteenth century, the contemporary documents themselves begin to speak of *Anglici*, this usage becomes inappropriate. I therefore use Anglo-Irish for those who had settled permanently in Ireland, English for those who were born in England, reserving the name Irish for those whose native language was Irish.

J.A.W.

ACKNOWLEDGMENTS

It is a great pleasure to have the opportunity to express formally my debt to many people. This book has its origins as part of my university teaching on the subject of the history of the medieval papacy and its involvement in politics and the theory and practice of the relations of the ecclesiastical and temporal powers. It grew under the critical scrutiny of successive years of history students in University College Dublin. It profited much from exposure to the members of the Irish Historical Society by way of the four papers which at various times I have had the honour to read to that most stimulating and friendly band of scholars and lovers of history who meet in both University College and Trinity College.

I must mention individually Mrs Maureen Wall and Dr Geoffrey Hand whose different sorts of expertise in Irish history have been made freely available to me. I am grateful to Mr Derek Waite of the Brynmor Jones Library, University of Hull, for his help with the maps. Mr Neville Hadcock most generously allowed me to use the typescript of his forthcoming *Medieval Religious Houses, Ireland*. It is, however, Rev. Emeritus Professor A. Gwynn, s.j to whom I owe most, through his writings, through his never-failing enthusiasm for ecclesiastical history, through that mixture of trenchant criticism and generous encouragement with which he has always greeted my work whether publicly in meetings of historians or privately on innumerable occasions. Finally, I thank my wife, Marianne, for the very many ways she has helped me in the writing of this book.

J.A.W.

ABBREVIATIONS

Abbreviated references to the modern series of record publications are not included in the following list as these are thought to be self-explanatory.

ALC	*Annals of Loch Cé*
Anal. hib.	*Analecta hibernica*
Arch. hib.	*Archivium hibernicum*
AU	*Annals of Ulster*
Cal. Abp Alen's Reg.	*Calendar of Archbishop Alen's Register* ed. C. McNeill. (Royal Society of Antiquaries of Ireland 1949)
DNB	*Dictionary of National Biography*
EHR	*English Historical Review*
Gwynn Studies	*Medieval Studies presented to A. Gwynn, S.J.* ed. J. A. Watt, J. B. Morrall and F. X. Martin (Dublin 1961)
Hbk Brit. Chron.	*Handbook of British Chronology* (2nd. ed. ed. F. M. Powicke and E. B. Fryde 1961)
IER	*Irish Ecclesiastical Record*
IHS	*Irish Historical Studies*
Ir. MSS Comm.	Irish Manuscripts Commission
PL	J. P. Migne, *Patrologia Latina*
Pont. hib.	*Pontificia Hibernica: Medieval Papal Chancery Documents concerning Ireland* ed. M. P. Sheehy 2 vols (Dublin 1962–5)
PRIA	*Proceedings of the Royal Irish Academy*
Proc. ICHC	*Proceedings of the Irish Catholic Historical Committee*
Rep. novum	*Reportorium novum (Dublin Diocesan Historical Record)*

RS	*Rolls Series*
RSAIJn.	*Journal of the Royal Society of Antiquaries of Ireland*
TRHS	*Transactions of the Royal Historical Society*
Stat. Irel. John–Henry V	*Statutes and ordinances and acts of the parliament of Ireland, King John to Henry V* ed. H. F. Berry (Dublin 1907)
Vet. mon.	*Vetera monumenta Hibernorum et Scotorum Historiam Illustrantia* ed. A. Theiner (Rome 1864)

Chapter 1

THE CHURCH IN IRELAND ON THE EVE
OF THE INVASION

The twelfth century ranks along with the fifth and the sixteenth as one of the more momentous periods in the life of the Church in Ireland when the course of its development was fundamentally changed. It was altered in a double way. The first was as part of a natural process of healthy growth wherein Ireland shared in that common experience of Latin Christendom when for a century and perhaps more, from mid-eleventh to mid-twelfth century, vigorous reform called a new religious spirit to life. The *aggiornamento* of the twelfth century brought great change to Ireland too, and however one might choose to define the historian's label 'Gregorian reform', there can be no doubt that Ireland participated in it to a considerable degree. Some historians have spoken of this period as one of 'ecclesiastical revolution'[1] in the life of the Irish Church and it is hard to say that this is an exaggerated judgment. For its fruits can be seen in the propagation of a radical programme of moral and social reform, in the diminution of internal feuds and racial conflicts to permit the achievement of ecclesiastical unity, in a new diocesan structure which ousted the vested interests of centuries of steady family accumulation of ecclesiastical wealth and influence, in a zealously reforming episcopate. Harmonious relationships were established outside Ireland. There were introduced the most developed types of monasticism which in turn stimulated a revival of the older traditionally Irish Columban type. The connexion with Rome was inestimably strengthened.

H. J. Lawlor, 'The Reformation of the Irish Church in the Twelfth Century' *Irish Church Quarterly* 4 (1911) 216–28; *idem:* 'In default of a better word we may call the movement a Reformation, though it might perhaps be more accurately described as an ecclesiastical revolution' *St. Bernard of Clairvaux's Life of St. Malachy of Armagh* (1920); J. F. Kenney, *The Sources for the early history of Ireland: an Introduction and Guide* 1. *Ecclesiastical* (1929) 758. 'Reformation and revolution' is Miss Kathleen Hughes's description, *The Church in early Irish society* (1966), as the title of ch. 24.

I

Change of the second sort, however, came as a serious deflection of the regular course of the reform movement, as a result of the unexpected, the arbitrary and the violent. The Anglo-French invasion of Ireland in the second half of the twelfth century was essentially disruptive. It was possible to argue that Angevin lordship of Ireland would advance Church reform and accelerate its progress. At any rate Popes Adrian IV and Alexander III endorsed this argument and the Irish hierarchy initially acquiesced in it. For a time perhaps, it might have seemed that just as in England a papally approved invasion and conquest had brought a contact of native and foreigner which was, on balance, beneficial to the cause of reform, so it would be in Ireland. Ultimately, however, whatever the solidity of the foundations on which those hopes rested, foreign intrusion did not forward the best interests of the Church in Ireland. For the eventual consequence was the emergence of a division between the Church *inter Hibernicos* and the Church *inter Anglicos*. The antagonism of these sections ensured that Ireland remained throughout the middle ages what possibly by the turn of mid-twelfth century it was beginning to cease to be, a remote and backward province of the Church, stunted in its growth, distorted in its development.

Reform came slowly to the Irish Church. An archaic ecclesiastical organization, deeply entrenched in the whole social and political order, internecine warfare among the multitudinous political units into which the country was divided, near-isolation from external influences constituted major barriers to any restoration of the glory of the island whose saints and scholars and artists of former days were the admiration of Christendom. Any diagnosis of the root of the disease must inevitably emphasize the near-chaos of an ecclesiastical organization for which there was scarcely a parallel in eleventh century Europe and which even as late as the mid-twelfth century prompted St Bernard to say that 'it was unheard of from the very beginning of Christianity.'[1] The origins of this situation lay deep in Irish history. Ireland had been outside the Roman empire and hence

---

[1] *Vita Malachiae* (hereafter *VM*): 'Nam (quod inauditum est ab ipso Christianit at initio) sine ordine, sine ratione mutabantur et multiplicabantur episcopi pro libit metropolitani, ita ut unus episcopatus uno non esset contentus, sed singulae pen ecclesiae singulos haberent episcopos' *PL* 182. 1086.

2

there was no Roman civil administration to provide ready made, as in so many parts of the early Christian Church, a structure of provinces and dioceses. Nor was there any home-produced substitute. There was no political unity and no urban development. Ecclesiastical organization followed a prevalent political organization which was excessively particularistic and a social organization which was exclusively rural. The basic unit of society was the *tuath* or tribe under its *rí* or king. The exact correlation of this organization with the episcopate is far from clear. It has been suggested that at the very beginning of Christianity in Ireland St Patrick tended to appoint bishops for each *tuath* as it was converted.[1] But by the time of St Columbanus it was the monastery rather than any defined territorial area which was the basis of episcopal jurisdiction.[2] This situation has obvious parallels elsewhere in early medieval Europe, for the establishment of a monastery which was also a bishop's seat was an obvious technique of establishing Christianity in rural missionary areas. In the Irish system, however, it was the abbot, the heir or coarb of the founder of the monastery who emerged as the dominant figure, the real controller of the business and properties of the monastery. The coarb of Columcille, of Brendan, of Ciaran, and so on, may or may not at a particular time be a bishop. Even as early as the sixth and seventh centuries there were abbots who were only priests. The course of this development remains very obscure, but by the eighth century for the non-episcopal abbot to be the real administrator was the leading feature of ecclesiastical organization of Ireland as a whole.[3] Further, he would have obtained his office by

[1] Cf. J. B. Bury, *The Life of St. Patrick and his place in history* (1905) 171–86 and especially Appendix C.18 'The organization of the Episcopate' 375–9; L. Gougaud, *Christianity in Celtic Lands* (1932) 214. For a critical discussion of the more exaggerated numbers of episcopal ordinations attributed to Patrick, cf. J. Ryan, *Irish Monasticism, origins and early development* (1931) 83–90. For sixth and seventh century developments, Hughes, *The Church in early Irish society* 77–90.

[2] Cf. Ryan, *Irish Monasticism* 167–90 for the authoritative exposition of this matter. He concludes: 'Almost all jurisdiction in sixth century Ireland was exercised, therefore, from the monasteries. About half the leading abbot-rulers were bishops, about half priests, and the more illustrious names were to be found among the latter. In this way the essential connection between the episcopal order and ecclesiastical government bade fair to be lost to view.'

[3] The process of change over the centuries may be studied in the basic article of H. J. Lawlor and R. I. Best, 'The ancient list of the Coarbs of Patrick' *PRIA* 35 (1919) 316–62.

virtue of inheritance: he was coarb or heir by virtue of the customary Irish law of descent which operated for the chief ecclesiastical office in the same way as for succession to the chief secular power. By the eleventh century, following the turmoil and havoc of the Norse invasions, it had become common for the abbot to be a layman and for his selection to be primarily for the preservation of dynastic rather than ecclesiastical interests. The supreme example of this was the coarb of St Patrick himself, abbot of Armagh, in title at least the senior ecclesiastic of Ireland. For two centuries before 1134 when St Malachy finally succeeded in gaining possession of Armagh he was a layman of the Ui Sinaich family.[1] This was a common pattern.

The downgrading, so to say, of the episcopal status in favour of that of the abbot, the consequent absence of a defined metropolitan and diocesan system and the lay usurpation of abbatial positions, were the source from which sprang many of the evils denounced by foreign critics and attacked eventually in reforming councils. With an episcopate so enfeebled in authority, though not apparently lacking in numbers, it is not surprising to read complaints that clergy were few, that they led lives indistinguishable from laymen, that the administration of the sacraments was neglected, that preaching was in desuetude. Nor to find considerable sexual licence prevalent among the laity. With such a degree of lay control of ecclesiastical affairs, deterioration of the monastic idea was inescapable and simoniacal traffic in ecclesiastical office a recurrent evil.

Reform must begin in the minds and hearts of men. There could be no reform movement in Ireland until men appreciated that reform was needed and determined to accomplish it. Hence it is quite unnecessary to stress that 'the leading part in it was taken by Irishmen' and to emphasize that the movement for reform came from within.[2] Of course it did. Men cannot be reformed from outside against their will. But it was an essential feature of the movement that it was fostered by help sought and obtained from abroad in the different directions that were available to Irishmen in the eleventh and twelfth centuries. The reform developed with a renewal of contact with leading personalities and movements of the universal

---

[1] As St Bernard stated, *VM* 10. 1086; cf. Lawlor and Best, *art. cit.* 343; Kenney, *Sources* 353 for discussion of the Clann Sinaich grip on Armagh.

[2] E. MacNeill, *Phases of Irish History* (1920) 283.

Church which brought Ireland into closer conformity with the religious and ecclesiastical norms accepted elsewhere. In particular it was a drawing closer to Rome and to the life, law and institutions for which she stood in this period of vigorous papal leadership.

The reform movement had no simple origin nor did it follow any single path. It is possible to distinguish at least three main sources. They were never quite independent of each other but they began separately and for a time pursued different courses. At points there was even some hostility between them. One trend is to be associated with the Ua Briain (O'Brien) kings of Munster,[1] aspirants to the high kingship of Ireland—Toirdelbach or Turlough (*d.* 1085) who was in correspondence not merely with Archbishop Lanfranc of Canterbury but with Gregory VII himself, and especially his son, Muirchertach or Murtagh (1086–1116), who presided over the first two of the three reforming councils (Cashel 1101, Rathbreasail 1111), which mark the main stages of the whole movement. The second, roughly contemporaneous with the progress in Munster, concerns the participation of the Norse–Irish towns, which made of the dioceses of Dublin, Waterford and Limerick quasi-suffragan sees of Canterbury.[2] The connexion between Dublin and England was particularly close. The start of the third reform current can be dated precisely. With the accession of Cellach to the abbacy of Armagh in 1106 the coarb of Patrick was again a bishop. He was to prove a zealous reformer and the participation of the northern part of the country in the reform movement began with him.[3] It was due to his initiative that he was succeeded as primate by the leading personality of the whole reform movement, Malachy of Armagh.

From Cashel, Dublin and Armagh then, sprang the founts that are recognizably the main tributaries of what came to flow together in a

---

[1] The origins of reform in Munster have been best described by A. Gwynn in D. F. Gleeson and A. Gwynn, *A History of the Diocese of Killaloe* (1962) 90–127.

[2] There are differing views of the importance of this connexion; compare e.g. Kenney: 'But the whole history of Ireland made it natural that the Irish Church would in this crisis (of the reform movement generally) seek inspiration and help on the Continent rather than in England' *Sources* 758, with Gougaud: 'The work of reform was carried on in the Irish Church throughout the entire twelfth century. The impulse came from Canterbury' *Christianity in Celtic Lands* 398.

[3] His feast is still celebrated in the Irish dioceses on 7 April. There is no satisfactory study of his life, for which the main sources must be the various annals, especially *AU* and *ALC*. For a brief account cf. Gwynn, *Diocese of Killaloe* 113–18.

common stream. When these three were full archiepiscopal sees in the ordinary sense of that term, whose incumbents were willing to work together, the reform movement had achieved a signal success. This had occurred by the time of the third and most important of the three major reform councils, that of Kells–Mellifont, held in 1152.

Chronologically the reform movement falls into three main periods: that of its prologue, the period before 1101, a year which marks a real turning point and, in beginning a decade of outstanding decision in the history of the Irish Church, marks the true beginning of the reform movement proper. The third period corresponds to the working life of St Malachy of Armagh, 1119–1148, and the council of 1152 which was in many ways the logical conclusion of his career.

The origin of the diocese of Dublin is shrouded in obscurity.[1] The Donatus or Dunan who died in 1074 was apparently the first bishop of this see, but when and in what circumstances he was appointed is very uncertain. The earliest account from Dublin of diocesan origins (which is fourteenth century) gives a clue. It states that Sitric, the Norse king of Dublin, was cofounder with Donatus of the cathedral of Holy Trinity.[2] Sitric was in Rome in 1028,[3] and it is possible that the establishment of the diocese was part of the same manifestation of piety which took him on pilgrimage to the Confession of St Peter.[4] What is quite certain is that Donatus's successor, Patrick, was sent to Canterbury for consecration. Lanfranc stated that for him to consecrate a bishop of Dublin was but to follow the example of his predecessors.[5] It is thus possible that Donatus was also consecrated at Canterbury and thus that the see was initially established at least partly under Anglo-Saxon initiatives. However this may be, the second bishop of Dublin certainly had a firm link with

---

[1] The topic has been exhaustively discussed by A. Gwynn in a series of articles in *IER*, now conveniently summarized in *Rep. novum* 1 (1955) 1–26.

[2] 'Postea venit Sitrius rex Dubliniae, filius Ableb comitis Dubliniae, et dedit S. Trinitati, et Donato primo episcopo Dubliniae, locum ad aedificandam ecclesiam S. Trinitati …' *White Book of Christ Church Dublin* in Dugdale, *Monasticon Anglicanum* 6 (ed. J. Caley, H. Ellis, B. Bandinel 1830) 2. 1148.

[3] See the entries in *AU* and *Annals of Tigernach* at the relevant date.

[4] A suggestion made by M. V. Ronan, *IER* 43 (1934) 40.

[5] 'sacratum ad propriam sedem, cum testimonio litterarum nostrarum, more antecessorum nostrorum remisimus' Ep. 37 *PL* 150. 535.

the Anglo-Saxon world since he was a monk trained in Worcester in the school of St Wulfstan himself.[1]

With Bishop Patrick began a constitutional connexion between the Norse–Irish sees and Canterbury which lasted until 1140. Four archbishops of Canterbury were thus involved in Irish affairs, more especially the great Anselm. Four, possibly five, bishops-elect of Dublin, one bishop of Waterford and one of Limerick were canonically examined and consecrated by the archbishops of Canterbury and swore canonical submission to them as their primates.[2] There began also with Patrick a link between the Norse–Irish episcopate and monasticism in England. His successor, Donngus (1085–95) was also a monk, one of Lanfranc's own at Canterbury,[3] Samuel (1096–1121) was a monk of St Alban's,[4] whilst the first bishop of Waterford, Malchus (1096–1135), was a monk of Winchester.[5]

Irish historians have sometimes been prone to indignation at the alleged pretensions of Canterbury to a primacy in Ireland. 'Ecclesiastical imperialism' is a recurrent description of this claim,[6] and Lanfranc in particular has come in for some rough handling as one whose interest in Ireland was 'hardly innocent of ulterior purposes'.[7] It must be remembered however that canon law required that a bishop-elect should be examined by his metropolitan as to his suitability for office. As has been seen, the situation in Armagh in the eleventh century with laymen in complete control was not such as to inspire confidence in those who wished to adhere strictly to the law. Moreover there is evidence that the form of episcopal consecration in use in Ireland was not in conformity with the canons.

---

[1] For his life and writings, A. Gwynn, *The Writings of Bishop Patrick, 1074–1084* (*Scriptores Latini Hiberniae* 1. 1955).

[2] The texts of the submissions of Bishops Patrick, Donngus, Samuel and Gregory of Dublin, of Bishop Malchus of Waterford and of Bishop Patrick of Limerick are printed in *Veterum Epistolarum Hibernicarum Sylloge* ed. J. Ussher (1632) in *Whole Works* (ed. C. R. Elrington and J. H. Todd 1847–64) 4. 564–8.

[3] 'Lanfrancus archiepiscopus Cantuariensis ad regimen Dublin' ecclesie sacravit Donatum monasterii sui monachum ...' *Annals of St. Mary's Dublin* ed. J. T. Gilbert, *Chartularies of St. Mary's Abbey, Dublin* (RS 1884) 2. 250.

[4] Eadmer, *Historia novorum in Anglia* ed. M. Rule (RS 1884) 73. Eadmer is a very valuable source for the relations between Anselm and Irish sees.

[5] Eadmer, *Hist. nov.* 76.

[6] Kenney, *Sources* 758 would appear to be originator of the judgment.

[7] A. Gwynn, 'Lanfranc and the Irish Church' *IER* 57 (1941) 500.

Overtures from Dublin to the most accessible metropolitan should be seen as at least as much the result of the shortcomings of ecclesiastical organization in Ireland as of any other reason. In any case, Lanfranc clearly based his claim to be 'Britanniarum primas' in the genuine belief that this was the traditional position of Canterbury,[1] without arousing opposition in Ireland. St Anselm, who described himself as 'totius Britanniae primas' and whose attitude to Ireland was not substantially different from Lanfranc's, must surely be acquitted of any inordinate ecclesiastical ambition. However this may be, the primacy was not very onerous in practice, for if on the one hand the archbishops of Canterbury did not summon Irish bishops to their provincial councils, their intervention in Irish affairs other than canonical examinations and consecrations was confined to counsel and admonition.[2]

There can be little doubt that the Canterbury link was valued in the more advanced reforming circles, namely those of Munster. Dublin came under O'Brien tutelage in 1072 and under the direct rule of Turlough in 1075. He was the recipient of two of the five letters Lanfranc is known to have sent to Ireland and the senior bishop of Munster, Domnall Ua h-Énna, a third. These are letters from an acknowledged spiritual father to his sons. Further, Turlough was associated with the selection of Donngus to be bishop of Dublin in 1085, and with the request to Lanfranc for his consecration.

The bond between Turlough's son Murtagh, and Anselm, Lanfranc's successor, was not less close. Murtagh was involved in the establishment of the new diocese of Waterford and in 1096 the former Winchester monk was sent to Anselm for consecration. Also associated with this request were three bishops. That besides the bishop of Dublin, the bishops of Meath and Leinster petitioned Anselm is further evidence that the Canterbury connexion was wider than merely Dublin itself. There is a suggestion of a personal

---

[1] Canterbury's claim to a primacy is examined in Appendix 1.

[2] For a calendar of Lanfranc's and Anselm's letters, Kenney, *Sources* 758–61. It should be noted, however, that the letters have been more accurately dated in a number of cases by Fr Gwynn in his analyses of the relations of Lanfranc and Anselm with the Irish Church. Also it should be noted that though Kenney only cites Ussher's *Sylloge* for the complete texts they are also printed in the more generally accessible *PL* 150 (Lanfranc) and *PL* 159 (Anselm). Cf. also *Anselmi Opera Omnia* 4 (ed. F. S. Schmitt 1949) Epp. 198, 201, 207, 277, 278; 5 (1951) Epp. 426, 427, 435.

relationship between Anselm and Murtagh in a letter where the King thanks the Archbishop for succouring his son-in-law, the Norman Arnulf of Montgomery, who had been in revolt against Henry I.

If all the evidence points to recognition of Canterbury's claim to superiority among reformers, what is the evidence that the nexus was fruitful? The letters of Lanfranc and Anselm are primarily admonitory. In urging the kings of Munster and their clergy to attend to certain evils, they were suggesting the main trends of a reform programme: elimination of simony, proper administration of the sacraments (for example, in baptism and orders), correction of a marriage law that allowed divorce and marriage within degrees of kindred forbidden in canon law, assurance that no bishop should be consecrated except to a fixed see. Further they suggested a method of procedure—the council of senior clergy summoned and protected by the king, with his aristocracy also being encouraged to participate.[1]

Just such a council, issuing legislation concerned with some of these abuses, was to meet on Murtagh's initiative at Cashel in 1101. It is possible that this was a following-up of reform already begun at a council which had met under his father's auspices in 1084.[2] Of course, reform councils might have met in Munster at this time had there been no Canterbury connexion. The exact impact of Canterbury cannot be measured. It is clear, however, that there existed a channel of communication between men who ranked as major reformers, now working in Canterbury, and rulers and prelates in key positions in Ireland. That there was an important traffic in reforming ideas can hardly be doubted even though the evidence does not allow us to say very much about the precise nature of receptivity in Ireland.

Whilst trying to assess the results of the contact between Ireland and Canterbury, it is perhaps not altogether without significance to notice a few details of the careers of each of the leading personalities of the second and third periods of the reform. Gilbert, bishop of

---

[1] The most important letter on this score is that of Lanfranc to Turlough O'Brien in 1074, Ussher, *Sylloge*, 27. 492–4; a generally similar letter of Anselm to Murtagh O'Brien in 1100 is probably based on Lanfranc's, *Sylloge* 36. 523–5. These letters are also *PL* 150. 536–7 and *PL* 159. 178–80.

[2] *Ann. St. Mary's Dublin*, in *Chart. St. Mary's* 2.250

Limerick, the papal legate who presided over the important council of Rathbreasail in 1111 and sometimes spoken of as the initiator of the reform movement,[1] had known Anselm in Rouen and though not consecrated to Limerick by him, certainly was in close touch with his successor in Canterbury.[2] Again, the channel of communication opened by Malachy of Armagh, the acknowledged paragon of Irish reformers, was directly to Rome itself through Arrouaise and especially Clairvaux. His contact with Canterbury was not apparently direct, but it had its part in his monastic formation. In *c.* 1121–2 he was of the community of the reformed monastery of Lismore where he had sought out a spiritual director of recognized eminence, Malchus, former monk of Winchester, consecrated bishop of Waterford by Anselm in 1096. It was to be his first contact with men with experience of monasticism other than Irish. We cannot know exactly how important this was to him nor how many others of his contemporaries were affected by personal contact with men who had moved in reforming circles abroad. But these details of Gilbert and Malachy remind us that reforming ideas can circulate through personal connexions which leave no documentary trace for the historian. The prosperity of the reform movement was not merely a matter of receiving and putting into practice the correct rules of ecclesiastical law. It was also a matter of profiting from the example of men of sanctity, and their influence can work in ways that an historian cannot trace. It would surely be unwise to minimize the influence, direct and indirect, of an Anselm.

It has been said earlier that the reform movement proper began in 1101, a year which constituted a turning point in the history of the Church in Ireland. It is time to justify this statement.

The appointment of Maol Muire Ua Dúnáin, formerly bishop of Meath, now chief bishop of Munster, as papal legate, the first such known in Irish history, marks with formality that closer bond between Ireland and Rome which is one of the most important changes that occurred in the twelfth century.[3] It opens a new era of

---

[1] For example by Gougaud, *Christianity in Celtic Lands* 399.

[2] 'Quoniam autem olim nos apud Rothomagum invicem cognovimus, dilectione sociati sumus' Anselm to Gilbert *PL* 159. 174; Ussher, *Sylloge* 32. 513–14. For his presence at an episcopal consecration at Canterbury in 1115, Eadmer, *Hist. nov.* 235–6.

[3] On the authority of St Bernard, Gilbert of Limerick is usually credited with being

Hiberno-papal relations and virtually uninterruptedly thereafter, throughout the whole of the first half of the century the papacy had a legate at work in Ireland. The apostolic see was thus in some sense the recognized reform leader. This first legate presided over a council whose decrees stand out as the first real evidence of a more radical approach to the Church's ills. The legislation of this council is sufficiently original for it to be considered a point of new departure. A third point of significance of the year 1101 concerns the place, Cashel, where this important council was held. It was in this year that Murtagh O'Brien, in a splendid gesture, made over Cashel 'of the kings' to the clergy.[1] The council thus inaugurated the ecclesiastical career of what was shortly to become the metropolitan see of Munster. The conversion of this historic centre of political power to ecclesiastical purposes perhaps symbolized that change in men's thinking about the place of the Church in Irish society which betokened the arrival of the reform movement proper.

The eight decrees of the first council of Cashel[2] are partly of a type familiar enough to students of the Gregorian reform on the Continent and partly of a type to remind us that in certain ways, Irish society and the Irish Church had features that were *sui generis*. Thus the decrees forbidding simony, prohibiting clerical marriage, insisting on clerical immunity from lay financial or equivalent exactions and from trial before a lay judge, are of the first category. The decree concerned with marriage between near-relations recalls the strictures of Lanfranc and Anselm[3] about the laxity of the Brehon[4]

---

the first papal legate to Ireland, *VM* 10. 1087. Fr Gwynn restored the honour to Ua Dúnáin, 'Papal Legates in Ireland during the Twelfth Century' *IER* 63 (1944) 361–70 at 365–6.

[1] As recorded in various Annals *s.a.* 1101: *Chronicon Scotorum, Annals of the Kingdom of Ireland by the Four Masters* (hereafter *AFM*), *Ann. Tigernach.*

[2] They exist only in an early modern version of the Senchas Sil Bhriain, published by S. H. O'Grady, *Irish Texts Society* 26. 174–5 (In Irish: translation *ibid.* 27. 185). For the dating of the council, Gwynn, 'Papal Legates' 365–6 and for an analysis of the decrees themselves, *idem* 'The First Synod of Cashel' *IER* 66 (1945) 81–92; 67 (1946) 109–22.

[3] References on p. 8 n. 2 above.

[4] Native Irish law was customary and in the keeping of *breithemain* (lawgivers) whose function was to declare what the law was. When in the early modern period English officials wished to find out what was the customary position in any Irish legal matter they naturally had recourse to these men. The word *brehon* is their anglicization of *breithemain*. I owe this explanation to the late Professor

law in this respect.[1] The *erenagh* or abbot, that figure of unique importance in the unreformed constitution of the Irish Church, figured prominently in the condemnation of lay usurpation of clerical office and of clerical marriage. But most surprising to anyone unfamiliar with the Celtic world was the position accorded to the professional class of poets. Like the clergy itself, it was a privileged caste, exempt from the ordinary lay courts.[2]

This first reforming council had nothing to say about episcopal government or the constitution of a diocesan hierarchy. As yet there was no sign from inside Ireland that men's minds were turning towards the achievement of that feat of ecclesiastical engineering, so to say, which would equip the country with a constitutional structure of the type common to Latin Christendom. But this sign was forthcoming within a few years, and is to be connected especially

Gerard Murphy whose cyclostyled lecture course *Introduction to Irish Studies* was available to me in University College, Dublin. See also n. 2 on this page for Camden's note about the brehons.

[1] For a discussion of Irish marriage law and twelfth century criticisms of it, Gwynn, 'First Synod of Cashel' 109–21. It is clear that it was primarily the practice of inter-marriage between near relations and the instability of marriages ('It is said that men exchange their wives as freely and publicly as a man might change his horse', said Anselm) which, among the ills of the Irish Church and society, most shocked opinion outside Ireland.

[2] The decree reads (in O'Grady's translation: for a different translation substantially modifying O'Grady's interpretation, Gwynn, 'First Synod of Cashel' 109): 'That neither cleric's nor poet's mis-demeanour should be brought before lay authority.' This interesting feature of Irish society survived throughout the middle ages to be noted by English observers of the early modern period. In the early seventeenth century, the Irish historian Keating wrote: 'Camden says it is a system among the Irish for their nobles to have lawgivers (*breithemain*), physicians, historians, poets and musicians, and for endowments to be bestowed on them, and also *for their persons, lands and property to enjoy immunity*. Here is what he says, speaking of them: 'these princes', he says, 'have their own lawgivers, whom they call "brehons", their historians for writing their actions, their physicians, their poets ... and their singing men and land is assigned to each one of these, and each of them dwells on his own land and moreover, every one of them is of a certain distinct family; that is to say, the brehons are of one special race and surname, the historians of another race and surname, and so for each one from that out; they used to bring up their children and their kinsfolk each one of them in his own art, and they have always successors drawn from their own family in these arts' G. Keating, *History of Ireland* ed. D. Comyn and P. S. Dineen (Irish Texts Society) 4 (1901) 71. I owe this reference to G. Murphy, *Introduction to Irish Studies* (p. 11 n. 4 above). The prevalence of these hereditary castes in a country of small population, relatively isolated, is surely at least part cause of the inbreeding about which reformers protested so vigorously.

with the name of Gilbert, first bishop of Limerick. Gilbert has a threefold claim to a place in the history of the reform: for his connexion with Canterbury, imperfect though our knowledge of this is; because he was a papal legate and in that capacity presided over the council of Rathbreasail which carried forward the work begun at Cashel ten years earlier; because he is the only known theorist of reform in Ireland.

It is particularly in this latter capacity that he is a significant figure. The Gregorian reform was essentially a movement of ideas. In its fundamentals, it was a rethinking of the whole constitution of the Church, not perhaps so much in its theological as in its juridical aspects. This rethinking, which considered the place of the *sacerdotium* in society, of the laity, of political power, of papal power and so forth, called forth a considerable literature, especially of law but also of polemic. It is not known what of this work was being read in twelfth century Ireland. The only Irish work which can be accorded a place in the Gregorian literature is the *De statu ecclesiae* of Bishop Gilbert, written in the first decade of the twelfth century.[1] Perhaps by comparison with the work of the great Yvo of Chartres and other contemporary legal luminaries this is not a very sophisticated treatise. But its message, which concerned hierarchy, was an important one for the Irish Church.[2]

The treatise set out, literally with diagrammatic simplicity,[3] the

[1] Printed by Ussher, *Sylloge* 500–10 and *PL* 159. 997–1004. There is also a short letter of Gilbert's to the bishops of Ireland *de usu ecclesiastico*, printed before the *De statu ecclesiae* in each of these editions. This letter is, however, the preface to the treatise, see n. 3 on this page and p. 14 n. 2, below. A new edition would be welcomed.
[2] The best analysis is by A. Gwynn, 'St. Malachy of Armagh' *IER* 70 (1948) 961–78 at 971–6.
[3] Both the chief manuscripts of the treatise, Cambridge University Library MS Ff. I. 27 and Durham Cathedral Chapter Library MS B. II. 35 do have illustrative diagrams of Gilbert's presentation of the whole hierarchical structure of the Church. There is a reproduction of the Durham version in R. A. B. Mynors, *Durham Cathedral Manuscripts to the end of the twelfth century* (1939) Plate 32. Gilbert obviously wrote his treatise to explain an accompanying diagram. It begins: 'Imago ecclesie supra notata ...' and continues as an explanation of the structure and nomenclature of the diagram. The prefatory nature of the so-called letter *de usu ecclesiastico* is demonstrable from this sentence taken from it: 'Quantum ergo deberet morum unitas servari a fidelibus, quamvis ex multis locis sacre scripture manifestum sit, *presens tamen ecclesie depicta imago oculis subiecta patenter ostendit*' (*PL* 159. 996). This sentence has to be read with the incipit of the treatise cited above.

structure of the Church from Christ, his Old Testament figure, Noah, and his earthly representative, the pope, through all grades of the ecclesiastical hierarchy, down to the traditional three grades at the basis of society; those who pray, those who plough and those who fight. Each grade has its duties recalled to it, thereby giving a homiletic note to the treatise. There is much to recall the writing of a less advanced period than the twelfth century.[1] But there was much in the structure of the Irish Church reminiscent of more primitive societies. Reading the work with a particular eye to its relevance for specifically Irish conditions,[2] it is impossible not to be struck by the particular aptness of Gilbert's words (even if he is only reiterating an earlier as yet unidentified continental source) concerning monasticism. The diocese and the monastery were clearly distinguished. Bishops and parochial clergy were not in the same hierarchy as abbots and monks. Right order was clearly laid down: 'it is not the duty of monks to baptize or to administer communion or to minister to the laity in any ecclesiastical matter unless by chance necessity demands *that the bishop should order them to do so:* their purpose is to abandon all worldly pursuits and serve God alone in prayer.'[3] A platitude no doubt in the universal Church, but a different premise from that of the constitutional logic governing ecclesiastical organization in Ireland. Its propagation at this time reads like an ominous warning of changing times to the coarbs and *erenaghs* of Ireland.

As with the earlier council, it was Munster initiatives which were primarily responsible for the summoning of the council of Rath-

---

[1] The one author cited by name is Amalarius of Metz, though it is not clear which of his works he had in mind, *ibid.* 997, 1001.

[2] There is no direct reference to Ireland in the treatise proper but the mention of a particular practice 'apud nos' (1001) makes it clear that he was addressing specific people—'Episcopis et presbyteris totius Hibernie' of the prefatory so-called *de usu ecclesiastico*.

[3] 'Quoniam non est monachorum baptizare, communicare, aut aliquod ecclesiasticum laicis ministrare; nisi forte, cogente necessitate, imperanti episcopo obediant. Quorum proposito est soli Deo, relictis secularibus, in oratione vacare' (*ibid.* 998). Another general norm would seem especially novel in Ireland at this period: 'Tenet quoque (episcopus) synodum bis in anno, in aestate et in autumno. Hoc modo congregatis omnibus presbyteris totius episcopatus ...' (*ibid.* 1002). Another was eventually to be fulfilled at St Malachy's insistence: 'Utrumque enim archiepiscopum et primatem, oportet Roma ab apostolico ordinari, aut a Roma eis a papa pallium afferri ...' (*ibid.* 1003).

breasail (co. Tipperary, situated near Cashel).[1] Murtagh O'Brien, Ua Dúnáin, senior bishop of Munster, Gilbert, papal legate and bishop of Limerick (now the centre of the O'Brien lordship) were the chief figures of the council. But it was a more than merely southern affair, for Cellach of Armagh was present. Two independent sources give fifty as the number of bishops present.[2] It was clearly an assembly representative of most of the Church in Ireland and its work was to affect the whole country.

This council has its place in history as marking the first step towards that creation of a national diocesan hierarchy which was to be virtually completed in 1152 at the council of Kells–Mellifont. That it decreed reform legislation of other sorts '[enacting] discipline and law better than any previously promulgated in Ireland' is known from the cryptic statements of the Annals. But nothing is known of its precise character as the decrees themselves have not survived; how far and in what ways they expanded or modified the decrees of Cashel cannot be known.[3]

The basis of the new system of territorial dioceses was a division of the country into two provinces (Map 1). This reproduced in ecclesiastical terms an ancient political division of Ireland.[4] That Armagh, traditionally the pre-eminent Church in Ireland, should take the northern half was only to be expected, while the selection of Cashel for headship of the southern half was the logical consequence of the new status conferred on it in 1101. The overall superiority of Armagh was recognized in the specific designation of its archbishop as primate. Already in 1106, he had made visitation of Munster where his superiority was recognized in payment of the customary

1 The main source for this council is an extract from a now lost Annals of the Church of Clonenagh, preserved by Geoffrey Keating in his *History of Ireland* (Irish Texts Society) 9 (1908) 296–307. That part of his text which dealt with diocesan boundaries had been re-edited with an invaluable *Index locorum* by J. MacErlean, 'Synod of Rath Breasail. Boundaries of the dioceses of Ireland' *Arch. hib.* 3 (1914) 1–33. The best account of the council is by Gwynn, in Gleeson and Gwynn *Diocese of Killaloe* 116–27.
2 *AU* (*ALC* derivatively?); *Ann. Inisfallen.*
3 That lay investiture was on the agenda is clear from Keating's otherwise enigmatic statement (from the Annals of Clonenagh): 'It was at this synod that the churches of Ireland were given up entirely to the bishops free for ever from the authority and rent of the lay princes' *History of Ireland* 299.
4 Cf. MacErlean, 'Synod of Rath Breasail' 5.

offerings throughout the kingdom. The Annals record similar recognitions after Rathbreasail in Connacht and Meath.[1] There can be little doubt that it was the major achievement of Cellach to have this primacy unambiguously recognized, with the one major exception of Dublin, throughout Ireland.

Yet if the positions of Armagh and Cashel were assured by this council, there was the mark of impermanence on some of the remaining diocesan dispositions. To each archbishop was assigned twelve suffragans. There seems to have been a Canterbury influence behind the selection of this quite arbitrary number. Just as Augustine on his mission to England had been instructed by Gregory I to set up two provinces each with twelve suffragans, so now, it appears, the model was to apply in Ireland.[2] Obviously this was a very uncertain basis for the work in hand. The existence of both a multiplicity of rulers, each conscious of the administrative convenience and of the status value of a bishop for his territory, and of numbers of long-established monasteries, each now the nub of a complex of vested interests, demanded of the new system flexibility and a regard for existing circumstances above all else. The framers themselves seem to have been aware of this, however, for the clergy of both Connacht and Leinster were left free to change the boundaries, though not the number, of the five dioceses allotted to each of these kingdoms.[3] Though the decisions of the council of Kells–Mellifont were to reveal the imperfections of the work of this council, the vital first step towards the setting-up of a new constitution for the Irish Church had been taken. The principle of freedom of the episcopate from lay control had been solemnly proclaimed: of the twenty-five dioceses named and defined, nineteen were to survive and keep their identity throughout the middle ages: the future division of Ireland into four ecclesiastical provinces was adumbrated. It was, in the event, a very successful first venture into an area of very delicate political and ecclesiastical sensitivities. It provides good evidence that the reform movement in Ireland had already achieved its maturity.

The most striking of the imperfections of the Rathbreasail scheme

[1] See *AU* and *ALC* for the period 1105–29.
[2] Keating, *History of Ireland* 299. It is of course possible that there was here a consequence of the Canterbury connexion of the head of this council, Gilbert of Limerick.
[3] *Ibid.* 303–5, 307.

Map 1. Monasteries selected by the council of Rathbreasail (1111) to be diocesan centres.

was undoubtedly the absence of any mention of Dublin. The Dublin area was comprehended within the diocese of Glendalough. The fact that Dublin had been a diocesan centre for over half a century was ignored. Dublin was still regarded with suspicion and itself regarded the rest of the Irish ecclesiastical world with more than a little reserve. There is not much positive evidence to set along with the negative evidence of the absence of Dublin's name from the acts of Rathbreasail which would throw light on the real nature of Dublin's relations with what, after 1111, can be properly called the Irish hierarchy. Such as it is, it points to a particular animosity between Dublin and Armagh, which revealed itself especially after the death of Bishop Samuel in 1121. There is a letter extant, professedly from all the townspeople and clergy of Dublin to Archbishop Ralph d'Escures, Anselm's successor, asking for the consecration of Gregory, their bishop-elect, protesting abiding fidelity to the traditional bond of Dublin and Canterbury and declaring that 'the bishops of Ireland are very jealous of us, because we are unwilling to be subject to them but wish always to be under your rule'.[1] Gregory was duly consecrated bishop, but on returning to Dublin found Cellach, the archbishop of Armagh, in his place. Eadmer leaves no doubt that Cellach enjoyed more support in Dublin than Gregory could command. The champion of the Canterbury connexion had perforce to withdraw.[2] Whether Cellach himself ruled Dublin and if he did, for how long, is obscure. Gregory did in due course return and

---

1 Eadmer recounted the circumstances of the arrival of Gregory bishop elect of Dublin in Canterbury and cited in full the letter from 'omnes burgenses Dublinae civitatis cunctusque clericorum conventus' which included these statements: 'Antecessorum enim vestrorum magisterio semper nostros libenter subdimus, a quo recordamur nostros accepisse dignitatem ecclesiasticam. Sciatis vos revera quod episcopi Hiberniae maximum zelum erga nos habent, et maxime ille episcopus qui habitat Archmachae, quia nos nolumus obedire eorum ordinationi, sed semper sub vestro dominio volumus' *Hist. nov.* 297. Eadmer then records how Gregory twice made his profession 'de subiectione sua et obedientia sanctae matri ecclesiae Cantuariensi et eius pontificibus'—once at Lambeth before he was consecrated bishop and again four days later when he placed a text of this oath on the high altar of Canterbury cathedral. *ibid.* 298.

2 'Post haec ipse episcopus Hiberniam regressus pontificem Archmachiae, Caelestinum nomine, in loco suo substitutum invenit, cui et nobilitas generis, et maior abundantia terrenae facultatis, et in hos atque illos profusior manus, homines patriae ipsius in sui favorem, pulso Gregorio, conglutinavit. Qui Gregorius inde discedens ad archiepiscopum qui eum sacraverat reversus est' *ibid.* 298.

survived in possession of the see to become its first archbishop at the council of Kells–Mellifont in 1152. The Canterbury link was quietly severed and the breach between Armagh and Dublin was apparently healed, at least for the time being.

Between the outbreak of this controversy in 1121 and the formal reconciliation of the chief native Irish see and the chief Hiberno-Norse see in 1152, lay the working life of the man who stands without peer as the foremost personality of the Irish reform movement, Maol Maodoc Ua Morgair. St Malachy of Armagh personifies the reform as a whole because he was its noblest spirit and because there is not a facet of the reform that his career does not illuminate. From whatever angle one views the reform, the figure of Malachy dominates the scene; whatever the issue involved—subjection to Rome, the revivification of the episcopate through emancipation from lay control and constitutional reorganization, apostolic endeavour among the people, communication with men of intellectual and spiritual stature at home and abroad, monasticism in both its traditional and newer forms—the name of Malachy is inseparable from its history.

It is of course possible that the overwhelming dominance of the personality of Malachy is something of a distortion of perspective, inescapable because he is the one man of whom there exists a contemporary biography. And it is a biography of considerable power. Malachy died at Clairvaux in 1148. Shortly after his death, the abbot of the Cistercian house of Inislounaght (co. Limerick) wrote to St Bernard asking him on behalf of the Cistercian communities in Ireland, of whose birth Malachy was the spiritual father, to write the saint's life. Using information supplied by the Irish Cistercians and drawing on his personal knowledge of one whom he revered as a master of the life of the spirit, Bernard produced a *Vita Malachiae* which is at once a unique tribute to a medieval Irishman and a major source for twelfth century Irish history.

Abbot Comgall had asked Bernard for a *narratio* of Malachy's life, not an *eloquium*—for history rather than for panegyric. Irish historians have on the whole tended to be somewhat sceptical about Bernard's assertion that 'historical truth is safe in my keeping'.[1] For Bernard

---

[1] 'Libens obedio, presertim quod non eloquium exigitis, sed narrationem. Dabo vero operam, ut ea sit pura et luculenta, devotos informans, fastidiosos non onerans. Sane narrationis veritas secura apud me est ...' *VM* Praef. 1075.

has presented Malachy as the *lucerna ardens et lucens*[1] amid some very Stygian gloom.[2] The main theme of the *Vita* and of the sermons preached on the anniversaries of Malachy's death concerns the taming of Irish 'barbarism'[3] by the apostolicity of the saint.[4] Bernard did not in fact confine himself to sober history but held up his subject for wonder and for imitation.[5] He was painting the portrait of an ideal monk and bishop: a figure of light who shone the more in the encompassing darkness. It is not surprising that historians have found his descriptions of conditions in Ireland some-what rhetorical. Bernard had no first-hand experience of Ireland and both his sources and his imagination are under suspicion of excessive severity.[6] Certainly Bernard's language has all its wonted vigour for the denunciation of evils.[7]

It is of course very proper to look critically at any historical

[1] 'Virum vere sanctum, et nostrorum quidem temporum singularis sapientiae et virtutis. Iste erat lucerna ardens et lucens: nec exstincta est, sed submota' *ibid.* 1074.

[2] 'Inde tota illa per universam Hiberniam de qua superius diximus, dissolutio ecclesiasticae disciplinae, censurae enervatio, religionis evacuatio: inde illa ubique pro mansuetudine christiana saeva subintroducta barbaries, imo paganismus quidam inductus sub nomine christiano.' St Bernard saw the defects of the episcopate as the root cause. He continued: 'Nec mirum: nam quomodo tam morbidi capitis membra valerent' *ibid.* 10. 1086.

[3] 'Posuit sine sumptu evangelium, replevit evangelio patriam, suorum maxime feralem edornuit barbariem Hibernorum' Bernard of Clairvaux *Sermo II in transitu S. Malachiae episcopi PL* 183. 486.

[4] 'O virum apostolicum, quem tot et talia nobilitant signa apostolatus sui' *VM* 19. 1098.

[5] 'Habes, diligens lector, in Malachia quid mireris, habes et quid imiteris' *ibid.* 29. 1112.

[6] See the judicious appraisal of A. Gwynn, 'St. Malachy of Armagh' 968. His final estimate: 'Stripped of the rhetoric which is so characteristic of Bernard's style when he is denouncing evil, the charges that he makes against the people of Connor are, without exception, the same as those that he and other contemporary witnesses bring against the Irish people as a whole. There were too few priests; the sacraments were neglected; the native Brehon law had corrupted the observance of the Church's matrimonial law; the Roman liturgy was unknown; the duty of paying tithes was not recognized by either clergy or laity' *IER* 71 (1949) 143.

[7] For example: 'Cum autem coepisset pro officio suo agere [i.e. as bishop of Connor], tunc intellexit homo Dei, non ad homines se, sed ad bestias destinatum. Nusquam abhuc tales expertus fuerat in quantacunque barbarie: nusquam repererat sic protervos ad mores, sic ferales ad ritus, sic ad fidem impios, ad leges barbaros, cervisosos ad disciplinam, spurcos ad vitam. Christiani nomine, re pagani' *VM* 8. 1084.

source. But reservations about accepting literally everything Bernard wrote should not allow us to overlook the very remarkable quality of the work. Its place in the *corpus* of St Bernard's writings does not concern us here except to notice that it is a high one.[1] That it was a successful piece of hagiography is attested by Pope Clement III's acknowledgment of its witness to Malachy's sanctity in the bull announcing the canonization of Malachy.[2] As biography it presents a reasonably clear outline of the main events of his life,[3] allowing also some glimpses of his personality. As a source for the history of the reform movement, whatever reservations may have to be made, it is without equal.

With Malachy the centre of the reform moved northwards. He was himself very much an Armagh product. His father was a teacher in the abbatial school there and it was there that he began his ecclesiastical life in the monastery of SS Peter and Paul. It was Cellach, archbishop of Armagh who ordained him deacon, then priest and finally bishop and designated him as his successor at Armagh,[4] and who with the Armagh monk Imar Ua h-Aedhacain, was his spiritual director during his young manhood. It was in Armagh as deputy in Cellach's absence that he gained his first major pastoral experience,[5] and his whole life as a bishop was spent in the northern province.

There is a second change in the character of the reform movement

---

[1] Cf. the opinion of E. Vacandard: 'La vie de S. Malachie est, avec le traité *De Consideratione*, l'un des écrits les plus achevés de l'abbé de Clairvaux. Son style y atteint un degré de pureté, de clarté, d'élégance et d'originalité, que nul écrivain de son siècle, pas même Jean de Salisbury, n'a surpassé' *Vie de S. Bernard* 2 (1920) 384–5.

[2] Clement III to the Cistercian general chapter 6 July 1190, *Pont. hib.* 1.23.

[3] There remain some problems of dating and of place-name identification. Fr Gwynn's study of Malachy (*IER* 70. 961–78; *ibid.* 71.134–48, 317–31) differs at a number of important points from the older standard account, H. J. Lawlor, *St. Bernard of Clairvaux's Life of St. Malachy of Armagh*, Introduction, and his 'Notes on St. Bernard's Life of Malachy' *PRIA* 36 C (1919) 230–64. Ch. 29 of E. Vacandard *Vie de S. Bernard* is, in the author's own words 'de la sorte, un abrégé de la *Vita Malachiae*' and is of value.

[4] 'ipse (Celsus) est qui Malachiam in diaconum, presbyterum, episcopum ordinauit: et cognoscens quia moreretur, fecit quasi testamentum, quatenus Malachias deberet succedere sibi, quod nullus alius videretur dignior, qui episcoparetur in sede prima' *VM* 10. 1086.

[5] *Ibid.* 3. (*Ordinibus initiatus episcopi vices gerit*) 1078–9.

discernible as due to Malachy. He himself was first and foremost a
monk and the specifically monastic side of reform became noticeably
more prominent in his lifetime. His monastic experience was wide
and the currents of monasticism which can be traced as undergoing
renewal in the second and third quarters of the twelfth century can
all be associated with Malachian endeavours. But the episcopal and
diocesan aspects of reform continued to hold an important place in
men's minds in the same period and here, too, Malachy's leadership
was of considerable significance.

Malachy's monastic life began at Armagh under Imar.[1] It developed, in two periods of the 1120s, at Lismore under Malchus,[2]
whilst in the same period he reconstructed the abbey of Bangor[3]
and built a new monastery in co. Kerry.[4] He was a bishop for twenty-
four years: six years from 1124, ruling Down and Connor from
Bangor, archbishop of Armagh from 1132 to 1137 when he resigned
his province to return to Bangor as bishop of Down. But he was a
bishop with reluctance. It was only the earnest entreaties of Cellach
and Imar that persuaded him of his duty to accept episcopal office;
he accepted Armagh with all the unwillingness of an Anselm and,

[1] 'Sedebat sibi invenculus secus pedes Imarii ...' Earlier St Bernard had described
Imar: 'homo ille sanctus et austerae admodum vitae, inexorabilis castigator corporis
sui, cellam habens iuxta ecclesiam' *ibid.* 2 (*Religiosae vitae tirocinium*) 1077–8.
[2] On Malchus and Lismore: 'Hic erat senex plenus dierum et virtutum, et sapientia
Dei erat in illo. Natione quidam Hibernus, sed in Anglia conversatus fuerat in habitu
et proposito monachali in Wintoniensi monasterio: de quo assumptus est in
episcopum in Lesmore civitate Mumoniae: et ipsa nobilior inter ceteras regni
illius. Ibi tanta ei desuper collata est gratia, ut non modo vita et doctrina, sed et
signis clareret. Quorum duo pono exempli causa, ut omnibus innotescat qualem
in scientia sanctorum Malachias habuerit praeceptorem ... nomen grande adeptus
est; ita ut ad eum Scoti Hibernique confluerent, et tanquam unus omnium pater ab
omnibus coleretur' *ibid.* 4. 1079. This was the Malchus consecrated by Anselm in
1096. Perhaps the part played by English influences on the formation of this man
was the most important single contribution of the Canterbury connexion to the
reform movement.
[3] *Ibid.* 6 (*Monasterium Benchorense desolata instaurat*) 1082–3. This work was done under
Imar's direction: 'Itaque ex mandato patris Imarii assumptis secum decem circiter
fratribus, veniens ad locum coepit aedificare ... Praefuit Malachias loco illi tempore
aliquanto, patre Imario ita constituente, ipse rector, ipse regula fratrum' 1083.
[4] *Ibid.* 9 (*Monasterium Ibracense construit*) 1085–6. The exact whereabouts of this
monastery is not clear. Fr Gwynn suggests the modern Ballinskelligs, where there is
trace in the later middle ages of an Augustinian house, following the Arrouaisian
rule, *IER* 71. 147. The Arrouaisian connexion of St Malachy is considered below.

like Malchus, resigned his metropolitan charge to return to the life
of a monk–bishop as soon as possible. In the spring of 1139 he visited
Clairvaux while on his way to Rome and was so attracted by the
Cistercian way of life that he asked Innocent II if he might resign his
bishopric and take the habit there.[1] This request was refused, but
Clairvaux retained its hold on his affections though he had close
contacts with houses of canons both in France and England, and it
was there that he was to die and be buried[2] and whence came in due
season the successful petition for his canonization.

There is nothing on record which enables us to follow the evolution of Malachy's monastic life. Since he served his noviciate under
Imar the assumption must be that he began by following the
Columban rule. Bangor was refounded with a community of Imar's
monks and Malachy's Kerry foundation was presumably with at
least some Bangor monks. It is not impossible, however, that these
houses followed the rule of St Augustine. What rule was followed at
Lismore in the time of the eminence of Malchus, formerly a monk of
Benedictine Winchester, is not known. Was it an amalgam of
traditional Irish monasticism and the rule of St Benedict such as was
not unknown on the Continent in earlier centuries? That it is not
possible to know any precise details of monastic régimes in this
period is not merely a commentary on the prevailing paucity of
source material; it suggests also that this was very much a transitional phase of monasticism in Ireland. It is not improbable that the
traditional Irish rules in Ireland were much more affected at this time
by external influences than our sources allow us to establish with any
degree of conviction. It is relevant to recall here that there is evidence
for the existence of a house of Irish monks in Rome at the end of the
eleventh century.[3] If, as is just possible, Lismore had become
Benedictine, this change would not have been unparalleled. There
was at this very time a lively development of Irish monasticism in
Germany, where the Irish community of St James at Ratisbon was
the chief monastery of a group which included Würzburg, Nurem-
burg, Erfurt, Eichstatt, Constance and Vienna. These were Bene-

[1] *VM* 17. 1094–5.
[2] *Ibid.* 31 (*Rursus Claramvallem venit, moriturus loco et tempore quo desideraverat*) 1114–8.
[3] Cf. A. Wilmart, 'La Trinité des Scots à Rome et les notes du Vat. Lat. 368' *Revue Bénédictine* 41 (1929) 218–30.

dictine houses.[1] There is evidence that German influences were felt in Munster in the lifetime of Malchus.[2] It is possible that the Benedictine monastery of Cashel was founded from Ratisbon before 1150.[3] Moreover it is possible that other new influences were at work on the practice of monasticism in twelfth century Ireland. It has been suggested that there was a foundation from Cluny of a monastery at Athlone before 1150.[4] It has also been suggested that two Munster houses, Holycross and Fermoy, later both well-known Cistercian houses, were originally Benedictine foundations of the congregation of Tiron, established in the first decade of the twelfth century. To this external influence must be added two more Benedictine foundations, also later to become Cistercian houses: Erenagh and St Mary's Dublin, monasteries of the congregation of Savigny.[5] The first of these was established in Malachy's own diocese of Down when he was bishop.

These details do not unfortunately add up to any coherent picture of the nature of the reform which Irish monasticism was undergoing. But they certainly indicate that the ground was to some extent prepared for the acceleration of monastic reform which received its impetus from Malachy. The change for which he was especially responsible concerned the introduction into Ireland of the monastic usages of houses of acknowledged fervour from abroad, Cistercian and Augustinian.

The story of the introduction of the Cistercians into Ireland is among the best known in Irish medieval history. The credit belonged unambiguously to Malachy. St Bernard recorded that Malachy left four of his companions behind at Clairvaux and others 'at other places' for training in Cistercian discipline and that further aspirants

[1] Cf. D. A. Binchy, 'The Irish Benedictine Congregation in medieval Germany' *Studies* 18 (1929); A. Gwynn, 'The continuity of the Irish tradition at Würzburg' *Herbipolis jubilans* (Würzburg 1952) 57–81.

[2] German influence has been detected on the architecture of Cormac's chapel at Cashel (1134). The contemporary abbot of St James's Ratisbon, Christian MacCarthy, was a close kinsman of Cormac. Cf. A. Gwynn, 'Ireland and the Continent in the eleventh century' *IHS* 8 (1953) 192–216 at 208–9 with references to the architectural literature.

[3] Cf. Introduction to *Map of Monastic Ireland* (2nd ed. Ordnance Survey 1964) 6.

[4] *Ibid.* 6.

[5] Cf. H. G. Richardson, 'Some Norman Monastic Foundations in Ireland' *Gwynn Studies* 29–43.

were sent from Ireland to join them.[1] In due course, these monks, reinforced with some Frenchmen, and under the leadership of Gillacrist (Christian) were sent in 1142 to establish the first foundation, that of Mellifont, near Drogheda. After some early setbacks, Mellifont established itself and the order spread rapidly.[2] Between 1147 and 1153 Mellifont had produced seven daughter houses in different parts of Ireland. All but one proved to be permanent establishments.[3] Abbot Christian became bishop of Lismore in 1151 and was appointed papal legate.[4] Another abbot, Peter, of Boyle abbey, became bishop of Clonfert about this time.[5] The Cistercian impact on Ireland made itself felt very quickly.

It is of course quite natural that St Bernard should highlight St Malachy's Cistercian connexions and achievements. The absence of any very explicit reference to his connexions with the Canons Regular is not necessarily of much significance. But such brief snatches of his biography as appear in Irish writings—obituaries in the different Annals—credit Malachy with the introduction of the canons as well as of the Cistercians.[6] Were there any houses of canons in Ireland before St Malachy's time? Further problems concerning the introduction of the Canons Regular arise from some evidence of a different kind. In 1179, Gualtier, abbot of the Augustinian canons of Arrouaise, near Arras, stated that Malachy had visited the abbey, approved of the rule and liturgical practices of the order, had them copied and persuaded most of the clergy in cathedral churches and other places in Ireland to adopt them.[7] There is nothing intrinsically

[1] *VM* 15. 1094; *ibid.* 16. 1095.

[2] Cf. C. Conway, *The Story of Mellifont* (1958) 6–12 for an account of the establishment of the house and the tensions between Irish and French monks.

[3] They were: Bective, Baltinglass, Inislounaght, Monasteranenagh, Kilbeggan and Newry. Grellachdinach (co. Roscommon?) was the temporary foundation; the final choice of this community was Boyle. I follow here the findings of N. Hadcock in Gwynn and Hadcock, *Medieval Religious Houses, Ireland* (1970).

[4] *Ann. St. Mary's Dublin* 2. 263. 265.

[5] *Hbk Brit. Chron.* 346.

[6] For example *Chronicon Scotorum s.a.* 1148. On the whole question of Malachy's introduction of canons, see P. J. Dunning, 'The Arroasian Order in Medieval Ireland' *IHS* 4 (1944–5) 297–315.

[7] 'Sanctae memoriae Malachias, Hiberniensium archiepiscopus per nos iter faciens, inspectis consuetudinibus nostris et approbatis, libros nostros et usus ecclesiae transcriptos suam in Hiberniam detulit, et fere omnes clericos in episcopalibus sedibus et in multis aliis locis per Hiberniam constitutos, ordinum nostrum et

unlikely in Malachy's visit to this house of canons which lay near to his route through France to Rome. Careful reading of the Annals makes it probable that Malachy was responsible for the introduction of the Augustinian rule in seven houses.[1] The inclusion of Bangor and Down among this number gives a degree of plausibility to Gualtier's statement that Malachy induced the clergy of cathedral churches to adopt Arrouaisian customs. But when he says that this was in most of the cathedral churches the statement surely exaggerates Malachy's influence since outside the northern province no connexion can be established between Malachy and the change of rule to that of St Augustine in any house.[2] Nor is there any internal Irish evidence to suggest that the customs of Arrouaise were the preponderant model. Indeed it would seem very likely that Malachy himself did not confine himself rigidly to the acceptance of but one set of Augustinian customs. St Bernard noted that Malachy had an intimate and long-standing connexion with the canons of the Yorkshire priory of Guisborough,[3] which makes it certain that this knowledge of the rule of St Augustine was not confined to Arrouaise and almost certainly ante-dated his visit there.

The introduction of the Cistercians happens to be the best documented part of the history of monasticism in twelfth century Ireland. This does not make it the most important part, significant as a development though it was. It might be thought that the supplantation of the traditional Irish monastic rules by the rule of St Augustine was ultimately the most fundamental change in medieval Irish monasticism. It has been estimated that there were sixty-three houses of canons established before 1170.[4] This process is very obscure indeed. But it was too widespread a phenomenon to stem from a single source and proceed according to a single pattern. Malachy did not originate this movement though he forwarded it

habitum et maxime divinum in ecclesia officium suscipere et observare praecepit' *PL* 217. 68, where it is printed with a letter of Innocent III concerning the attendance of Irish canons at the annual chapter at Arrouaise (*Pont. hib.* 45. 112–13)

[1] Dunning, *art. cit.* 301–9.

[2] *Ibid.* 303.

[3] 'Et pertransiens Scotiam, in ipso introitu Angliae divertit ad ecclesiam Gisiburnensem, ubi habitant viri religiosi, canonicam ducentes vitam, ab antiquo familiares ei pro sua religione et honestate' *VM* 30. 1113–14.

[4] Information kindly given me by Mr Neville Hadcock.

in the north. Nor was Arrouaise its sole parent, though it did have daughter houses in Ireland.

Cistercians and canons were not, however, the only religious with whom Malachy was associated. It will be recalled that he began his life as a religious in what was almost certainly a Columban community, part of that *familia S. Columbae* whose history goes back to the sixth century and which now in the twelfth, under the coarbs of Columcille at Derry, was showing signs of new life. The *Annals of Ulster* provide a bare sketch of this reform, particularly when Flaithbertach Ua Brolchain was abbot in the quarter century after 1150.[1] Throughout this period the archbishop of Armagh was Gille mac Liag (Gelasius) who had himself ruled the *familia* from Derry for sixteen years (1121–37). The link between Gelasius and Malachy was a very close one. For it was in favour of the saintly abbot that Malachy had resigned the primacy.[2] There can be little doubt that Malachy was at least as concerned in the promotion of Columban as of Augustinian or of Cistercian monasticism. There was nothing narrow or restrictive in the all-embracing encouragement of those who sought the monastic life by one, 'qui quasi unus omnium parens vivebat omnibus.'[3]

There is a second incident of the life of Malachy as well known as his introduction of the Cistercians. This concerns his journeys to Rome seeking *pallia* for the metropolitan sees of Ireland. The first, in 1139, saw the replacement of Gilbert of Limerick by Malachy as papal legate, but the main object of the mission was not accomplished. St Bernard has a summary of what Innocent II ruled concerning the palls:

Malachy prayed that the constitution of the new metropolis [i.e. Cashel] be confirmed, and that palls be given for both sees [i.e. Armagh and Cashel]. The privilege of confirmation was granted at once; but as for the

---

[1] The evidence, such as it is, has been discussed by A. Gwynn, 'Raphoe and Derry in the Twelfth and Thirteenth Centuries' *Donegal Annual* 4 (1959) 84–100.

[2] 'Igitur Malachias intra triennium reddita retributione superbis, et libertate ecclesiae restituta, pulsa barbarie, et reformatis ubique moribus christianae religionis, videns omnia in pace esse, coepit cogitare et de sua pace. Et memor propositi sui, constituit pro se Gelasium, virum bonum, et dignum tali honore, conniventibus clero et populo ...' *VM* 14. 1092.

[3] 'quasi gallina pullos suos sic fovebat omnes, et in velamento alarum suarum protegebat' Bernard, *Sermo II in transitus S. Malachiae PL* 183. 483.

palls the supreme pontiff told him that more formal action must be taken. 'You must call together the bishops and clerks and magnates of the land, and hold a general council; and so with the assent and common desire of all you shall then demand the palls by persons of good repute, and it shall be given you.'[1]

The holding of this council was long delayed. It did not meet until nine years later. Quite why it was delayed is yet another of the enigmas of this period, and seems insoluble. Its clarification might throw light on whether, when the council was finally held on Inis Pádraig and agreed that Malachy should return to Rome on a similar errand, he was briefed to ask again for two palls as in 1139 or for the four that Eugenius III in the event despatched. But Malachy died at Clairvaux before reaching Rome[2] and thus the *Vita Malachiae* does not cover the consummation of this aspect of Malachy's work at the council of Kells–Mellifont in 1152.[3]

The sources for the history of this council are of very much the same type as those for Rathbreasail—some rather general and laconic observations in the Annals, with the main bulk of the story, such as it is, deriving from Keating's reproduction of the 'old book of Chronicles which was written in Clonenagh.'[4] In sum, these

[1] *VM* 16. 1095. The translation is Lawlor's, *St. Bernard's Life of St. Malachy* 73.

[2] What happened between the death of Malachy and the dispatch of the legate Cardinal John Paparo in 1151 with the palls is unknown. That there was a further petition from Ireland, with which rulers as well as churchmen were associated is known from the one existing reference to this matter, John of Salisbury: 'Nuntii regulorum et ecclesie Hiberniensis iam altera uice redierant ut legatum quem petierant optinerent' *Historia pontificalis* (ed. M. Chibnall 1956) *s.a.* 1151. 36. 70.

[3] It is customary to speak of this council as 'of Kells'. The authority for this assignation is the Annals of Clonenagh cited by Keating. Since Keating tells nothing of the nature of this now lost work there is no incontrovertible reason for according it any more authority than other non-contemporary sources which speak of the council being held at Drogheda (*AFM* and *Fourth Fragment of Ann. Tigernach*) or at Mellifont (*Ann. St. Mary's Dublin*). Fr Gwynn has argued, successfully in my view, that the first sessions of the council were held in early March at Kells and the concluding session at Mellifont (sometimes called Drogheda in the sources; it was very near) at the end of the month, cf. 'The centenary of the Synod of Kells' 161–76 at 164–7. For a detailed proof that 'the abbey of Drogheda' in this context was Mellifont, Conway, *The Story of Mellifont* 286–303.

[4] G. Keating, *History of Ireland* 312–17, 356–7. Paparo's mission was fairly widely recorded by chroniclers in Britain for it was an interesting event of Anglo-papal relations. Stephen refused the Legate passage unless he first took an oath that he would do no harm to the kingdom. The Cardinal refused and, after delay, reached

The eve of the Invasion

sources make it clear that this council undertook a reforming programme of a nature which makes it reasonable to see it as the logical complement of Rathbreasail. There are no decrees extant[1] but general indications from various sources allow it to be said that they concerned marriage law, simony, usury and the payment of tithe.[2] The most important business, however, for contemporaries was with

Ireland under the safe conduct of the King of Scotland. All record the purpose of the legation as being to distribute palls in Ireland (Roger of Howden *RS* 1. 212, deriving from the Melrose Chronicle; Ralph Diceto *RS* 2.295; John of Hexham in *Symeonis monachi Dunelmensis opera RS* 2. 326; John of Salisbury, *Hist. pont.* 6). There was another reason why his embassy might attract interest in England—its effects on the primatial claims of Canterbury. Robert of Torigny recorded it from that point of view, though it would seem he is the only one to do so: 'Eugenius papa Iohannem Romanae ecclesiae cardinalem presbyterum, cognomento Paparo destinavit legatum in Hiberniam, cum quattuor palliis, quorum unum dedit episcopo Duvelinae; et reliqua tria tribus aliis episcopis eiusdem insulae; subiiciens unicuique eorum qui pallia acceperunt quinque alios episcopos. Et hoc factum est contra consuetudinem antiquorum et dignitatem Cantuariensis ecclesiae, a qua solebant episcopi Hiberniae expetere et accipere consecrationis benedictionem' *Chronica* in *Chronicles of the reigns of Stephen, Henry II and Richard I RS* 4.166.

[1] There were: 'Iohannes ... constituit canones qui et in terra illa et in archivis apostolice sedis habentur' John of Salisbury, *Hist. pont.* 72. Keating's quotation from the Latin Annals of Clonenagh is the best account: 'mclii. anno ab incarnatione domini nostri Iesu Christi bissextili et embolismali anno, nobile concilium in vernali tempore ad dominicam "Laetare Ierusalem" apud Ceanannus celebratum fuit, in quo presidens dominus Iohannes cardinalis presbyter beati Laurentii in Damasco inter viginti duos episcopos et quinque electos et inter tot abbates et priores ex parte beatorum apostolorum Petri et Pauli et domini apostolici Eugenii, simoniam et usuram omnibus modis extirpavit et damnavit, et decimas dandas apostolica auctoritate praecepit. Quattuor pallia quattuor episcopis Hiberniae, Dublinensi Caselensi Tuamensi Armachano tradidit. Insuper Armachanum archiepiscopum in primatem super alios prout decuit ordinavit. Qui etiam Ioannes cardinalis protinus post peractum concilium iter arripuit et nono kalendas aprilis transfretavit' *History of Ireland* 314–16.

[2] In addition to the text cited in the previous note, Keating recorded that the council considered ways of 'putting down robbery and rape and bad morals and evils of every kind' *ibid.* 357. *AFM* record rules establishing 'that kinswomen and concubines must be dismissed; that payment must not be sought for anointing or baptizing ...; that church property must not be sold; that tithes should be given punctually' *s.a.* 1152; John of Hexham: 'Profectus inde in Hyberniam quatuor pallia certibus sedibus distribuit, gentemque in ea, legi nuptiarum non assuetam plurimum correxit' *Historia* 2. 326. John of Salisbury recorded only the unusual among the decrees: 'et ordinauit inter cetera ne abbatisse sancte Brigide in conuentibus publicis de cetero ante episcopos habeant presessionem; solebant enim sedere pro pedibus eius' *Hist. pont.* 72.

Map 2. Diocesan centres, council of Kells (1152).

the ordering and adjustment of dioceses, and in terms of abiding effect, this was the most significant issue on which decisions were made at this council (Map 2). What was agitating some contemporaries was the fact that the papal legate, Cardinal John Paparo, had arrived with four palls, for Dublin and Tuam, in addition to Armagh and Cashel, signifying that they too were to enjoy metropolitical status. It is not perhaps surprising to find Armagh named as among the discontented,[1] for though the legate confirmed the place of Armagh as the primatial see, the advancement of Tuam was at its expense. Possibly, too, there was still suspicion of Dublin. But whatever the validity of these conjectures, there can be no doubt that the creation of four archbishoprics in Ireland, and the final affirmation of the primacy of Armagh, which have endured down to our own day, was the first major achievement of this council. Its second was to amend and improve the diocesan structure created at Rathbreasail and to produce an organization which, in essentials, was to endure in all four provinces throughout the middle ages.[2]

So lasting have been these aspects of reform substantially accomplished at Kells that it is understandable that the view should be

[1] Keating: 'For Ireland thought it enough to have a pallium in Armagh and a pallium in Cashel and particularly it was in spite of the church of Armagh and the church of Down that other pallia were given besides, as the book of annals of the church of Clonenagh in Leix which gives a summary of the transactions of this council, explains the matter' *History of Ireland* 314–15.

[2] With the loss of the Kells decrees there was lost also any text which detailed the diocesan structure envisaged by Paparo. Keating is here no guide. There is extant, however, a twelfth century list of provinces and sees which is apparently drawn from a text of the Kells decree. It is headed: 'Tempore domini Eugenii pape iii facta est tocius hibernie in quattuor metropolos per iohannem paparo presbyterum cardinalem tituli sancti laurencii in damaso apostolice sedis legatum [hoc] modo.' The manuscript, formerly of the Cistercian monastery of Pontigny is now Montpellier Medical School MS 92 and has been edited and analysed by H. J. Lawlor, 'A fresh authority for the synod of Kells, 1152' *PRIA* 36 (1922) 16–22. It is known from later evidence that Paparo ruled that on the deaths of present bishops smaller and poorer sees should be suppressed and become units of larger consolidated dioceses (cf. the council held in 1216 by Simon de Rochfort, bishop of Meath where this ordinance was put into effect, *Concilia Magnae Brittaniae et Hiberniae* ed. D. Wilkins i. 547 and the instruction of Innocent III for the incorporation of Glendalough into Dublin, *Pont. hib.* I. 93. 171–2). When the Montpellier list is compared with the diocesan position in 1216, the reductions for each province are: Armagh, remained at ten suffragans; Dublin, from five to four; Cashel, from twelve to ten; Tuam, from seven to six. In addition two sees, Ardmore and Mungret, which the list names as having claimed to be episcopal seats, have not been established.

expressed that 'the work of reform and reorganization was indeed complete in 1152; after that date nothing remained to be arranged but matters of detail'.[1] This is, however, only true if the reform movement is wholly equated with the diocesan reorganization, though even here some of the details still to be arranged were of substance. There are certain indications that there was still much to be done in other aspects of the movement, notably in the crucial matter of lay control of ecclesiastical life,[2] while the monastic reforms, though impressive, were not without serious problems of adjustment to Irish society.[3] Another basic matter of Church organization, the establishment of parishes, has been as yet too little studied for it to be possible to make any confident judgments as to whether Kells was an end or a beginning.[4] Nevertheless, these qualifications made, the judgment which lies behind the one cited, namely the rejection of the view that the progress of reform demanded the intervention of Henry II and Anglo-French control of the Irish Church, is certainly correct. To look back over what had been accomplished in the first half of the twelfth century is to appreciate both the great strength of the movement and the fact that it was still gathering momentum. It had produced a hitherto un-

[1] J. Ryan, *Ireland from 800 to 1600* (n.d.) Cf. also J. F. O'Doherty: 'The ecclesiastical reform may be regarded, as we saw already, as completed in 1152. There remained only such matters as liturgy in need of reform.' 'St. Laurence O'Toole and the Anglo-Norman Invasion' *IER* 50 (1937) 600–25 at 606.

[2] Particularly in Connacht where reform came later. Cf. *Annals of Clonmacnoise*: 'In the year 1170 (*recte* 1179) there was a great convocation of the clergy of Ireland at Clonfert ... where it was laid down that no layman should have the rule of any church or church matters ... that holy orders should not be given to bishops' or priests' sons and for example of these their constitutions, they took the livings of seven bishops that had bishoprics and were laymen.' These Annals (ed. D. Murphy, 1896) are known only in a seventeenth century English translation. I have here modernized the spelling. Cf. also Innocent III to his legate John de Monte Coelio in 1203: '... intelleximus evidenter quod inter alias enormitates quas in ecclesiis Yberniensibus invenisti hanc detestabilem abusionem presertim in ecclesia Tuamensi et in partibus aliis cognovisti vigere quod non solum in minoribus prelaturis verum etiam in archiepiscopatibus et episcopatibus immediate filii patribus succedebant' *Pont. hib.* 1. 53.

[3] Conway, *The Story of Mellifont* 9.

[4] The assumption must be that it was not very far advanced in 1152 since parochial organization could only come after dioceses had been properly established. This topic has been well studied for the Killaloe diocese by D. F. Gleeson, 'The coarbs of Killaloe diocese' *RSAIJn.* (1949) 160–9 and Gleeson and Gwynn, *Diocese of Killaloe* 307–15.

achieved measure of ecclesiastical unity; a new diocesan structure; an increasing degree of cooperation from lay rulers at the same time as the grip of lay families on ecclesiastical office was being weakened; leaders of acknowledged sanctity; a marked renewal of monastic fervour; a signal advance in overcoming isolation from outside influences, of which advance the evolution of a new distinctive architectural style, Hiberno-Romanesque, integrating native and foreign elements, is the symbol;[1] a significant amount of new church building in a wide spread of the country.[2] It had begun to attack matrimonial laxities. It had subordinated itself to Rome to an extent unknown in previous Irish history. There is no suggestion here that the Church in Ireland was incapable of reforming itself.

This, however, was apparently the view that came to prevail in Rome. There is a certain rather bitter irony here. The Roman theme sounds insistently throughout the whole reform movement. First announced in characteristic strength by Gregory VII to Murtagh O'Brien when in 1076 he reminded the king and all the clergy and people of Ireland of the *principatus* of the see *super omnia mundi regna* and bade them ever to revere and obey it,[3] it had its most concrete manifestation in the appointment of three Irish prelates as papal legates, a succession which virtually covered all the first half of the twelfth century.[4] It had a prominent place in the treatise of Bishop Gilbert of Limerick: its message concerning hierarchy is especially Roman.[5] It was very emphatic in the lifework of Malachy. Here particularly, in reverence and devotion to Rome, did he personify the reform as a whole. His pastoral work was characterized by insistence

---

[1] Cf. G. Petrie, *The ecclesiastical architecture of Ireland anterior to the Norman invasion* (1845); A. C. Champneys, *Irish ecclesiastical architecture* (1910).

[2] Cf. the account, with map, of L. and M. de Paor, *Early Christian Ireland* (1958) 178–82.

[3] 'Beato igitur Petro eiusque vicariis inter quos dispensatio divina nostram quoque sortem annumerari disposuit orbis universus obedientiam similiter et reverentiam debet quam mente devota Sancte Romane ecclesie exhibere reminiscimini' *Pont. hib.* I. 2.

[4] They were: Maol Muire Ua Dúnáin (*c.* 1101); Gilbert of Limerick (before 1111 to 1139); Malachy of Armagh (1139–48).

[5] 'Namque omnia ecclesie membra uni episcopo videlicet Christo, eiusque vicario beato Petro apostolo, atque in eius sede presidenti apostolico, subiici et ab eis manifestat gubernari' *De statu ecclesiastico* Praef. 996; in the concluding paragraph: 'Soli tamen Petro dictum est, "Tu es Petrus ..." Papa ergo solus universali pre-eminet ecclesie; et ipse omnes ordinat et iudicat ...' 1004. See also 998–9.

on the canons and the practices of Rome, whilst his journeys to ask for the granting of palls were a clear acknowledgment of the primacy of jurisdiction. Whether it was the establishment of new sees or a decision affecting his personal life, Malachy's respect for the papacy was unquestioning.[1] His attitude was reflected at the council of Kells when the Irish hierarchy, through its four archbishops, made clear its collective obedience to Rome.[2] When the Roman Church changed its attitude to Ireland, the reason cannot have been because of any failure to heed the Gregorian admonition to revere and obey the apostolic see. This change came within a few years of the solemn submission at Kells when Pope Adrian IV decided to approve Henry II's invasion of Ireland on the grounds apparently, despite the evidence to the contrary, that Ireland was incapable of reforming herself.

[1] *VM*: 'Sed et apostolicas sanctiones ac decreta sanctorum patrum, praecipueque consuetudines sanctae Romanae ecclesiae, in cunctis ecclesiis statuebat' 3. 1079. C. 16 treats of his relationship with Innocent II. As well as recounting the request to resign his bishopric to become a monk of Clairvaux and the decisions about the *pallia*, it mentions Malachy's respect for Rome as a pilgrimage centre: 'Mensem integrum fecit in Urbe, loca sancta perambulans, et frequentans causa orationis' 1095. Malachy's mentor, Imar, had died in Rome five years previously, *AFM s.a.* 1134.
[2] *Ann. St. Mary's Dublin*, 263.

Chapter 2

THE ESTABLISHMENT OF THE NEW ORDER

THE PERIOD OF THE INVASION

Papal policy concerning Ireland had changed by the late summer of 1155. John of Salisbury has recorded this change of heart in the well-known passage of his *Metalogicon* wherein he claimed for himself the credit for inducing Adrian IV to entrust the country to Henry II and his successors. John related how the Pope fell in with this suggestion, involving as his warrant for sanctioning the change of rulership, the curious but by no means novel principle that the Donation of Constantine had given him sovereignty over all islands. He therefore sent Henry II a handsome emerald ring in testimony of his concession.[1]

John of Salisbury offered no comment on the motives of the principals concerned in this transaction. Robert of Torigny has written of Henry II's interest in securing Ireland as an appanage for his brother William.[2] As for Adrian IV, it has been argued in Ireland

---

[1] 'In response to my petition the pope granted and donated Ireland to the illustrious English king, Henry II, to be held by him and his successors, as his letters still testify. He did this by that right of longstanding from the Donation of Constantine whereby all islands are said to belong to the Roman Church. Through me the pope sent a gold ring set with a magnificent emerald as a sign that he had invested the king with the right to rule Ireland; it was later ordered that this ring be kept in the public treasury.' Latin text in *Metalogicon* 4. 42 ed. C. C. J. Webb (1929) 217–18.

For a reading of this passage which would have the 'iure hereditario' refer, not to the future, but to Henry's *already* held hereditary right, see W. Ullmann, 'On the influence of Geoffrey of Monmouth in English history' *Speculum Historiale: Geschichte im Spiegel von Geschichtsschreibung und Geschichtsdeutung* ed. C. Bauer *et alii* (Freiburg–München 1966) 257–76 at 272–3. The ingenious suggestion is that Adrian IV, likely enough through John of Salisbury, had accepted Geoffrey of Monmouth's fictions that Ireland had already in the distant past been subjugated by kings of England (by Arthur in particular). Thus papal recognition of Henry's lordship was 'in substance though not in form, a confirmation'.

[2] 'Circa festum S. Michaelis (1155) Henricus rex Anglorum habito concilio apud Wincestre, de conquirendo regno Hiberniae et Guillelmo fratri suo dando, cum optimatibus suis tractavit' *Chronica RS* 4. 186.

at least from the early fourteenth century, that his main idea was to accommodate the sovereign of his native land.[1] Irish historians have also probed John of Salisbury's mind for the *arrière-pensée*. He was the devoted secretary of the archbishop of Canterbury. The council of Kells had deprived Canterbury of any last vestiges of its primatial pretensions in Ireland. Canterbury now urged this grant upon the Pope, it is argued, as a means of regaining her lost right. Thus Archbishop Theobald is given paternity of the appeal to Adrian IV, with his secretary, a personal friend of the Pope, as go-between, to sanction the Invasion of Ireland in the cause of an ecclesiastical reform under the primacy of Canterbury.[2]

If the celebrated *Laudabiliter* be in fact Adrian IV's, as Giraldus Cambrensis, Ralph Diceto and the consensus of modern historical scholarship would have it,[3] the Pope professed his mind quite without ambiguity. He thought that the Irish were an uncivilized and ignorant people, that Henry II should be encouraged to help to teach them the truths of the Christian religion and that in return for this service the Irish people should receive him with honour and reverence as their lord. Adrian IV had obviously decided, and some might think had decided very irresponsibly, that the future of Christianity in Ireland depended on its political and ecclesiastical subordination to the Plantagenet. That Archbishop Baldwin and John of Salisbury shared this view is easy to believe but there is no evidence to warrant the linking of the Invasion with any plot to resurrect the primacy of Canterbury in Ireland.

There is no need, however, to seek a religious motivation for Henry II's decision to invade Ireland. The circumstances in which

---

[1] As in the 'Remonstrance' of the Irish princes to John XXII in 1317, E. Curtis and R. B. McDowell, *Irish Historical Documents, 1172–1922* (1943) 38–46 at 39.

[2] J. F. O'Doherty, 'St. Laurence O'Toole and the Anglo-Norman Invasion' 449–77 at 459; 600–25 at 601; 51. 131–46 at 139.

[3] The text of *Laudabiliter* is invariably associated with the name of Giraldus Cambrensis, *Expugnatio Hibernica* 2. 5 ed. J. F. Dimock *Giraldi Cambrensis Opera RS* 5 (1867) 317–18; *De rebus a se gestis* 11 ed. J. S. Brewer *Opera* 1 (1861) 62–3; *De instructione principum* 2. 19 ed. G. F. Warner *Opera* 8 (1891) 196–7. It is not generally appreciated that its publication by Ralph Diceto, *Ymagines historiarum RS* 1. 300–1 is almost certainly independent of Giraldus Cambrensis. Stubbs made a careful examination of Ralph's debt to other extant histories of the time, *ibid.* 2. xxx, without finding any evidence that he knew Giraldus's works and from detailed comparison it seems quite evident that he did not draw his Irish material from them.

Henry was led to transport an expeditionary force to Ireland were quite secular in nature and had no more to do with Church reform or the primacy of Canterbury than had the Donation of Constantine or a ring from the pope in authorizing his assertion of lordship over Ireland. These circumstances were totally political and were of a type familiar enough in their general pattern to students of colonialism in many countries in many historical periods. The dispossessed party in a tribal feud sought help from abroad in reviving his cause. The successful intervention of soldiers of fortune and their settling permanently, seeking what they might devour, became an embarrassment to their own government. Central government, in the person of Henry II, hitherto disinclined to intervene, was now constrained to take action to ensure that elements already notoriously lawless should not be encouraged to further excess and possible virtual political independence by their sudden and considerable accessions of power. Ireland must not be allowed to upset the always precarious balance of power which Henry hoped to hold over the south Welsh marcher lords.

This consensus has been reviewed by L. Weckman, *Las bulas alejandrinas de 1493 y la teoría política del papado medieval. Estudio de la supremacía papal sobre islas, 1091–1493* (1949) 48 ff. The old battleground has been revisited most recently, to argue in favour of authenticity, by M. Sheehy, 'The bull *Laudabiliter:* a problem in medieval *diplomatique* and history' *Journal of the Galway Archaeological and Historical Society* 29 (1961) 45–70.

At the risk of oversimplification, it is suggested that the main elements in the authenticity issue stand as follows:

The intrinsic probability that *Laudabiliter* is a genuine papal letter is based (a) on John of Salisbury's evidence in the *Metalogicon*, cited on p. 35 n. 1 above. This testimony has not been seriously impugned since Kate Norgate's reply to the objections to it in 'The bull *Laudabiliter*' *EHR* 8 (1893) 18–52 at 25–31. (b) On the conformity of its composition to the style of the papal chancery. On this cf. especially J. F. O'Doherty, 'Rome and the Anglo-Norman invasion of Ireland' *IER* 42 (1933) 131–45. (c) On the conformity of its political logic—Donation of Constantine, Peter's Pence, sun of justice—to antecedent papal tradition and also to Adrian IV's policy and ideas as papal legate in Scandinavia before he became pope. This is the theme of Weckman, *Las bulas alejandrinas, passim.* (d) On the fact that papal policy to the English lordship of Ireland continued to be based on the principles of *Laudabiliter.* (e) On its explicit acceptance by all parties in medieval Ireland, cf. my '*Laudabiliter* in medieval diplomacy and propaganda' *IER* 87 (1957) 420–32; though pointing out that the papacy remained noncommittal in the thirteenth and fourteenth centuries about whether the bull had in fact been issued by Adrian IV.

None of these arguments is in itself conclusive but together they make a formid-

Henry's Invasion then was not primarily a religious crusade.[1] But
it might be allowed that he saw the tactical possibilities of exploiting
a position as a champion of the Church in the diplomacy that was to
come with Pope Alexander III in the aftermath of the Becket murder.
At any rate, once he had established his rule in Ireland he quickly
threw a religious aura round his new position. That ecclesiastical
issues held a prominent place in his calculations can be seen from the
care he took to secure oaths of submission not merely from secular
rulers but from the whole Irish hierarchy, from his successful bid for
the leadership of the reform movement by causing a reform council
to be summoned and from his care to seek the approval of the
Pope for what he had done.[2]

able body of circumstantial evidence for authenticity. On the other hand, there
would seem to be two considerations against, still worth taking seriously.

Firstly, there is no satisfactory explanation as to why, if Henry II had the bull,
none of the chronicles mentions his using it in the context where it was so obviously
most appropriate, namely when he was demanding submissions from Irish kings
and prelates. As Cardinal Moran put it: 'It is extremely difficult, in any hypothesis,
to explain in a satisfactory way this mysterious silence of Henry II, nor is it easy to
understand how a fact so important, so vital to the interests of Ireland, could remain
so many years concealed from those who ruled the destinies of Ireland': 'Bull of
Adrian the Fourth' *IER* 9 (1872) 49–64 at 55. Secondly, Giraldus Cambrensis
accompanied *Laudabiliter* with an alleged confirmatory letter of Alexander III,
Quoniam ea. The authenticity of this letter is highly suspect on paleographical
grounds and for lack of any confirmatory evidence. Even Giraldus himself appears
to have had his doubts as he introduces it with the admission that some people have
denied that it was ever promulgated by the Pope, *De princ. instruct.* 2. 19. 196. If the
confirmation is suspect, is it unreasonable to suspect the grant itself?

[1] For the suggestion that it was an appeal from Irish kings which took Henry to
Ireland, J. Otway-Ruthven, *A History of Medieval Ireland* (1967) 48–9.

[2] There are four main narrative sources for the ecclesiastical issues raised during
Henry's stay in Ireland: Howden in *Gesta* 1. 26–8 and *Chron.* 2. 30–2; Giraldus, *Exp.
hib.* 1. 34–5. 280–1 and 2. 5. 315; Diceto, *Ymagines hist.* 1. 350–1. They are clearly
independent accounts and while there are some inconsistencies, for the most part
they supplement and confirm each other. The chief points raised by the inconsistencies are:

(a) *The submissions of the Irish bishops.* Giraldus does not mention these. Diceto
says simply (*ibid.* 348): 'Lismorensis episcopus et apostolice legatus, archiepiscopi et
episcopi receperunt eum in regem et dominum et fidelitatem ei iuraverunt.'
Howden has a much fuller account, stating that the bishops accepted Henry as their
lord and king, swore fidelity to him and to his heirs for ever and that each bishop
formally rendered submission in the form of a charter carrying his seal. A list of all
the bishops who submitted is given in *Gesta* 1. 26–7, *Chron.* 2. 30–1: substantially
the same account.

(b) *The date of the council of Cashel.* Diceto places the council at Lismore without

The Irish bishops readily associated themselves with Henry II and actually told Alexander III they had thrown in their lot with the new order in praising his efforts for reform and for the preservation of the liberty of the Church. Together, papal legate (Christian, bishop of Lismore), episcopate and Henry II, presented to Alexander III an account of what had happened militarily and politically. They spoke of the moral evils besetting Ireland, of Henry's declared intention of subjugating the Irish people to his lordship in order 'to extirpate the filth of their abomination', of the hierarchy's appreciation of Henry's services and their willingness to support him politically.[1]

Alexander's reply came in letters to the bishops, to Henry and to the kings and princes of Ireland—documents as well known as the *Metalogicon* passage quoted above and *Laudabiliter*, so that it is not necessary to narrate their contents at any length. But it was a reply of very great consequence for the future of Hiberno-papal relations. The Pope professed himself overjoyed by the success of this 'devoted son of the Church', accounted his purpose the subjugation of Ireland,

specific date but implicitly assigning it to 1172 (*Ymagines hist.* 351). Giraldus simply dates it 1172 (*Exp. hib.* 281). Howden at least, in the *Gesta*, is very specific about the whole chronology of Henry's itinerary from his arrival at Pembroke *c.* 14 September 1171 to his arrival back in Wales at Milford Haven on 16 April 1172. It is as part of a very detailed timetable that he says: 'Praeterea rex circa festum Sancti Leonardi [6 November] misit Nicolaum capellanum suum et Radulfum archidiaconum de Landaf clericum suum, archiepiscopis et episcopis Hiberniae. Et ipsi cum praedictis archiepiscopis et episcopis magnum celebraverunt concilium apud Cassellensem civitatem' (*Gesta* 28; date omitted in the account, *Chron.* 31).

(c) *The canons of the council.* All four narratives are consistent here but differ very much in emphasis. Diceto's is the least informative and Giraldus easily the fullest. These two both refer to the principle of bringing the practices generally of the Irish Church into conformity with those of the English Church (see below, p. 41 n. 1) which Howden does not mention in either of his versions.

(d) *The notification of these proceedings to the Pope.* Diceto makes no reference to the Pope being informed of what had happened in Ireland. Giraldus Cambrensis, *Exp. hib.* 2. 5. 315 and *De prin. instruct* 2. 19. 195, mentions that letters were sent from the council of Cashel concerning abuses in Ireland but again without reference to the submissions. *Gesta* 28 states that the charters of submission were sent to Alexander III before the council. *Chron.* 31 also says that these letters of submission were sent to the Pope but there is an implicit suggestion in the order in which the material is arranged that they were sent after the council.

[1] The evidence for the attitude of the Irish bishops is Alexander III's statements of what they had told him given in his reply to them. Texts of the three papal letters, *Pont. hib.* 1. 5–7; English translation, Curtis and McDowell, *Irish Historical Documents*, 19–22.

in order to tame a 'barbarous people, undisciplined, uncivilized and ignorant of the divine law', good; commanded the episcopate to underwrite his efforts and to excommunicate those who rebelled against him; admonished secular rulers to be submissive to him 'in all humility and meekness'. As far as the papacy was concerned, for the future, the king of England was lord of Ireland and the Church was committed to upholding his *dominium*. It may have been Adrian IV, if *Laudabiliter* be accepted as his, who gave this principle its first official enunciation. But it was Alexander III who gave it real meaning by promulgating it after Henry's rulership had already gained some recognition in Ireland. His successors continued to uphold it, even if they might from time to time express disapproval of particular acts. The position was made the clearer, if that were necessary, when in March 1215 Innocent III granted Ireland as a vassal kingdom to King John and his successors at an annual fee of 300 marks.[1] For the papacy the formal position was thus that Ireland was a papal fief granted to the kings of England. That Alexander III had approved so wholeheartedly of what Henry had done marked a turning-point in the relations of Ireland and the papacy. Henceforward all relations were conditioned, if not determined, by the fact that the king of England was papally approved as lord of Ireland. Hiberno-papal relations *tout court* did not exist. They were a branch of Anglo-papal relations.

This was not of course the only reason which made Henry II's Invasion the most important event in the history of the Irish Church between the fifth and the sixteenth centuries. The new order established in Ireland introduced new and far-reaching problems into the structure of a Church, hardly itself as yet constitutionally mature. The introduction of Anglo-Angevin feudalism made of the bishop a tenant-in-chief of the Crown and as such in a special relationship to it.[2] Inevitably, the composition of the episcopate, from one point of view a section of the baronage, was of importance to the Crown. Who became a bishop, and by what methods, was thus a matter of

---

[1] Text and English translation, C. R. Cheney and W. H. Semple, *Selected letters of Pope Innocent III concerning England* (1953) 67.
[2] Though 'in Norman Ireland the lands of the Church were held in frankalmoign, or sometimes in fee farm, with certain quite unimportant exceptions' J. Otway-Ruthven, 'Knight Service in Ireland' *RSAIJn.* 89 (1959) 1–15 at 2.

Crown policy, and recruitment to the episcopate and electoral procedure were henceforth to be subject to royal scrutiny and intervention. But this was merely one facet of what was to be the introduction of a relationship of the ecclesiastical and temporal powers which was quite new to Ireland. The council of Cashel had proclaimed the general principle that for the future the Irish Church was to be guided in every way by the customs and practices of the Church in England.[1] These usages included a view of what power kings had in Church affairs, of what was allowed churchmen in the way of privilege as to their persons and to their property, of what areas of cognizance was permitted to ecclesiastical courts, of the principle that should rule the cooperation of the spiritual and temporal powers.

These, and many other related principles, were to be the new basis of much of Irish ecclesiastical life, the features moulding the organization of the Church in Anglo-Ireland. They were not of course fully operative immediately, for their implementation followed on the progress of conquest and settlement. But already by the beginning of the reign of John, a substantial part of Ireland had been subdued and occupied. Conquest and settlement were to continue steadily throughout the thirteenth century. By the end of the reign of Edward I, the whole island was affected to a greater or lesser extent by the anglicization—in men and in institutions and ideas—of the Church in Ireland.

HENRY II AND THE IRISH CHURCH

Henry II hurried from Ireland in April 1172 to meet the papal legates about the death of Thomas Becket. Ireland was not again to loom so large in the governance of the Angevin empire as to demand the King's presence there. Nothing transpired politically of sufficient

[1] Giraldus: 'Itaque omnia divina, ad instar sacrosanctae ecclesiae iuxta quod anglicana observat ecclesia, in omnibus partibus ecclesiae amodo tractentur' *Exp. hib.* 1. 35. 283. Later he says that Henry asked successfully of Alexander III that 'Hibernico populo tam dominandi, quam ipsum, in fidei rudimentis incultissimum, ecclesiasticis normis et disciplinis iuxta Anglicanae ecclesiae mores informandi' *ibid.* 2. 5. 315 and similarly *De prin. instruct.* 2. 19. 195. Diceto: 'Et ut in singulis observatio similis regnum colligaret utrumque, passim omnes [i.e. the Irish prelates] unanimi voluntate communi assensu, pari desiderio, regis imperio se subiciunt' *Ymagines hist.* 1. 351.

importance to promote again that country to a major position in the order of the King's priorities. He was not unmindful of it, however, and the chroniclers in England continued to record a succession of events of Anglo-Irish relations for the rest of the reign. Some of these had ecclesiastical relevance.

The first of them, in order of time and possibly also of importance, concerned relations with the papacy about Ireland. After the death of Richard de Clare (Strongbow) in 1176, the King decided to make of Ireland an appanage for his youngest son John.[1] He also decided that with the change of lord should go an uplifting of the status of the lordship. It should become a kingdom and the *dominus Hiberniae* should be *rex Hiberniae*. Quite properly, Henry considered that papal consent was necessary for this promotion.[2] Alexander III, however, was not apparently in favour of this scheme nor was his successor Lucius III who, Howden says, had resisted the idea with vigour. The next pope proved more accommodating. Immediately on hearing of the election of Urban III, Henry II despatched an urgent embassy to ask of him the many things which Lucius III had refused. Among these petitions was one that Henry should be allowed to have a son consecrated king of Ireland. Pope Lucius signified his assent by sending a crown.[3] Shortly after the Christmas of 1186 the legate Cardinal Octavian arrived in England, empowered to perform the ceremony which was to be held in Ireland. The archbishop of Dublin was at Dover to meet him.

The scheme for an Irish monarchy petered out, however. Neither the King nor the archbishop of Canterbury (the *legatus natus*) was really very keen to have *legati* despatched *a latere*. When the Cardinal

---

[1] Roger of Howden, *Chron. RS* 2.100.
[2] *Gesta Regis Henrici secundi Benedicti Abbatis RS* 1. 161. Lady Stenton has shown that this work is in fact the first draft of Howden's Chronicle, 'Roger of Howden and "Benedict"' *EHR* 68 (1953) 574–82.
[3] Howden does say, *Chron.* 2. 133, that Henry made John king of Ireland 'concessione et confirmatione Alexandri summi pontificis' though he had not said this in noting the appointment in *Gesta* 1. 162. But this seems inconsistent with his narrative *s.a.* 1185: 'Henricus rex Angliae misit nuncios suos ad Urbanum papam, et multa ab eo impetravit, quibus papa Lucius fortiter resistebat; quorum unum hoc fuit, quod ab eo impetravit, quod unus quem vellet, de filiis suis coronaretur de regno Hyberniae; et hoc confirmavit ei dominus papa bulla sua, et in argumentum voluntatis et confirmationis suae misit ei coronam de penna pavonis auro contextam' *Chron.* 2. 306–7; substantially the same version, *Gesta* 1. 339.

showed signs that he intended a general embassy of some significance and comported himself as a man of no little authority, Henry II allowed Archbishop Baldwin to persuade him that it was in the best interests of the country to be rid of this legate. Cardinal Octavian was shepherded out of England, ostensibly to help the King to negotiate with Philip Augustus in Normandy.[1] No more was to be heard about the kingship of Ireland.

The negotiation about it has significance, however. When placed in its due chronological sequence it helps to demonstrate the continuity of papal support for the new régime in Ireland after Alexander III's initial approval of it. In 1177 Alexander III had sent his legate Vivian to Ireland. In a council at Dublin the Legate formally confirmed the papal authorization of Henry's lordship and threatened anathema on those who should dare to defy it.[2] In 1182 Lucius III had confirmed Henry's appointment of an Englishman for the vacant see of Dublin and had even, apparently, made him temporarily a cardinal.[3] And now in 1186 Urban III was willing to sanction a kingship for Ireland to be conferred on a son of Henry's. The papacy, having approved the establishment of English rule over Ireland, was consistent in underwriting its maintenance.

The second issue in the field of Irish ecclesiastical affairs in which Henry II showed some interest concerned the composition of the episcopate. It was in 1175 that a king of England was for the first time involved in the appointment of a bishop to an Irish see. Henry II had been receiving the submission of Rory O'Connor, king of Connacht and nominal high king of Ireland at a council at Windsor. The see of Waterford being then vacant, there came to him a certain Master Augustine, an Irishman to whom Henry 'gave and granted' the bishopric. The bishop-elect was then sent in the company of the archbishop of Dublin, Laurence O'Toole, to Cashel, there to be

---

[1] The fuller of the two versions is *Gesta* 2. 3–4; *Chron.* 2. 317 omits any reference to the view of Archbishop Baldwin and his suffragans, as also to the behaviour and intentions of the legate.

[2] Giraldus Cambrensis: 'Interea Vivianus legationis vice per Hiberniam fungens, convocato Dubliniae episcoporum synodo, ius Anglorum regis in Hiberniam, et summi pontificis confirmationem, viva voce publice protestatur; tam clero quam populo, sub anathematis interminatione districte praecipiens et iniungens, ne ab eius aliquatenus fidelitate, ausu temerario, resilire praesumant' *Exp. hib.* 2. 19. 345–6.

[3] The appointment of John Cumin is discussed below, pp. 45 ff.

canonically examined and consecrated by his metropolitan.[1] Roger of Howden's narrative does not say whether or not, as seems likely, Augustine was the choice of the Waterford electors, sent to England for royal assent. There is significance in the rôle of Archbishop Laurence, now the outstanding figure of the Irish hierarchy, in the making of this bishop. His participation was consent to this exercise of the royal prerogative in the English usage. It shows something of what was demanded in the way of practical cooperation with the King in consequence of the ecclesiastical submission to him and the council of Cashel's resolve to organize the Church in Ireland according to the practices of the Church in England.

That the King sent Augustine to his metropolitan, the archbishop of Cashel, for consecration, is also of significance. At the origins of the diocese of Waterford lay a connexion with Canterbury. Its first bishop had been among those from Ireland who in swearing obedience to Canterbury had acknowledged its primacy. If there was in fact any element of ambition on Canterbury's part to reassert its Irish primacy, this was surely a promising occasion to do so. But no advantage was taken of the precedent and of the opportunity. If it is true that Archbishop Laurence was worried by the danger of 'the restoration of the metropolitan jurisdiction of Canterbury'[2] (though there is no evidence at all of his anxiety on this score), his fears were surely allayed by Henry's decision to observe correct canonical procedure after he had given his assent to Augustine.

The appointment of Augustine was the first step in the anglicization of the episcopate in Ireland. As yet, however, it did not go beyond the adoption of the English electoral procedure. The next step, the first appointment of a foreigner to an Irish see, came *c*. 1178, with the promotion of Reginald to the see of Connor. It does not seem, however, that Henry II was in any way involved in the selection of this man. Conclusive evidence is lacking, but it seems all but

---

[1] Howden: 'In eodem vero concilio dominus rex Angliae dedit (et concessit) magistro Augustino Hiberniensi episcopatum Waterfordiae, qui tunc vacabat, et misit eum in Hiberniam cum Laurentio Duvelinensi archiepiscopo, ad Donatum Cassellensem archiepiscopum ad consecrandum' *Gesta* I. 103-4, *Chron.* 2. 85 (the words in parentheses were omitted in *Chron.*). The significance of the event was not lost on English observers: one of the two manuscripts of the *Gesta* has rubricated this passage: 'Primus episcopus constitutus in Hibernia per regem Angliae' *Gesta* 103. 9.

[2] J. F. O'Doherty, 'St. Laurence O'Toole and the Anglo-Norman Invasion' 142.

certain that this appointment was due to John de Courcy whose invasion of Ulster began early in 1177 and who was securely established in the area of this diocese not many months later.[1]

Henry II was not, however, wholly content to leave the composition of all the Irish episcopate to initiatives originating in Ireland, whether Irish or Anglo-French.

The other occasion on which he was concerned with an Irish episcopal appointment was altogether more important than the Waterford choice. The election of John Cumin to Dublin in 1181 was a major event in the history of the Irish episcopate on a double count. For this was the first time that an English king was both to use the full accepted electoral procedures of English custom and to cause an Englishman to be appointed to an Irish see.

Laurence O'Toole died in November 1180. Speedily there arrived in Ireland a royal clerk and (significant detail of papal support) a clerk of the papal legate then in England, to take the not unsubstantial possessions of the diocese of Dublin into the King's hand.[2] At about the same time there arrived at the royal court 'some clergy of the metropolitan church of Dublin who had come to the King in England in order to obtain a pastor'. It was at Evesham on 6 September 1181 that Henry 'granted the archbishopric of Dublin to his clerk and member of his household, as was agreed by the bishops and clergy of England and the clergy who had come from the metropolitan church of Dublin'.[3]

The taking over of the temporalities of the see during the vacancy

---

[1] Cf. *AU s.a.* 1177; Giraldus Cambrensis, *Exp. hib.* 2. 17. 338–44; G. H. Orpen, *Ireland under the Normans* 2. 5–23; E. Curtis, *Medieval Ireland* 77–9.

[2] Howden: 'Misit etiam rex Angliae Gaufridum de Aeya clericum suum et clericum Alexii legati, in Hiberniam ad saysiendum archiepiscopatum Duvelinae in manu sua' *Gesta* 1. 270; *Chron.* 2. 253. For the lands of the see at the time, J. Otway-Ruthven, 'The Medieval Church Lands of County Dublin' *Gwynn Studies* 54–73 at 58–60.

[3] Howden: (at Evesham, 6 September 1181): '(rex) concessit Johanni Cumin, clerico et familiari suo, archiepiscopatum Duvelinae ad electionem episcoporum et clericatus Angliae, et quorundam clericorum metropolitanae ecclesiae Duvelinae, qui in Angliam venerant ad praefatum regem pro pastore habendo' *Gesta* 1. 280–1. *Chron.* omits reference to any churchmen participating and states baldly that the King 'gave' the archbishopric to John, 2. 263. Giraldus Cambrensis gave a somewhat differently emphasized account: 'Successit eidem Johannes, cognomine Ciminum, vir anglicus natione, et in Anglia apud Evesham a clero Dublinensi, regia procurante industria, consone satis et concorditer electus' *Exp. hib.* 2. 24. 358.

and this method of episcopal appointment was precisely the application to Ireland of the standard English practice. This form was set out clearly enough in clause 12 of the Constitutions of Clarendon:

When an archbishopric is vacant or a bishopric, or an abbey, or a priory of the demesne of the king, it must remain in his hand; and he shall receive all the revenues and incomes from it, as if they were revenues and incomes of the demesne. And when it comes to providing for the church, the lord king shall summon the chief persons of the Church and the election shall be held in the king's chapel with the assent of the king and with the counsel of the persons of the realm whom he shall have called upon to do this. And there the elect shall do homage and fealty to the king as to his liege lord for his life and his limbs and his earthly honour, saving his order, before he is consecrated.[1]

Here then in Ireland was in operation the full customary English procedure at episcopal vacancies: taking of the *temporalia* into the king's custody (this had not happened at Waterford in 1175), appointment *coram rege* or at least with royal assent to the elect, taking of fealty before canonical examination and consecration.

The application to Ireland of the English custom in this respect, with papal approval, was, from 1181 onwards, a central feature of the Irish ecclesiastical policies of the kings of England. That Pope Lucius III himself consecrated him archbishop (21 March 1182)[2] shows that the papacy was not hostile to this procedure.

Relations with the papacy and involvement in episcopal appointments are two of the main ways in which Henry II's attitude to the Irish Church can be studied. There is a third. The outstanding churchman and the natural leader of the Irish hierarchy after the council of Cashel was Laurence O'Toole, archbishop of Dublin from 1162 to 1180 and papal legate in Ireland (1179–80), who was to be canonized by Pope Honorius III in 1225.[3] Some comment on this

[1] Latin text, W. Stubbs, *Select Charters* (9th ed. 1913) 166; English translation, S. Z. Ehler and J. B. Morrall, *Church and State through the Centuries* (1954) 59–60.
[2] Both Howden and Giraldus Cambrensis state that Cumin was ordained priest (13 March 1181) and consecrated bishop (21 March) by Lucius III, *Gesta* 1. 287, *Chron.* 2. 267; *Exp. hib.* 2. 24. 358. The *Gesta* and Giraldus both say that he was also made cardinal, but the *Chron.* does not. Presumably Howden has here corrected an original error which Giraldus had copied. There is no other evidence that Cumin was made cardinal nor that he was ever described as such.
[3] The chief source for the life of St Laurence is the *Vita* written soon after the canoni-

man and his relationship with Henry II is obviously called for.

There is nothing new about associating the name of Laurence of Dublin with Malachy of Armagh. The comparison was suggested by one of the witnesses in the canonization process. There are superficial resemblances which occur readily to anyone who considers the sources of the lives of each. Whilst neither apparently found a biographer in Ireland, each found one in France (where both men died) and their canonization causes seemed to have owed more to French initiatives than to Irish ones. The comparison will, however, bear matters of more weight. These were the outstanding two of the sort of churchman who typified the spirituality of the twelfth century Irish reform movement. Both men were reformers who were first and foremost products of native Irish monasticism with its especial love of poverty and austerity, who were yet much influenced by monasticism as practised abroad. Both became bishops with reluctance and continued to live the life of a religious as far as episcopal duties permitted. But perhaps the essential point about linking these two men lies in the reflexion that a reform movement which could produce spiritual leaders of such calibre, deserved better of the papacy than it was to get.

Laurence has not been as well served by his biographer as has Malachy. The canon of Eu, like Bernard, had collected information from Ireland, but he had not himself known Laurence nor was he as interested as Bernard in setting his subject in the context of his own society. *The Life and Miracles of St Laurence* is unfortunately mostly about miracles. Hard facts about the saint's life are sparse and often

zation by a canon of the Augustinian house of Eu, Normandy, who was possibly Jean Halgrinus of Abbeville, later archbishop of Besançon. It has been edited by C. Plummer, 'Vie et miracles de S. Laurent, archevêque de Dublin' *Anal. Boll.* 33 (1914) 121–86. A. Legris, *Saint Laurent O'Toole, archevêque de Dublin* (1128–1180) (1914) is a good biography, written close to the sources and is better informed on the chronology of Laurence's life than Plummer. The political activities of the Archbishop have been examined by J. F. O'Doherty, *Laurentius von Dublin und das irische Normannentum* (1933) and in the articles listed below, p. 238. This work should be treated with caution as it often makes too much of too little source material, as the author himself seems to admit, 'St Laurence O'Toole and the Anglo-Norman Invasion' *IER* 51 (1938) 142. St Laurence as reform leader is the theme of A. Gwynn, 'St. Laurence O'Toole as legate in Ireland', *Mél. P. Peeters Anal. Boll.* 68 (1950) 223–40. Cf. also, M. V. Ronan, 'St. Laurentius, archbishop of Dublin: original testimonies for canonization' *IER* 27 (1926) 347 ff.; 28 (1926) 247 ff.; 467 ff.

inaccurate and impressions of his personality no more than purely conventional. Nor is there much to be gleaned from other sources. His biography can be no more than a glimpse. Of a family of minor kings whose territory included the great monastery of St Kevin at Glendalough, Laurence became abbot there *c.* 1152, refused its see in 1157 and was appointed to Dublin in 1162. That he was well known to Henry II is quite clear. He played an important rôle in negotiations between the king and the high king, Rory O'Connor.[1] Little is known in detail, however, about this relationship which if fully documented would tell so much about the problems and attitudes of politicians and churchmen in the first years after the ecclesiastical submission. But it is clear that though there was some cooperation on the ecclesiastical and political level between the King and the Archbishop, Laurence was to incur Henry's enmity.

On two occasions when writing about the Archbishop, Giraldus Cambrensis mentioned the common report that Laurence was a man of excessive partiality for his own people.[2] Clearly this was another way of saying that many held the Archbishop to be politically unreliable. Certainly Henry II held him suspect on some such score. The King's animosity showed itself after the third Lateran council. Like the English bishops attending it, the Irish bishops had been compelled to swear an oath that they would not attempt anything prejudicial to the King, before they were allowed to go to Rome.[3] Henry alleged that the Archbishop had violated this oath in seeking privileges of the pope, which were injurious to him. It is not absolutely clear which privileges Henry had in mind. But Laurence had secured two privileges from Alexander III in 1179 which were confirmations of the rights and privileges of his own province and

[1] On at least two occasions: 1175, at Windsor in negotiating the *concordia* between the two kings, *Gesta* I. 102, *Chron.* 2. 83, and in Normandy in 1180, *Gesta* I. 270, *Chron.* 2. 253; Plummer, *Vita S. Laur.* 152.
[2] The first occasion is an entry for the year 1171 when Dublin was besieged by an Irish army said to have been collected by Archbishop Laurence who was moved 'zelo suae gentis, ut ferebatur' *Exp. hib.* I. 22. 265. The second is in the notice of his death in 1180: 'Interea Laurencius Dublinensis archiepiscopus, vir bonus et iustus, ob privilegia in Lateranensi concilio, cui interat, contra regiae dignitatis honorem, zelo suae gentis, ut ferebatur, impetrata, Anglorum regi suspectus, et ob hoc tam in Anglicanis quam transmarinis Galliae partibus diu detentus ...' *ibid.* 2. 24. 357.
[3] *Gesta* I. 221, *Chron.* 2. 171.

diocese of Dublin and of Glendalough.[1] If these were the documents objected to, Henry's complaint was presumably against the implicit suggestion that the pope had any power to confirm the temporalities of dioceses subject to a king of England. Such matters, in English custom, were for the king alone and it was therefore an injury to royal right for Laurence thus to transgress the distinction of the spheres of the spiritual and temporal powers as it was understood in England.

It was perhaps this quarrel, which kept Laurence on the Continent in exile, which strengthened the King's resolve to promote an Englishman as the next archbishop of Dublin.

Certainly he chose a man with a long record of loyal royal service. There could hardly be a more striking contrast between the background of the two successive archbishops of Dublin, Laurence O'Toole and John Cumin. Each in some degree personifies an episcopal type representative of his own society: the one a monk of the stony remoteness of Glendalough, who left the cloister for the active life with regret; the other who had pursued a successful career in the world, to whom the devotion of all his attention to religion came quite late.

For nearly twenty years before he was made archbishop, John Cumin had held senior positions in royal service.[2] It had taken him into a variety of governmental occupations, in the chancery and exchequer and on the bench. As a diplomat, it had taken him to a variety of places: to the courts of pope and emperor and of other rulers. Through it, he had suffered excommunication by the pope and incurred the hostility of Becket's supporters. If consistent loyalty to the king and successful application to his business was a criterion for promotion to the episcopate, John Cumin was exceptionally qualified.

[1] The Dublin privilege is dated 20 April 1179: text, *Pont. hib.* I. 9, that for Glenda-lough is 13 May 1179, *ibid.* 10.

[2] There is a good summary account of Cumin's career in *DNB s.v.* Comyn, John, by T. F. Tout (1887). It has been superseded as far as his origins and early career is concerned by J. A. Robinson, *Somerset Historical Essays* (1921): 'Early Somerset Archdeacons, Appendix C. The early career of John Cumin, archbishop of Dublin' 90-9, expanded in certain respects particularly about his important provincial council of 1186, by A. Gwynn, 'Archbishop John Cumin' *Rep. novum* I (1956) 285-310, and also concerning his foundation of St Patrick's, by G. J. Hand, 'The rivalry of the cathedral chapters in medieval Dublin' *RSAIJn* 92 (1962) 193-206 at 194-7.

The bureaucrat–bishop owing his promotion to royal favour, and whose appointment was at least in part political, cuts an unsympathetic figure, especially when contrasted with a monk–bishop of outstanding sanctity. But for all that, and despite absenteeism, avoidable or otherwise,[1] John Cumin did not make a bad archbishop. Indeed he has claims to be accounted a significant figure in the reform movement. He was reformer of his own diocese. The canons of his Dublin council of 1186 stand in the tradition of Cashel and earlier reforming legislation in ordering that the sacraments be administered in the forms observed generally in the universal Church, that benefices be out of lay control, that respect for Christian marriage be strengthened, that tithe be duly paid.[2] He followed his predecessor's example in making clerical incontinence a special target of attack.[3] He established the collegiate church of St Patrick in Dublin to combat the backwardness of learning in Ireland.[4] He was prepared to give battle to the justiciar and resist King John when in his view the liberties of his Church were threatened.[5] He played his part in promoting the canonization of his predecessor.[6]

Of more dubious value for reform purposes but nevertheless of great significance, was Lucius III's grant to the archbishops of Dublin that they should be for the future exempt from the jurisdiction of any other prelate.[7] Autonomy for Dublin was to be the prologue to its primatial claims.

Reviewing Henry II's interest in Irish ecclesiastical issues, it cannot be said that he pursued any very vigorous ecclesiastical policy. But he was not indifferent to what happened in Ireland; the political logic which had taken him to the country kept him concerned with

---

[1] It is possible that Cumin was only intermittently in Ireland before 1190, *DNB*, Comyn, 912; Hand, *art. cit.* 195. For his periods of exile, see below p. 69.

[2] The text of these canons is given by A. Gwynn, 'Provincial and diocesan decrees of the diocese of Dublin during the Anglo-Norman period' *Arch. hib.* 11 (1944) 39–44 and he has discussed them, 'Archbishop John Cumin' 303–6.

[3] Giraldus Cambrensis was present at the council and has described it and has given the text of the sermon he delivered at it, *De rebus a se gestis* 13–15 *Opera* 3. 65–72. The allusion to the Archbishop's attack on clerical incontinence after the issue had been raised against the foreign clergy by the Irish abbot of Baltinglass is p. 66. For St Laurence's severity and zeal in this matter, Plummer, *Vita S. Laur.* 146.

[4] Hand, 'The rivalry of the cathedral chapters in medieval Dublin' 196.

[5] See below, p. 69.

[6] Cf. Legris, *Saint Laurent O'Toole* 109–10.   [7] See below, pp. 109–10.

numerous Irish issues throughout his reign. Much that was happening in the country at this time was provisional and transitory. At least Henry's attitude to the Irish Church constituted a policy and not a mere bundle of expedients. It was a simple policy and it had been stated at the council of Cashel. The Irish Church was to conduct its affairs according to the organizational norms of the Church in England. A corollary had been asserted with the appointment of Cumin to Dublin. Where judged necessary, the ecclesiastical official would be English. If these principles had not as yet been put into practice on any wide scale they had certainly been implemented in the critically important diocese of Dublin. They took root and flourished. Their further implementation, always with papal approval, continued apace after the death of Henry II.

Chapter 3

THE NEW ORDER CONSOLIDATED

Distribution maps of motes and bailies and of castles show how quickly and penetratively the invaders had swarmed over the country by the beginning of the reign of John.[1] Similar maps of chartered towns and of religious houses founded by the conquerors would indicate to some degree the areas where settlement was most secure. 'By the end of the twelfth century', it has very justly been concluded, 'the whole of Leinster, the ancient kingdom of Meath including not only Meath and Westmeath but also south Longford and the north west part of the modern co. Offaly, Ulster east of the Bann and a great part of Munster, were effectively dominated by the new power.'[2]

In ecclesiastical terms, this was domination of all the provinces of Dublin (Leinster) and almost all of Cashel (Munster), of the Armagh (Ulster) dioceses of Meath, Down and Connor, with such dioceses as Dromore, Ardagh and Clonmacnois overshadowed by the Anglo-French (Map 3). The Shannon at this time still remained a major frontier so that the province of Tuam (Connacht) was as yet outside the occupied area, though the first serious attack on it had been as early as 1177.

This dominance was not however very quickly manifested in an anglicized episcopate. At the end of John's reign in 1216 there were still after very nearly half a century of Anglo-French expansion only

---

[1] Cf. G. H. Orpen, 'Motes and Norman Castles in Ireland' *EHR* 22 (1907) 228–54, 440–67 and *Normans* 2 (1911) 343 f. (with map). The most instructive administrative record in this context is 'The Irish Pipe Roll of 14 John 1211–12' ed. O. Davies and D. B. Quinn, *Ulster Journal of Archaeology* 4 (suppl. vol. 1941).

[2] J. Otway-Ruthven, 'The Character of Norman Settlement in Ireland' *Historical Studies* 5 (1965) 75–84 at 75, a more satisfactory summary than Orpen's *Normans* 2. 323–4. Cf. also A. G. Richey, *A short history of the Irish people* 173–4.

Map 3. The diocesan structure in the thirteenth century.

nine of the thirty-six sees held by foreign bishops. They were:[1]

ARMAGH

Connor	Reginald (*c.* 1178–1225/6)
Meath	Simon Rochfort (1192–1224)
Down	Ralph, O.Cist. (*c.* 1202–?24)

DUBLIN

Dublin	Henry of London (1213—28)
Leighlin	Herlewin, O.Cist. (*a.* 1202–17)
Ossory	Hugo Rufus, O.S.A. (*c.* 1202–18)

CASHEL

Emly	Henry, O.Cist. (1212–27)
Limerick	Edmund (1215–23)
Waterford	Robert (1210–23)

The general lack of precise information about the dates of these episcopates is indicative of how very little information there is either about these men themselves or about how they became bishops. What seems virtually certain is that with the exception of Dublin and possibly of Waterford, John had very little to do with any of these creations. They were due to local initiatives. Connor and Down were in the Ulster lordship of John de Courcy; Meath in the de Lacy lordship; Ossory and Leighlin in the Leinster liberty whose heiress, Strongbow's daughter, had married William Marshal in 1189. Trim, Kilkenny and Downpatrick, the seats of the bishops of Meath, Ossory and Down, were palatinate chief towns. It is no coincidence that anglicization came earliest in the best organized of the lordships. This is what is expected, just as it would be expected that the main voices in the making of these bishops would be local ones: newly installed canons of foreign race on the formal level of election and, not less insistent for being extra-juridical, the influence of the local magnate. Local initiatives in the making of bishops in the Anglo-French area of Ireland were strong in the beginning and were to continue to be so.

The prominence of religious among these first bishops is also perhaps not very surprising. The new rulers were liberal in establishing new houses, and colonies of imported monks and canons were

[1] Details from *Hbk Brit. Chron.*

obvious reservoirs of episcopal talent.[1] Hugo Rufus was of the Augustinian house founded at William Marshal's suggestion by the lord of Kells (co. Kilkenny), Geoffrey Fitzrobert. This was apparently the first house of English canons in Ireland (1183), an offshoot of Bodmin, Hugh being one of the four canons brought to Ireland to found it.[2] Little is known about the Cistercians who became bishops in this period. Abington in the diocese of Emly was a foundation (1205) of Theobald Walter and was colonized from Furness. William Marshal founded a Cistercian monastery which after two changes of site settled at Graiguenamanagh (1202–7) not far from Kilkenny, just inside the Leighlin diocese. It was founded from Stanley in Wiltshire. Dunbrody in the neighbouring diocese of Ferns founded *c.* 1182 from St Mary's, Dublin is another possible source of Cistercian bishops in the Dublin province. There were three Cistercian monasteries in the Down diocese.[3] Bishop Ralph was a former abbot of Melrose.[4] As the colonists consolidated and cathedral chapters developed a sense of self-identity the number of monk–bishops was to decrease.

All the indications, then, are that it was not John or his justiciars (in England or Ireland) who were primarily responsible for the first phase in the anglicization of the personnel of the episcopate in Ireland. This is not to say, however, that the royal government was indifferent to the making of bishops there. The appointment of Henry of London to Dublin, though information is lacking, must surely have been, like John Cumin's, a royal one.[5] On at least six other occasions John is known to have been interested in an Irish episcopal appointment. Significantly, in only one of them was he successful. But then his candidate would almost certainly have secured Waterford even without the King's help. For, as cousin of the justiciar, he had what was in the circumstances much more telling backing.[6]

1 For details of the newly established houses cf. A. Gwynn and N. Hadcock *Medieval Religious Houses, Ireland.*
2 Cf. Dugdale, *Monasticon Anglicanum* 6. 2. 1142 (*Ex regist. Coenobii S. Mariae de Kenlis*).
3 Comber, Grey Abbey, Inch.
4 Cf. J. Lynch, *De praesulibus Hiberniae* ed. J. F. O'Doherty 1 (1944) 224.
5 There is a short summary of Archbishop Henry's career in *DNB s.n.* Loundres, Henry de, by J. T. Gilbert.
6 *Rotuli Litterarum Patentium, 1201–1216* ed. T. D. Hardy (Record Comm. 1835) 47a.

In all five of the other cases, John was promoting the candidature of an Englishman to a see still in Irish hands. Two of those in question, Armagh (1201) and Cashel (1206), as metropolitan sees, were obviously of unusual importance. Two others, Limerick (1207) and Cork (1214), had long been of personal interest to John for they were of his domain when he was lord of Ireland and he had granted charters to these towns. In the last see, Killaloe (1216), the invaders had made progress into Clare and the attempt to appoint an Englishman reflects this.[1]

In the event only Limerick of these five sees was to become in any real sense a safe English seat in the thirteenth century. Why John's nominee, whom he had earlier promoted to the rectorship of his borough of Dungarvan, was not appointed is not known, nor is anything known about the circumstances of the successful candidate.[2] He was to prove to be the first of an uninterrupted succession of English or Anglo-Irish bishops.[3]

John's failure elsewhere does not surprise, though the prospects of his success were not without hope. It is not unlikely that he was supporting candidates at the instance of his justiciar in Ireland and was therefore underwriting with his authority what his Irish government thought it possible to achieve.

The royal candidate for Cashel and Killaloe was the same man. He was the Cistercian Ailbe O Maelmuidhe, bishop of Ferns since *c.* 1186.[4] That he had royal backing shows beyond question that the King was not inflexible about demanding Anglo-Frenchmen as bishops if he was satisfied about the loyalty of an Irishman. But the chapter of Cashel (apparently fortified by the Cashel suffragans

---

[1] The candidate, Robert Travers, was the nephew of the justiciar, Geoffrey Marsh. The story of his intrusion and eventual ejection is told by Gleeson in Gleeson and Gwynn, *Diocese of Killaloe* 225–35.

[2] The King's assumption that the bishopric was within his giving comes out clearly in his letter to the justiciar: 'Sciatis quod concessimus Magistro Gaufrido parsone ecclesie de Dungaruan episcopatum Lymeric. qui vacatum et volumus et assentimus ut preficiatur episcopali sedi Limeric. Et ideo vobis mandamus quod episcopatum illum ei habere faciatis et moneatis et inducatis clerum illius episcopatus quod ipsum eligant et recipiant in episcopum'. *Rotuli Litterarum Clausarum, 1204–27* ed. T. D. Hardy (Record Comm. 1835) 97.

[3] *Hbk Brit. Chron.* 330–1; G. J. Hand, 'The Medieval Chapter of St. Mary's Cathedral, Limerick' *Gwynn Studies* 74–89.

[4] His *curriculum vitae* may be read in *Pont. hib.* I. 139.

as co-electors)[1] had other ideas which prevailed. There was no divided election and the intervention did not lead to strife.

This was not the case in Killaloe. Bishop Conchobhair died in 1216 and was replaced as candidate by Robert Travers, a kinsman of the justiciar, Geoffrey Marsh. There was a protracted struggle over this see. Robert was consecrated but was deposed by Pope Honorius III in 1221 as 'intrusus per potentiam laicalem'. His replacement and all the bishops of Killaloe thereafter were native Irishmen, though there was a strong and continuous tradition of cooperation with the Crown.

The *cause célèbre* of John's interventions in Irish episcopal appointments, however, concerned Armagh. Its significance is that it was the first major clash of the two peoples in an ecclesiastical matter of primary importance: native Irish and Anglo-French met in head-on conflict in a struggle to decide who should be archbishop of Armagh and primate of Ireland. No doubt there had been earlier incidents and no doubt some of them were important. But none had been important enough, apparently, to leave its mark on the files of both the royal and papal chanceries. As it occasioned one of Innocent III's more notable clarifications of the law of episcopal elections it found a place in the *Corpus Iuris Canonici* and its fame was thus perpetuated in the law schools of Christendom.[2]

There were really two issues involved in the succession to Archbishop Tomaltach O Conchobair who had died in 1201. The first was whether the election should be conducted according to the forms of the English Church with the king's rights of custody of temporalities during vacancy, granting of permission to proceed to an election and of the giving of assent to an elect. This latter, often enough at this period, as has been seen in examining Henry II's interest in Irish episcopal appointments, fell only a little short of direct nomination.

[1] There was an important change in the method of election to Cashel in the thirteenth century. Originally election was by the suffragans of the province. With the establishment of a cathedral chapter at Cashel election was apparently shared by it and the suffragans. It was this practice which Innocent III confirmed in 1210, *Pont. hib.* 1. 68 at p. 142. The participation of the suffragans became a subject of controversy after the death of Archbishop David O'Kelly in 1253. Innocent IV had the claims of both parties thoroughly investigated by judges-delegate in Ireland. The suffragans, however, admitted that by that time the chapter was in possession of the right to elect and withdrew their claim. The pope made a definitive pronouncement in favour of the chapter *Pont. hib.* 2. 388 (17 Aug. 1254).

[2] *Corpus Iuris Canonici. Decretales* 1. 6. 28.

The second was whether or not the new archbishop should be of the native or of the foreign race. The two issues were of course very closely related. But it was not inevitable that the English procedure would produce an English candidate, as John's sponsorship of Bishop Ailbe of Ferns for the archiepiscopal see of Cashel shows.

The full detail of this highly significant case is best recounted elsewhere.[1] The intervention of the justiciar and of the king, the flaring of racial antipathy, prevented exact compliance with canonical forms of election. Each side in the dispute producing its own candidate, the controversy inevitably found its way to the papal curia. What is important to notice here is what is revealed of the attitudes of both King John and Pope Innocent III to a dispute which highlighted the antagonism of the nations and showed in microcosm many of the forces in play in the ecclesiastical politics of these early days of the colony.

John was obviously anxious to have a candidate of his own choosing. His first choice was one of his clerks, with experience in royal service and of high potential for further service in the government of Ireland. He was prepared to buy off Eugenius, the Irish choice of the majority of the electors and when this failed, to contest his claim at the curia and do what he could to prevent his taking *de facto* possession of the see. Though precise details are wanting, it is clear that there were some Armagh temporalities taken into the King's hand.

When the papal legate Cardinal John of Salerno arrived in Ireland, Eugenius had already been consecrated archbishop and King John was opposing him vigorously. The Legate was a little out of his depth amid the legal and political complexities enshrouding the issue and asked for Innocent's advice. The Pope gave a masterly delineation of the case for and against the quashing of the election, leaned heavily towards letting it stand, but left the final decision to the Legate. If the Legate were to decide against Eugenius, a candidate who was of neither race was recommended. The Legate did not in fact have to make a decision for Eugenius went to Rome in person. Innocent confirmed him as archbishop of Armagh.

This decision seems to have been quickly accepted by the English in

---

1 Appendix 2 below, where full references will be found.

the province itself. King John needed more time and a cash transaction before he withdrew his objection and restored the temporalities. There seems every reason to suspect that throughout John was more interested in exploiting this vacancy financially than anything else.

Here then racial animosity had divided men. But it had not driven them to extremes. It had proved possible to achieve a *modus vivendi* between the two peoples. There was no reason to deduce that the peaceful coexistence of both in the Church was impossible.

There was one other major sector of ecclesiastical organization where the papal and royal powers touched the episcopate of Ireland. This was in a very sensitive area, that of diocesan boundaries. It will be recalled that the establishment in Ireland of a territorial diocesan structure was still, in the reign of John, of relatively recent date. Cardinal Paparo and the architects of the new system at the council of Kells had envisaged emendations to be made in the future, particularly in the absorption of smaller dioceses into larger ones. It may be readily believed that the putting of these measures into practice might well prove controversial and be attended by strenuous and tortuous legal and diplomatic manoeuvrings of various degrees of success. Monastic communities, entrenched ecclesiastical dynasties, kinglings jealous of their power, were not always to be easily persuaded to accept a reduction of ecclesiastical status. When, however, to the ordinary human difficulties of the problem there was added the intervention of the invader, there were all the makings of some obdurate problems. Sometimes, however, there was the prospect of a relatively easy settlement of them because the invader was in a position of strength to impose one.

Four examples of diocesan reconstruction present themselves for scrutiny in any examination of the fortunes of the Irish episcopate in this period: a boundary dispute between Armagh and Clogher; the establishment of Meath; the completed union of Glendalough and Dublin; the unsuccessful attempt to unite Waterford and Lismore.

The origins of the first of these cases preceded even the council of Kells and the problem remaining unsolved at that time, continued to vex successive episcopal generations long after the Invasion.[1] It

[1] Cf. H. J. Lawlor, 'The Genesis of the Diocese of Clogher' *Louth Archaeological Society Journal* 4 (1917) 129–59; A. Gwynn, 'Armagh and Louth in the twelfth and thirteenth centuries' *Seanchas Ardmhacha* 1 (1954) 1–11 (1955) 17–37.

concerned the boundary of the Armagh diocese at the point where a part of the kingdom of Oirghialla (roughly the territory of the modern co. Louth) was allocated at Rathbreasail to the archiepiscopal see. From *c.* 1140, however, it was transferred to the diocese of Oirghialla (Louth). Having remained a part of that diocese for about half a century, its jurisdiction was once more resumed by Armagh. The circumstances of these changes remain very obscure. So also do those in which this transfer back to Armagh was being challenged by Bishop Donatus of Clogher at a date before 1227. Since his opponent was Archbishop Luke of Netterville, an Anglo-Frenchman, it is tempting to read the dispute as a racial one. But what significance, if any, racial antagonism played in the making of this challenge cannot be determined. If it did play a part, this did not prevent Donatus receiving the King's support for the new policy he adopted when he succeeded Luke at Armagh in 1227. Showing a sense of duty to his new see totally devoid of any nostalgic sentiment of loyalty to his former charge, he at once became as ardent a champion of the claims of Armagh as he had been of Clogher earlier. Taking advantage of the Clogher vacancy his promotion had occasioned, he secured Henry III's approval, 'so far as in him lay', for the union of Clogher to Armagh and petitioned Pope Gregory IX for approval.[1] This he did not get and the Primate was thwarted. So too was his successor who, likewise fortified with royal support, sought to bring about the union. The dioceses were not destined to be united. Nor were the bishops of Clogher ever to be successful in their intermittent attempts to recover Louth.[2]

Three of the great strongholds of the classical period of Irish monasticism—Kells, Clonard and Glendalough—which had become dioceses in the twelfth century reorganization were to lose their episcopal status through changes introduced by the Anglo-French.

In 1202 the see of Meath, apparently on the instruction of the papal legate Cardinal John of Salerno, was transferred from Clonard to the Newtown by Trim, chief town of the de Lacy lordship. Bishop Simon Rochfort instituted there an Augustinian priory with the cooperation of his metropolitan Archbishop Eugenius of

[1] *Calendar of Patent Rolls* 166 (10 October 1227).
[2] Gwynn, *art. cit.* 33–7; *Pont. hib.* 2. 70.

Armagh, who was of course a native Irishman.[1] The priory church was the Meath cathedral and the diocese did not have a chapter. In a second stage of the consolidation of his diocese, Bishop Simon, invoking a constitution of Cardinal John Paparo and the council of Kells that 'chorepiscopi' and bishops of very small dioceses should be replaced by rural deans on the death of the then occupants, divided his diocese into five such deaneries.[2] One of these was the former diocese of Kells, later to be one of the two archdeaconries into which the diocese of Meath was divided. If these changes aroused any hostility it was not vocal enough to make any impression on papal or royal or other records. It was clearly a peaceful operation brought about in one of the most settled areas of the colony.

The amalgamation of Glendalough and Dublin was altogether a lengthier affair. More than one Irish historian has considered that there were circumstances of doubtful morality about its achievement.[3] Its legality, however, cannot be doubted since the union was promulgated by Innocent III in February 1216[4] and confirmed later that year by Honorius III.[5]

In his decree of union, Innocent III referred to oral evidence that he had heard from many Irish prelates, in Rome in 1215 for the fourth Lateran council, concerning the intentions of Cardinal John Paparo for the future of Glendalough. On the death of the then occupant of the see the church of Glendalough and all pertaining thereto should fall to the metropolitan church of Dublin. This decision made, both Henry II and John had taken steps to do what it was appropriate for the secular power to do, to make it effective. There is evidence that Innocent III had been taking his information from the archbishop of Tuam and his suffragans from whom evidence concerning the papal Legate's decision and the royal support of it has survived. These prelates, like Simon Rochfort, spoke of the

---

1 This was the account given to Boniface IX in 1397 after Richard II had petitioned to have Meath made into a chapter of secular canons, *Calendar of papal letters* 5. 74–5.
2 *Concilia* I. 547 (1216).
3 Most emphatically by M. V. Ronan: 'In this intrigue, for a political purpose and for the aggrandisement of the see of Dublin, there was a deliberate suppression of truth and a suggestion of falsehood', 'The Union of the Dioceses of Glendaloch and Dublin in 1216' *RSAIJn.* 60 (1930) 56–62 at 62. P. J. Dunning has given an objective summary of the case, 'Irish Representatives and Irish Ecclesiastical Affairs at the Fourth Lateran Council' *Gwynn Studies* 90–113 at 101–2.
4 *Pont. hib.* I. 93.   5 *Ibid.* 103.

Legate's wish to suppress 'chorepiscopi' and said that Glendalough was now 'so deserted and desolate for almost forty years that from a church it has become a den of thieves and a pit of robbers, so that by reason of the deserted and naked wilderness there are more homicides committed in that valley than in any other part of Ireland'.[1]

The alleged grant of Henry II has not survived. John made two grants concerning Glendalough to Archbishop John Cumin: an abortive one of 1185, reiterated in 1192, and confirmed by Pope Celestine III, providing that the Archbishop might take the diocese into his hand and appoint a new bishop as his personal chaplain. This grant was confirmed *c.* 1199 by Matthew Ua h-Énne archbishop of Cashel in his capacity as papal legate. There was but one effective appointment to Glendalough within the terms of this grant, that of William Piro, 1192–1212. Innocent III's decision, then, was taken in the ensuing protracted vacancy. It was unchallenged and save for a brief reappearance of titular bishops of Glendalough in the late fifteenth century,[2] Glendalough was an archdeaconry of the diocese of Dublin throughout the rest of the middle ages.

The episcopal status of yet another of the great Irish monastic centres was under threat. For about half a century successive bishops of Waterford made a strong push to absorb the diocese of Lismore. Waterford, now a royal city, was a major Anglo-French stronghold and became of increasing political and economic importance as the thirteenth century advanced. Ecclesiastically, however, it was small and poor. That it sought union with Lismore is understandable enough and indeed the council of Rathbreasail had envisaged such a union. But the Anglo-French bishops of Waterford went about the business of uniting the dioceses with a degree of barbarism that makes a mockery of any claim that the foreigners came as reformers, at least as far as this part of Ireland was concerned. The violence of Waterford towards Lismore was the first sustained act of Anglo-French aggression in Ireland. It should be noticed, however, that it was not simply an issue of hostility to the native race. For the appointment of an Englishman to Lismore in 1219 was to do nothing to slacken the effort to suppress that diocese to the advantage of Waterford.

---

1 Text printed *ibid.* 172. *Cal. Abp Alen's Reg.* has summaries of most of the evidence.
2 *Hbk Brit. Chron.* 338.

It fell mostly to Innocent III to deal with the first phases of this episode. The sources are exclusively papal: two letters of Innocent III dated 5 November 1203, a third of 26 June 1212 and two of Honorius III's of 1219 which give details of the case heard by Innocent III at the time of the Lateran council of 1215 and his decision thereon.[1]

In 1202 Felix, bishop of Lismore resigned his see to Cardinal John of Salerno, the papal legate. The chapter of the diocese elected Malachy, Cistercian abbot of Midleton. The see at this time, however, was already occupied by Robert, bishop of Waterford, who was in fact merely continuing to hold what his predecessor had already seized. No information is available about this first seizure; even the name of the invading bishop is unknown. There is a suggestion in the evidence that the Legate had made a decision in Robert's favour and committed a joint diocese to him. However this may be, Malachy prepared to take his cause to Rome. But Robert had him abducted and cast fettered into prison and took a personal part in the beating administered to the unfortunate bishop-elect.[2] Somehow Malachy escaped and in due course was confirmed and consecrated by Innocent III. Robert of Waterford was excommunicated. Three Irish bishops were named by the Pope to publish this sentence and to secure possession of Lismore for Malachy. Malachy was in fact put in possession of his diocese, possibly because of the opportunity for so doing that occurred with Robert's death in 1204.

Conflict was renewed with the appointment as bishop of Waterford of David Breathnach, that cousin of the justiciar, Meyler Fitzhenry, who has been mentioned earlier in connexion with John's Irish episcopal promotions. He deprived Malachy of his see. Malachy again betook himself to Rome. Innocent III again appointed three judges-delegate in Ireland to take charge of the matter.

Bishop David defended himself before these judges on the grounds that Malachy was an excommunicate and proffered letters

---

[1] *Pont. hib.* I. 57, 58, 73, 128, 132. Cf. P. J. Dunning, 'Pope Innocent III and the Waterford–Lismore controversy' *Ir. Theol. Quart.* 28 (1961) 215–32, with lengthy extracts in translation.

[2] *Pont. hib.* I. 58. As Malachy was on his way to Rome the bishop arrested him, 'presumpsit capere violenter et nequiter spoliare et manibus propriis usque ad effusionem sanguinis iniectis in eum in carcere positum et compedibus alligatum, duris verberibus fecit affligi'.

of the legate, Cardinal John of Salerno, to prove it. Malachy, however, was able to convince the judges that these letters were forgeries. Before the case came to final judgment, however, David was assassinated (1209) by a member of the Ui Faolain family which ruled the small kingdom of the Deisi, an event apparently unconnected with the Waterford–Lismore dispute.[1]

By June 1210 there was a bishop-elect for Waterford, another Robert, also fired with ambition to possess Lismore. Backed by secular powers (whom the sources do not specify), he took possession of the diocese. The archbishop of Cashel, perhaps daunted by these strong forces behind Robert, refused to listen to Malachy's protestations that he could not confirm the appointment of such a man. The Archbishop said he was confirming him as bishop of Waterford, not of both Waterford and Lismore, and duly consecrated him.

Robert was summoned before the judges-delegate. He attempted to delay proceedings with the technicalities of the law and refused to appear. The judges found Malachy's claim to be canonical bishop of Lismore perfectly valid and ordered Robert to withdraw from Lismore and pay Malachy 160 silver marks in compensation.

Like his earlier namesake, Robert II then had recourse to force against Malachy personally. Malachy was beseiged in his own cathedral by Robert's seneschal, seized and assaulted and carried off to imprisonment in Dungarvan castle. The bishop of Waterford himself helped the smith to lock the iron fetters with which the hapless Malachy was secured.[2] Bishop Robert then joined the judges and his archbishop at Cashel in making common canonical denunciation of the perpetrators of this outrage. After seven weeks of suffering, Malachy escaped from his prison and once more Robert was summoned to account before the judges.

Robert's reply was to threaten them with the wrath of King John, and also again to have Malachy attacked. One Thomas, a clerk of

---

[1] *ALC* I. 241.
[2] *Pont. hib.* I. 73. The bishop of Waterford was waiting in Dungarvan castle for Malachy: 'Cuius pedibus idem Watefordensis deponens modestiam pontificis, et induens nequiter carnificis feritatem, compedes tradens ferreos manu sua, et iuvans fabrum clavos ipsis compedibus defigentem, sic ipsum carceris ergastulo mancipavit'. The sentence of excommunication of those who had attacked the bishop of Lismore was solemnly promulgated, 'presente Watefordensi episcopo et pariter assentiente'.

the bishop of Waterford, tried to cut off Malachy's head as he stood at the door of Limerick cathedral: 'but the bishop of Lismore through the divine power escaped the blow which smashed against the door to leave there marks which will ever endure'.

This attack took place in the very presence of the papal judges-delegate and Thomas was excommunicated on the spot. Robert ignored their stern injunction that he should have nothing to do with his clerk. He was finally excommunicated and suspended from office. It is clear, however, that this sentence was ignored in Waterford.

Innocent III confirmed the sentence, instructed Bishop John de Gray who was then justiciar to enforce it and to send Robert to Rome. What John de Gray and his fellow judges attempted and accomplished is not known. But it is certain that Robert made his peace with the Pope and that he continued to press his claim to Lismore, even after Innocent III had imposed 'perpetual silence' about the whole issue when pronouncing definitively in favour of Lismore's independence and autonomy.

Two vacancies at Lismore gave him opportunity to press his claims again.

The first occasion was in Rome at the Lateran council (1215). Robert was among the Irish prelates at the council, obviously his earlier crimes pardoned. Malachy, however, was dead and a successor Thomas, had been elected but was not yet consecrated. He too was at the council. Robert made objection to his appointment. Innocent III, taking full advantage of the presence of numerous first-hand witnesses and authorities in Irish Church matters, found in favour of Lismore, confirmed Thomas and had him consecrated by his metropolitan, the archbishop of Cashel.

Thomas's pontificate proved to be brief and Robert was not the man to lose the opportunity presented by the vacancy to renew his attack on the see of Lismore. This last phase of his long-sustained struggle, destined to be thwarted again, involving King Henry III and Pope Honorius III, may be more appropriately considered later.

It is not easy to generalize about the Irish Church as it was at the end of the reign of King John. The immense variety of local conditions and the speed of change after the Invasion make it difficult to discern any underlying patterns and trends over and above the complexities of particular situations, in themselves glimpsed only very partially because of the paucity of source material. Most historians have been content to stress the contrast between the two sorts of churchmen which now confronted each other. Edmund Curtis has perhaps portrayed the contrast in its starkest terms. On the one hand he presented an English 'state church' feudalized, urbanized, organizationally sophisticated, every bishop a baron and potentate. On the other side there stood, he thought, an administratively back-ward Irish Church whose simple peasant piety, apparently the stronger for its freedom from property and political involvements, was typified in Primate Gelasius who, in Giraldus's story, arrived at the council of Cashel with 'the one cow on which he supported his life'. The main feature of the new situation, Curtis argued, lay in the fact that the Crown introduced 'a new style of state prelate as opportunity allowed', to form a 'party' which the 'old Gaelic bishops feared and disliked'.[1]

That there is some truth in these judgments can scarcely be doubted. Obviously a prelate of the type of a John Cumin or a Henry of London, career diplomats and experienced royal servants, were a phenomenon new to the Irish Church, however common such types of prelate were in England. But this was not the only style of cleric favoured for advancement to the episcopate and it was by no means axiomatic that the new bishops were but miserable political append-ages of the Crown. Nor was it by any means the rule that it was the Crown which had promoted them at all. Such qualifications of Curtis's analysis of the situation spring inevitably from the scrutiny of the nine bishops of the invading nation who held office at the end of John's reign. Of these, four were monks; only two were royal officials. At most, only two were Crown promotions. The career of Bishop Ailbe, the Cistercian abbot of Baltinglass, shows that John was far from hesitant about supporting native Irishmen, even for a see of major ecclesiastical and political importance like Cashel. It is important, further, that the degree of freedom from political control enjoyed by the 'Gaelic' Church should not be exaggerated. The use of the tendentious description 'state church' about the new Anglo-French order suggests that the native order was in a happier position.

[1] Curtis, *Medieval Ireland* 107–8.

But it is quite apparent from any examination of the pre-Invasion Church in Ireland that it was in many ways much less clearly separated from the temporal than the Church in England. The degree of dependence of churchmen on lay rulers had tended to lessen as the reform movement began to make progress. Nevertheless the Register of Pope Innocent III (1198–1216) supplies clear evidence that in some parts of Ireland at least, the traditional over-involvement of the ecclesiastical in the temporal order continued. This appears from the Pope's concern as well to eradicate the hereditary tenure of ecclesiastical office which flourished in Connacht and elsewhere[1], as to curtail excessive intervention in episcopal elections by the king of that province.[2] There is similar evidence of clerical marriage and at least attempted hereditary succession of ecclesiastical offices, and of a king transgressing the limits of canonical freedom in episcopal elections in the kingdom of Cork.[3] It is not easy to be certain that the 'state church' of the colony was marked by a greater degree of subjection to lay control than was the case in the Irish kingdoms.

There is likewise something to be said for, and possibly rather more against, Curtis's opinion that 'fear and dislike' was the prevalent attitude of Irish bishops to the 'Norman party'. Obviously a Bishop Malachy whose resolute defence of his see of Lismore brought him a beating-up, brutal imprisonment twice and nearly cost him his head at the door of Limerick cathedral, was not likely to be an enthusiast for the new order. And as has been seen in the Armagh election dispute, there was no love lost between certain prelates of that province and the foreign clergy. But for that again, there is evidence enough to indicate a significant degree of cooperation between the

[1] His source of information was his legate, Cardinal John of Salerno: 'Litterarum perlecto tenore quas ad nostram destinasti presentiam intelleximus evidenter quod inter alias enormitates quas in ecclesiis Yberniensibus invenisti hanc detestabilem abusionem presertim in ecclesia Tuamensi et in partibus aliis cognovisti vigere quod non solum in minoribus prelaturis verum etiam in archiepiscopatibus et episcopatibus immediate filii patribus succedebant' *Pont. hib.* I. 53 (1203).

[2] *Ibid.* 92 (1215–16). There is a reference too, to hereditary tenure: 'Ad hec quia sicut audivimus quamplures in regno tuo cupiditatis tenebris obcecati contendunt hereditate sanctuarium Domini possidere non timentes ...'

[3] *Pont. hib.* I. 33 (1198). Cf. P. J. Dunning, 'Pope Innocent III and the Ross Election Controversy' *Ir. Theol. Quart.* 26 (1959) 346–59. A subsidiary theme of this dispute was the attempt of the dean of Cork to secure the archdeaconry for his son.

clergy of the two nations both great and small: in liturgical functions,[1] in joint participation in councils and assemblies, in Ireland[2] and at Rome,[3] in the conscious imitation of English institutional models by Irish prelates,[4] in confirmation by the Crown of grants of land made by Irish kings to Irish prelates,[5] in the support the king commanded from some Irish bishops.[6]

Fragmentary and difficult source material makes insistence on firm conclusions imprudent. But the evidence does suggest quite strongly that at the end of John's reign, 'fear and dislike' was not the inevitable attitude of Irish bishops to foreign prelates. The fact that all four metropolitans seem to have been able to work in harmony in this period would seem to make it clear that the possibility of achieving a *modus vivendi* between all sections of the Church in Ireland was not totally out of the question.

Nevertheless the future was shrouded in great uncertainty and the portents were not good. Early thirteenth century Ireland was a stormy place and its ecclesiastical world inevitably reflected the turmoil of its political instability. An instructive illustration of some

[1] For example the consecration in 1192 of Archbishop John Cumin's new collegiate church of St Patrick's, Dublin by himself, the archbishop of Cashel and the archbishop of Armagh. Cf. G. J. Hand, 'The rivalry of the cathedral chapters in medieval Dublin' *RSAIJn.* 92 (1962) 195.

[2] For example the Dublin council of 1192 presided over by the archbishop of Cashel, in his capacity as papal legate, *Ann. Inisfallen* 317. Cf. *Chart. St. Mary's, Dublin* I. 121 143–4. Cf. also the Mullingar meeting (council?) of 1205–6, *Register of the Abbey of St. Thomas, Dublin* RS (1889) 348–9.

[3] For example Felix of Tuam and his suffragans' support of the union of Dublin and Glendalough in 1215, *Pont. hib.* I. 172.

[4] For example, the establishment of a chapter for the diocese of Limerick by Bishop Donnchadh Ua Briain *c.* 1205, *Black Book of Limerick* ed. J. McCaffrey (1907) 142, explicitly with *anglicana consuetudo* in mind. Cf. G. J. Hand, 'The medieval chapter of St. Mary's Cathedral, Limerick' *Gwynn Studies* 75 for the apt comment: 'While the persuasive influence of political power was on the side of the English example, it none the less appears that the heirs of the great reformers were still, in John's reign, well-disposed towards the ecclesiastical institutions of the newcomers'.

[5] For example, of lands granted to the archbishop of Cashel by Donnchadh Ua Briain, confirmed by John in 1215, *Rotuli Chartarum, 1199–1216* ed. Hardy I. i. 219; *Pont. hib.* I. 140.

[6] The career of Ailbe, bishop of Ferns, already mentioned, is the most notable example. Cf. 'Irish Pipe Roll 14 John' (p. 52 n. 1 above) 12, 70 for some evidence of cooperation from the bishops of Clogher and Killaloe and the archbishop of Cashel. The bishop of Elphin was described by Archbishop Henry of London as always faithful to King John, *Cal. Docs. Irel. 1171–1251*, 733.

of the main types of tension to which the Church in Ireland was subject in these years is provided by the fortunes of three of its archbishops.

John Cumin of Dublin fell foul of his royal patron—was in the king's wrath, as the technical phrase of protocol had it—and was exiled from his see from *c.* 1202 to 1205.[1] In the same period and for somewhat longer, a vacant Armagh was wracked with a bitter electoral dispute. The election to Tuam in 1202 of an outsider and reformer in the person of Felix O'Ruadháin, Augustinian abbot of Saul (co. Down) was strongly resisted by the family of the defunct archbishop which fought to maintain its hereditary grip on the see.[2] The dispute meant that its archbishop held his see but precariously at all times and at some times was forced to take refuge outside it.

There were three quite different situations of strife here. One (Dublin) was peculiar to an English context and quite typical of it; its cause was a conflict between a prelate and the Crown about feudal rights. Another (Tuam) just as typical in its own context, was a struggle in the cause of reform to disinherit an entrenched ecclesiastical dynasty. The issue at Armagh was a power struggle occasioned by the mutual resentments and fears of native and foreigner.

These were typical conflict patterns. It remained to be seen how far the progress of Anglo-French arms and consequent settlement would conduce to an assuagement or a heightening of such tensions.

THE EARLY YEARS OF HENRY III

In calling King John the founder of the Anglo-Irish colony, Curtis no doubt exaggerates the personal importance of that ruler.[3] There can be no doubt, however, that the period of his reign knew significant development in the history of Anglo-Irish relations. John had

---

[1] *Pont. hib.* 1. 54–6, 62. There had been a serious quarrel earlier about ecclesiastical property with the justiciar Hamo of Valognes in 1197 when Cumin excommunicated him and imposed an interdict before quitting the Irish scene. The second quarrel, occurring when according to Innocent III, John was 'senex et decrepitus', seems to have been about the encroachments of the royal forest on the possessions of the see of Dublin, *DNB* Comyn, John (T. F. Tout).

[2] Innocent III's letter confirming his appointment spoke of these difficulties, *Pont. hib.* 1. 53. By 1213 the Archbishop had been forced to take refuge with Henry of London in Dublin, *Cal. Docs. Irel.* 481. It is an interesting detail that the costs of his maintenance were to be a charge on the royal exchequer at Dublin.

[3] Curtis, *Medieval Ireland* 96.

resolutely resisted any fissiparous tendencies on the part of the new colonial aristocracy and his insistence, on the occasion of his disciplinary visit to Ireland in 1210, that prelates and magnates should swear to observe the law and custom of England, was formal testimony of it.[1] From his reign there date the first practical steps towards the assimilation of the governments of the two countries, when the organization of royal justice on the English model was begun and the ground was prepared for the introduction of the governmental institutions and bureaucratic offices of Angevin England.[2]

The Church was here involved with no new principle. Henry II had stood by the maxim that in church affairs *in singulis similis regnum colligaret utrumque.* There was no reason why John should depart from this most convenient of arrangements. There had been changes, however, in the English law of the relationship between the hierarchy and the king since Henry II's time and one of them is of especial importance. It concerned the rôle of the king in episcopal elections.

The problem of balancing the churchman's claim that laymen should be excluded from episcopal elections and the king's claim to a voice in the selection of those who as bishops would become important members of his baronage received a new solution as a result of the long struggle between John and Innocent III. The procedure envisaged by the Constitutions of Clarendon and used by Henry II in choosing bishops for Ireland, was superseded by new arrangements, set out in a *concordat,* finally achieved in March 1215. Agreement had been reached on the general principles of the respective rôles of the spiritual and temporal powers in the making of a bishop in England and by extension, in Ireland. It was of course a compromise solution, fruit of a long, slow development which had begun over a century earlier when Anselm first challenged Henry I on the investiture and homage issue. Now at length the papacy formally accepted the principles that the electors, normally the diocesan chapter, should first obtain royal licence to elect, that the chosen candidate should be

[1] *Cal. Docs. Irel. 1171–1251* 1458, 1602.
[2] H. G. Richardson and G. O. Sayles, *The Irish Parliament in the Middle Ages* 21–3. Otway-Ruthven, *Medieval Ireland* ch. 5 'The government of the Norman–Irish state' esp. 158–9, 182–3.

70

presented to the king for his assent, that the king should take possession of episcopal temporalities during vacancy for which an oath of
fealty was to be sworn on restitution to the new bishop. On the other
side, the king accepted the principle that the election should be
confined exclusively to the canonical electors and should be conducted according to the procedure papally decreed for the universal
Church.[1] An episcopal election was no longer, as in Henry II's time,
a royal occasion. The electors were free to conduct the election in
accordance with the procedure of canon law as made and controlled
by the papacy. This agreement was enshrined in the first clause of
Magna Carta and was confirmed by Honorius III in 1219.[2]

This proved an endurable compromise and was the legal basis of
the capitular election of bishops in England throughout the middle
ages. It had of course been fashioned in the specifically English context without explicit reference to Ireland. But it was applied to
Ireland, like any other part of the common law understanding of
the relations of Church and State. Its implementation as the colony
expanded gave form and consistency to a major aspect of the Crown's
attitude to ecclesiastical affairs. For, to ensure it worked for Irish
episcopal appointments as it did for English ones, shaped Crown
policy along lines which it was to pursue very consistently, and
within the early Plantagenet period at least, not unsuccessfully.

Right from the period of Henry III's minority, the government
kept as sharp an eye as it could on the creation of the episcopate in
Ireland and on the correct observance of the electoral forms in so far
as they concerned the Crown. The regency government went early
into action in an important Irish episcopal election. This concerned
Armagh, and the events connected with the filling of this see in the
years 1217–19 are no less revelatory than the comparable dispute
which had begun in 1202.

Archbishop Eugenius died in late 1216. Temporalities were taken
into the custody of the chancellor of the Irish administration, Richard
Marsh.[3] The chapter of Armagh diocese and the suffragans of the

---

[1] Text of the agreement (30 March 1215) with translation in Cheney and Semple,
Selected letters of Innocent III concerning England 76, with references to Innocent III's
earlier letters concerning the conduct of ecclesiastical elections which form the
background to the final agreement at 198–9.
[2] *Pont. hib.* I. 122, 123.   [3] *Cal. Docs. Irel. 1171–1251* 745 (22 January 1217).

province were warned not to elect without royal licence to proceed to an election.[1] The justiciar, Geoffrey Marsh, was instructed to ensure that for the future no Irishman should be elected to any see in Ireland since, it was claimed, the promotion of native clergy had very frequently led to unrest.[2] For the future, the justiciar, with the help of Henry of London, the archbishop of Dublin, who at this very time was being urged by Pope Honorius III to do what he could to keep the Irish loyal to Henry III,[3] was to make sure that only *Anglici* should be promoted.

Apparently more heed was paid to the latter instruction than to the former. For in August 1217 there appeared in London as the archbishop-elect without licence to elect having been granted, Luke Netterville, an Oxford graduate who had been archdeacon of Armagh from *c*. 1206. He was to be the first and only Englishman to occupy the primatial see in the thirteenth century. He was not, however, permitted to short-cut the new electoral procedure. He was sent back to Armagh with licence for the election to take place.[4] It was almost a year later when he received royal assent.[5] His election and person were then submitted to Honorius III for the scrutiny of both required by canon law. The Pope duly confirmed the choice and allowed the consecration to be performed by Pandulf then in England as his legate.[6] Almost another year had passed before the government restored the temporalities, on certification of papal confirmation.[7]

[1] *Ibid.* 750 (23 January).
[2] *Ibid.* 736; *Cal. Pat. Rolls, 1216–25* 22. The precise wording is of interest: 'Cum per electiones factas de Hibernicis in terra nostra Hibernie pax ipsius terre nostre frequentius fuerit perturbata, vobis mandamus, precipientes, in fide qua nobis tenemini, ne permittatis de cetero quod aliquis Hiberniensis in terra nostra Hibernie eligatur aut promoveatur in aliqua cathedrali. De consilio vero venerabilis patris nostri domini H. Dublinensi archiepiscopi et vestro, modis omnibus procuretis quod clerici nostri et alii Anglici viri honesti, nobis et regno nostro necessarii eligantur et promoveantur in episcopatibus et dignitatibus cum vacaverint' *Cal. Pat. Rolls 1216–25* 23. In Oct. 1217, Archbishop Henry was to be given custody of Armagh and of other vacancies which might occur in that province, *Cal. Pat. Rolls* 106.
[3] *Pont. hib.* 1. 106 (17 January 1217). He was appointed papal legate the better to fulfil this mission, *ibid.* 108 (29 April) and was relieved of the office when the mission was allegedly completed, *ibid.* 135 (6 July 1220).
[4] *Cal. Docs. Irel.* 797. For his career, Emden, *Biographical Register, Oxford* 3.2199.
[5] *Cal. Docs. Irel.* 839 (6 July 1218).   [6] *Pont. hib.* 1. 118 (29 October 1218).
[7] *Cal. Docs. Irel.* 894 (16 September 1219).

This case reveals two principles in operation in Ireland for the first time. The first was the government's declared intention to operate a policy of national exclusivism in the making of bishops. Neither Henry II nor John had issued any instruction that Irishmen should be excluded from promotion. The second was the putting into practice of the new procedure giving the king his regular place in the routine process of selecting a bishop.[1]

In opting for a policy of discrimination the home government was apparently making its own a practice of the colonial government. For the Dublin administration was already prepared to take strong action to have Englishmen appointed in preference to Irishmen before ever the regency government issued its instruction. As justiciar, Geoffrey Marsh had been responsible for foisting his candidates, one of whom was his nephew, on the sees of Ardfert and Killaloe when local candidates, native Irishmen, had already been canonically elected. Both cases inevitably went to Rome, specifically on the complaint of the metropolitan concerned, Donnchadh of Cashel. Honorius III found the two Irishmen canonically elected, the two Englishmen intruders, *per potentiam laicalem* and ordered their removal. A papal legate sent to Ireland at this time was charged with the implementation of this sentence.[2] The Pope condemned in no uncertain language the principle of *acceptio personarum* as iniquitous and ordered his legate to see that it did not prevail against suitable Irishmen who had been canonically elected.[3]

Justice was done in these two cases, though in the event rather protractedly so, for the intruders were not to be easily dispossessed.[4] Whether or not the English government and the Dublin administration paid much heed to Honorius III's condemnation of the discrimination policy is another matter.

The Crown certainly upheld the papal decision about the two

---

[1] Whilst the Armagh election was in progress, the procedure was in operation for Ossory (in correct form) *Cal. Docs. Irel.* 855 and for Lismore (election without licence rectified before royal assent given) *ibid.* 856.

[2] *Pont. hib.* I. 111 (Killaloe); 112, 126 (Ardfert); 127 (Killaloe).

[3] *Pont. hib.* I. 140, 158. The phrase quoted is from *ibid.* 141: '... in iudicio divinitus interdicta sit acceptio personarum'. The source is Rom. 2. 11: 'For God shows no partiality' (cf. also Gal. 2. 6; Eph. 6. 9; Col. 3. 25; Deut. 10. 17, etc.). The text is to recur as a melancholy refrain through the next century and a half of Irish medieval ecclesiastical history.

[4] *Pont. hib.* I. 165, 166 (Ardfert: 18 June 1224) 178, 179 (Killaloe: May 1226).

intruders and the justiciar was ordered to cooperate with the papal legate to remove the usurping foreigners from Killaloe and Ardfert.[1] But it was not prepared to drop its policy of excluding Irishmen altogether, for in 1225[2] and 1226[3] two further cases occurred where it intructed the electors to appoint an Englishman.

The year 1223 was an important one for the making of bishops in Ireland. No less than eight sees had fallen vacant. Five of these— Limerick, Lismore, Waterford, Ferns, Kildare—were dioceses where the promotion of English bishops was virtually certain. All save Ferns, occupied for so many devoted years by the faithful Bishop Ailbe, were already held by Englishmen. The government had a list of candidates, all English.[4] Three of these got sees, though in two cases not the ones for which they had been initially designated.[5] The other two, choices of the chapters concerned, received royal assent without apparent difficulty.[6] We can be sure that there was no intention of allowing an Irishman to be bishop, though in only one case, Waterford, did the government find it necessary to say so explicitly.[7]

It could only have been expected that when Cashel became vacant with the resignation of Archbishop Donnchadh in 1223, a renewed attempt would be made to secure this major see, by now very much within the boundaries of the colony. The Cashel chapter was apparently of mixed national composition. There was at this time a move to enlarge it, almost certainly for reasons of electoral tactics. The proposed increase in size, was, however, forbidden by Honorius III.[8] The Pope also reissued his condemnation of the prevention of

---

1 *Cal. Docs. Irel.* 1026.

2 *Ibid.* 1251 (Waterford).

3 *Ibid.* 1442 (Cloyne). 'Decanus et capitulum Clonensis habent licenciam eligendi, dum tamen talem eligant qui Anglicus sit' *Cal. Pat. Rolls 1225–32* 59. The instruction follows an earlier royal assent to a native Irishman who did not get possession, *Cal. Docs. Irel.* 1207, 1236.

4 *Cal. Docs. Irel.* 1092 (12 March 1223); *Cal. Pat. Rolls* 1223. Henry of London, then justiciar, was empowered to give assent in the king's name.

5 Hubert de Burgh was appointed to Limerick as planned, John of St John went to Ferns instead of Lismore, Ralph of Bristol to Kildare instead of Ferns.

6 William Wace to Waterford, *Cal. Docs. Irel.* 1094 and Griffin Christopher to Lismore, *ibid.* 1143–4.

7 The instruction came after Wace's premature death in 1225, *ibid.* 1251.

8 *Pont. hib.* I. 160.

Irish clerics for promotion to prelacies on grounds of nationality.[1]
The decree was phrased in general terms but it may be legitimately
suspected that he had the Cashel situation more particularly in
mind.

The chapter had postulated as its elect that Marianus O Briain who
had become bishop of Cork in 1215 despite the presence in the field
of a protégé of King John. The Pope refused him because of defect
in the election procedure and then provided the well-known
scientist, Michael Scot. When he declined on the grounds that he
did not know the language of the country, Honorius then approved
the election of Marianus.[2] Royal assent was requested and granted
without trouble. Marianus was a good compromise candidate. He
had earlier been accepted by John and in his new office he was to be
quickly accepted by the administration.[3]

The remaining two vacancies of 1223 were in Cloyne and Ross,
both Irish dioceses, but sufficiently within the sphere of English
influence for the Crown to have an interest in their occupants.

The detail of the respective situations of these cases is not available,
but sufficient of the outline of events can be known to throw some
light on the parts played by king and pope in episcopal appointments
at this time. In August 1224 the King gave his assent to one Florence
for Cloyne.[4] This was undoubtedly an Irish candidate. He had not,
however, been consecrated by February 1225 when Archbishop
Marianus was given custody of temporalities and the royal assent to
Florence was reiterated.[5] In July 1226, however, royal assent was
given to an English Cistercian.[6] These assents were clearly given in
advance of the election.[7] This candidate was not elected either and in
the following month the dean and chapter of Cloyne were given
licence to elect 'providing that they elect an Englishman'.[8] But the
man who finally became bishop of Cloyne was a native Irishman.[9]

[1] '... sane nostris est iam frequenter auribus intimatum quosdam Anglicos inaudite
    temeritatis audacia statuisse ut nullus clericus de Ybernia, quantumcumque honestus
    et litteratus existat, ad aliquam dignitatem ecclesiasticam assumatur' *Pont. hib.* 1.
    158. The 'frequenter' is significant.
[2] The relevant letters are *Pont. hib.* 2. 163–4, 167–9.
[3] *Cal. Docs. Irel.* 1206, 1209, 1233–5, 1258.   [4] *Ibid.* 1207.
[5] *Ibid.* 1235–6.   [6] *Ibid.* 1432–3.
[7] *Cal. Pat. Rolls 1225–32* 55.   [8] *Ibid.* 59.
[9] There is apparently no record of any royal assent being granted.

This was the last occasion of which record has survived where the Crown issued a specific instruction forbidding the appointment of an Irishman.

It was very unusual for a case with complications of this order not to go to Rome. There is, however, no trace of it in the papal registers. The Ross case reveals a phenomenon of exactly contrary trend: the referring of an elect straight to the pope even though there were apparently no complications. Papal ratification was of course the best guarantee of the validity of an election and this precedent was to be followed on a number of later occasions when chapters and bishops-elect had reason to anticipate trouble.[1]

That the Crown was now in a position to take episcopal temporalities into custody during vacancy obviously strengthened its position when it came to supporting particular candidates. There was an official charged with custody of escheats (not yet called an escheator, apparently)[2] but episcopal temporalities were not in this early period given into his charge. Individual arrangements were made for individual cases, sometimes to suit the diocese in question, more often in favour of particular individuals. In these early decades of Henry III's reign there was a good deal of variation of practice.[3] One tactic was frequently used. Custody of temporalities would be granted to the man whom the Crown had selected for promotion to the see.[4] This ploy did not always work, however, even when the see was English. It did not work, for example, when the government was anxious to have Walter of Brackley promoted to Meath[5] nor at Armagh when it wanted Hubert de Burgh, bishop of Limerick, to be

---

[1] In this case the pope appointed three Cashel suffragans to conduct canonical examination, *Pont. hib.* 1. 161. There is no record of the king being party to this procedure.

[2] On this period of the origins of the office in Ireland, H. G. Richardson and G. O. Sayles, *The Administration of Medieval Ireland* (1963) 28–9.

[3] Sometimes the justiciar was given custody, *Cal. Docs. Irel.* 846 (for all vacancies), sometimes the chancellor, *ibid.* 745 (Armagh only), sometimes an ecclesiastic who may have been also an official, e.g. Henry, bishop of Emly, *ibid.* 1057 (all vacancies) or one who certainly was, e.g. Henry of London, *ibid.* 807 (all vacancies in Armagh province), 1182 (Cashel: 'in payment of debt'), 1507 (Armagh), 1613 (all vacancies: 'to discharge what was owed to him').

[4] For example Hubert de Burgh, custody of Limerick (*ibid.* 1090); John of St John, Ferns (*ibid.* 1099); Luke, Dublin (*ibid.* 1818).

[5] *Ibid.* 1853, 1855.

the new primate in 1227.[1] It is noteworthy, however, that in all these cases where the Crown did not successfully place its man, it did not make an issue of it but gave royal assent with apparent good grace, even when, as in this Armagh case, the successful candidate was a native Irishman.[2]

Another element in the electoral proceedings of this time was the part played by the justiciar. He and the Crown did not always see eye to eye on what his rôle was. The Crown considered that the granting of licences and assents was a special prerogative reserved to it. The justiciar was not above usurping the prerogative as he thought fit.[3] Since to use him would save a chapter the expense and delay of journeys into England, his services were in demand. Further there was another prerogative connected with episcopal vacancies. The Crown claimed that it had the right to collate to such benefices as were in the bishop's gift which fell vacant during vacancy of the see. There were repeated complaints from England that the king was not being informed of such vacant benefices and that his right of collation was being usurped.[4] The justiciar had taken over this sector of royal patronage for himself.

In 1227 an attempt was made to make a regular arrangement about the justiciar's use of the prerogative in giving licences to elect and royal assents. Because of the poverty of the clergy and of the bishoprics of Ireland, the justiciar was to act for the king in all dioceses except the four archbishoprics; Kildare, Ossory, Leighlin and Ferns (all the dioceses of the Dublin province); Meath (Armagh province); Emly, Limerick, Killaloe, Cork, Waterford, and Lismore (Cashel province).[5] This list of exceptions gives a very good indication of the actual extent of the Crown's influence at this time; the remaining dioceses are still marginal. Within ten years another five dioceses can be added to give a general notion of the dioceses where the king or his justiciar would normally be asked for licence or assent. After some uncertainty, the rôle assigned to the justiciar seems to have been

[1] *Cal. Docs. Irel.* 1531. Another unsuccessful case was that of Ralph of Norwich (Emly, 1228), *ibid.* 1589.
[2] *Ibid.* 1557–8.
[3] *Ibid.* 1493, 2318.
[4] *Ibid.* 969 (1220), 1416 (1226), 1871 (1231).
[5] *Cal. Pat. Rolls 1225–32* 125. The summary of the same text in *Cal. Docs. Irel.* is defective.

decided by allowing him the exercise of royal prerogative only when specifically delegated to him in individual cases.

These five dioceses were Clogher, Down, Ardagh (Armagh province), Cloyne and Ardfert (Cashel province). Thus by 1237 some twenty dioceses were within the English sphere of influence[1] and of these, some eight or nine, including three archbishoprics, would be native Irish. Within another decade or so, seven more dioceses can be added: Connor, Dromore and Kilmore (Armagh province), Elphin, Kilmacduagh, Annaghdown and Achonry (Tuam province).[2] All save the first of these were native Irish dioceses. Irish chapters often had their own reasons for attaching themselves to the Crown by conforming to this procedure. The classic example of this was Annaghdown, whose autonomous existence was constantly threatened by Tuam. The link with the Crown was insurance against extinction.

The Crown, for its part, had settled for a compromise on the question of national exclusivism. It had been shown that chapters were prepared to comply with the established electoral rules and through them, an elect was subject to a security check. There were no further attempts to force Englishmen into native sees. It was not necessary. Events had shown that in the heavily settled areas, chapters inevitably became English and appointed from their own nation. In other areas racial discrimination could not be made to work in practice, especially with the papacy acting as watch-dog against this abuse. Cashel and Killaloe were the classic examples of dioceses that successfully resisted anglicization yet nevertheless produced bishops who, for the most part, cooperated with the Crown.

Thus the key to Crown policy towards the episcopate lay in great vigilance over the maintenance of the prescribed electoral forms. The chapter must formally notify the king that its bishop is dead and ask him for licence to elect; its candidate must be presented

---

1 See the list of dioceses from which it was expected to levy an aid in 1237 on the marriage of the king's daughter to Emperor Frederick II, *ibid.* 2410.
2 References in the order of dioceses as given in the text: *ibid.* 2739; 2774 (but see also 1500 for a royal assent in 1227); 3046; 2769. The archbishop of Tuam had refused to consecrate a papally provided candidate without his first obtaining royal assent; 2933, with pardon for not asking for licence to elect; 3048, 3130; 3113, 3156.

for royal assent, in person unless specially dispensed; if assent were granted, he would be sent to his metropolitan (or to the pope, in the case of a metropolitan) 'to do what is his', i.e. for canonical confirmation; when the metropolitan or pope certified to the king that there were no canonical objections to the person of the elect or to the way the election had been conducted and that he might be consecrated, the elect might have restitution of temporalities after swearing fealty to the king.

Judging by the attempts to evade it, chapters frequently found this procedure irksome.[1] It was expensive, protracted and laborious. Nor was the escheator or his equivalent more popular in Ireland than elsewhere and custody of temporalities during vacancy could be particularly galling when dioceses were so poor. But the government stood firm, as of course it had every incentive to do. It was secure in the knowledge that the papacy had agreed to the principles involved and was prepared to support it against electors and bishops-elect who tried to dodge them. The king was prepared to pardon failures to secure licence to elect or assents, if the chapter swore that the offences would not be repeated and (probably) made fine. Occasionally if circumstances seemed suspicious, restitution of temporalities might be conditional on giving security for good behaviour.[2]

All in all, the system worked harmoniously enough. It was at least a *system*, a structure of order and stability in a very insecure ecclesiastical world. Much the most important voice in the making of a bishop in Ireland was the local one, that of the chapter, or its equivalent. No doubt there were pressures on electors and no doubt private interests often played an excessive part in an election. Such imperfections are often enough the ordinary accompaniment of such

---

[1] The following examples of cases of infraction may be noted: Armagh, 1217 (*ibid.* 797); Lismore, 1218 (856); Meath, 1224 (1212); Leighlin, 1228 (1629); Emly, 1230 (1838); Meath, 1231 (1862); Killaloe, 1231 (1908). Custody of temporalities during vacancy was also unpopular with bishops and in 1231 the Irish bishops proposed to complain to the pope about it, with Hubert de Burgh, bishop of Limerick as their spokesman, *Cal. Cl. Rolls 1227–31* 588. Nothing seems to have come of the project.

[2] For example Killaloe, 1231. Security was wanted lest the bishop should hand over the castle of Killaloe to the king's enemies, *Cal. Cl. Rolls 1227–31* 547. The sum was found by Donnchadh, king of Thomond. The transaction was later to be held against the bishop as simony, *Pont. hib.* 2. 266, Gleeson and Gwynn, *Diocese of Killaloe* 240; Emly, 1238, *Cal. Cl. Rolls 1237–42* 111–12. There is apparently no case of security being taken from an English or Anglo-Irish bishop.

occasions. But we can say nothing of them in this context for lack of documentation. What, however, does seem reasonably clear from the available evidence is that electors in Ireland, on the whole, enjoyed the canonical freedom of election enjoined by the law of the universal Church. In the early years of Henry III, both king and justiciar were active in promoting their protégés. Occasionally they were successful, sometimes they were not. If they broke the canon law the papacy saw to it that they did not get their way. In any case, after *c.* 1230 the Crown stopped trying to promote its own candidates, though very occasionally it would suggest a name. Because local initiatives were dominant, some dioceses were invariably ruled by English bishops, others invariably by Irish bishops and others again sometimes by bishops of one nationality, sometimes of the other. The Crown had an established place in the electoral routine and insisted on its being recognized. It offered an opportunity to influence electors and especially of rejecting those thought to be disloyal or enemies of the Crown. Henry III seems to have objected only once to a candidate, but accepted the pope's confirmation of him.[1]

The part of the papacy in episcopal appointments was a significant one. It had a regular part in the ordinary routine of episcopal elections in two ways. Firstly, since archbishops were not subject to any prelate other than the pope, they went to him for canonical confirmation. So too, secondly, did candidates who had been postulated by a chapter but who were already bishops. The breaking of the bond between a bishop and his diocese whether by postulation, resignation or deposition was in canon law reserved to the pope's jurisdiction. Such cases of postulation brought many aspirants to Irish sees to papal attention.

More cases, however, came because things had gone wrong or were thought to be about to go wrong and a superior judge was required to decide where the right lay. In this appellate capacity the popes had an important part to play.

These papal interventions in circumstances when the ordinary legal machinery was not functioning properly were very various. One noteworthy type of case concerned the actual composition of the electoral body.

[1] The objection was to David MacCarwill, Cashel (1254), on political grounds, *Pont. hib.* 2. 388 at p. 213.

Some instances of this are worthy of remark. For Cashel in 1252, Innocent IV was called on to decide between the claims of the suffragans of the province to have a part in the election of their metropolitan, which seems at an earlier stage to have been the custom here as it was in Armagh, and of the Cashel chapter to be sole electors. The Pope's decision in favour of the chapter seems to have settled the matter immediately.[1] Two other cases proved more obdurate, however. In the diocese of Down, the abbot of the Augustinian house of Bangor, formerly the seat of St Malachy, contested the electoral right of the prior and chapter of the Benedictine St Patrick's, Down. The metropolitan, with the advice of his suffragans, had found for the Down house and Innocent IV confirmed this decision. But this ratification did not prevent a double election in 1258, which took no little time to compose.[2] More protracted still was the dispute between the chapters of the two Dublin cathedrals. Their rivalry was endemic and repeated papal attempts to effect a compromise were unsuccessful.[3]

Diocesan unions were also among the papal *iura reservata*. In this category of case it is the attempt of Waterford to absorb Lismore, not less unscrupulously pursued even when the latter had become anglicized, which holds pride of place.

In 1218 the Lismore chapter selected an Englishman, Robert of Bedford, an Oxford graduate, as their bishop. Its failure to obtain royal licence to elect brought them rebuke but, the fault rectified, the King gave his assent and despatched the elect to his metropolitan Archbishop O Longargain, then in England, for canonical confirmation. Robert of Bedford was duly consecrated in London by the archbishop of Cashel, the temporalities of Lismore were restored to him and the faithful of his diocese ordered to obey him as their canonically and legally appointed bishop. This was in December 1218.[4]

At this time Robert, bishop of Waterford was also in England, but at the other end of the kingdom, in Carlisle, whence he had been

---

[1] *Ibid.*

[2] *Ibid.* 259, with references for the events of 1258, p. 101 n.

[3] Hand, 'Rivalry of the cathedral chapters in medieval Dublin' 201–4.

[4] *Cal. Pat. Rolls 1216–25* 183; Harris, *Collectanea de Rebus Hibernicis, Anal. hib.* 6 (1934) 263; *Dunstable Annals* in *Annales Monastici RS* 3. 53; Emden, *Biographical Register, Oxford* 1. 146.

sent by the papal legate Pandulf to consecrate a bishop. When this Robert returned to London and found that a new bishop of Lismore had been installed he lodged the claim that he and his predecessors had long been in possession of that see. He produced letters of Cardinal John of Salerno to prove that Waterford and Lismore had been canonically united. This evidence was accepted by the regents. Robert of Bedford's restitution of temporalities was cancelled and the justiciar and the archbishop of Cashel were ordered to prevent him ruling a see now considered to have been obtained by fraud.[1]

What followed was by now a familiar pattern. Robert of Bedford went to Rome. He had no difficulty in convincing Honorius III that he had been wronged, for, papal registers apart, there were still cardinals at the curia who could recollect personally Innocent III's 'definitive judgment' concerning the autonomy of Lismore and the censure of Robert of Waterford. The pope decided that it was Robert who was guilty of deceit in defying Innocent III's ruling and concealing it from the King. Robert of Bedford was to be restored and Robert of Waterford sent to Rome.[2]

In due course the royal government reversed its earlier attitude to the bishop of Lismore and Robert of Waterford was ordered to pay him 300 marks in compensation.[3] It is not clear whether or not Robert went to Rome, whether he paid the compensation, whether Robert of Bedford enjoyed secure possession of Lismore. But he remained bishop of Waterford down to his death in 1224. When the other Robert died in 1228, the King approached Gregory IX about uniting the dioceses because of their poverty, but he apparently changed his mind and nothing came of this project.[4] These dioceses were to be united finally, however, by Urban V in 1363.[5]

The papal rôle in the actual selection of the episcopate was not very great. Capitular election at this period and throughout the century was the rule in practice as well as in theory. The popes administered the law primarily as a court of appeal, acting when things had gone wrong at the request of others, not inhibiting local electors and nominating men of their own choice, as became quite

[1] *Rot. Litt. Claus.* 392a; *Cal. Docs. Irel.* 878.
[2] *Pont. hib.* I. 128 (10 November 1218).
[3] *Rot. Litt. Claus.* 425b, 475b–476a; *Cal. Docs. Irel.* 948, 991; *Dunstable Ann.* 65.
[4] *Royal Letters, Henry III RS* I. 273 (16 July 1228).   [5] *Hbk Brit. Chron.* 332.

common in the fourteenth century. In this appellate capacity, the popes administered both the canon law of elections as it had developed in the thirteenth century and was incorporated in the *Corpus Iuris Canonici* and also those agreements made with individual rulers. Thus the popes abided by the compromise established by John and Innocent III between the canon and English laws relating to the secular aspects of the episcopal office.

Cases of disputed election investigated at the papal curia were solved where possible by adherence to the principle of capitular election. This might be done simply by establishing who in fact was the chapter's real nominee. Or it might be done by the pope, supplementing *ex plenitudine potestatis* any electoral defect, as happened in the case of Florence MacFlynn (Tuam, 1250). Though the pope had found the election to be uncanonical, he provided this candidate to the see. In cases where it was found that provision seemed the only solution the popes associated the electors, in the persons of their proctors at the curia, with the provision.

The anglicization of the episcopate, so far as it had proceeded in this period, constitutes the major part of the history of the introduction of the relations between the ecclesiastical hierarchy and the central government in Ireland. Anglicization of personnel was the essential precondition of any anglicization of institutions and practices. Other common law principles which related ecclesiastical and royal interests were of course introduced at this same time as part and parcel of the policy of constructing the legal and administrative system of the colony on the English model. Because of the rather sparse nature of the records for this period, however, these aspects can only be glimpsed rather than analyzed in any very systematic way. Hence it is preferable to study the detail of this segment of the law at a later stage in its history. Here it is sufficient to say that there is no reason for believing that the Crown envisaged either the functioning of the ecclesiastical courts or the cognizance by the secular courts of cases touching ecclesiastical persons and causes, in any way differently in Ireland from English practice.[1]

---

[1] Cf. especially the solemn public declaration that by English law, pleas concerning advowsons, lay fees and chattels not of matrimonial or testamentary jurisdiction were not to be heard in the ecclesiastical courts, *Cal. Docs. Irel.* 2069 (28 October

The papal attitude to the composition of the episcopate constitutes the most significant part of Hiberno-papal relations in this same period. Because the issue was of such a fundamental nature, it reveals in microcosm the whole papal attitude to the English lordship of Ireland and to the Irish Church. It shows the consistency of papal policy: acknowledgment of the validity and reality of the king of England's lordship in Ireland, support of his policies, in the interests of reform, wherever they did not deviate from the principles of ecclesiastical law.

In one major respect the bond between England and the papacy concerning Ireland was strengthened in this period. Papal recognition of, and support for, English lordship was put on a new and more clearcut legal basis. In May 1213, King John acknowledged that he held his kingdom as a fief from the papacy, performed fealty and homage for it, bound his successors to recognize this as a 'perpetual obligation and concession' and contracted to pay an annual sum of 1,000 marks as recognition of his vassalage.[1] This status did not envisage only the kingdom of England, but the 'kingdom' of Ireland too and 300 marks of the annual payment was for Ireland. The Crown now held that country as a papal fief. The vassal was entitled to the protection of his lord and the papacy was to recognize its special obligation in this regard. Thus, after 1213, *Laudabiliter* offered no temptation to either king or pope to employ it as a legal title for English lordship of Ireland. This alleged papal letter did indeed continue to circulate in thirteenth and fourteenth century Ireland and was used by both Irish and Anglo-Irish petitioners to both king and pope to strengthen their requests. Whilst it was not repudiated by the papacy, it was not acknowledged by it as a genuine product of the papal chancery.[2] As far as the popes were concerned, the authentic legal basis of the claims of the papacy and English Crown to Ireland was in the submission made by John to Innocent III.

1233). In 1227 the justiciar was ordered to make use of the English practice of caption of excommunicates, *ibid.* 1481.
[1] Cheney and Semple, *Select. letters, Innocent III* 67.
[2] Cf. my '*Laudabiliter* in medieval diplomacy and propaganda' 431–2.

Chapter 4

THE CRISIS OF THE CISTERCIAN ORDER
IN IRELAND

The seed planted in Ireland by St Malachy and St Bernard bore good fruit. In the thirty years that separated the foundation of Mellifont from the council of Cashel, the number of Cistercian houses effectively established had risen to fifteen, all save one of the *filiatio Mellifontis*.[1] New rulers meant new patrons and nine Anglo-French houses were established in the half century or so after the Invasion.[2] Within this same period there were ten further native Irish foundations[3] (Map 4).

This was encouraging progress. Naturally it brought its problems. Chief of these was the one which faced the whole of the Irish Church at this time: the integration of the old with the new, the achievement of a *modus vivendi* between Irish and Anglo-French. The particular Cistercian experience of this general problem was to prove especially bitter.

The Irish Cistercian province, however, had its difficulties, even without the invader. In general terms, these problems were not in kind dissimilar from those which attended the exportation of a new and highly sophisticated monastic system from the relatively ad-

---

[1] In approximate chronological order: Bective, Inislounaght, Dublin (Savigny: Buildwas), Monasteranenagh, Baltinglass, Newry, Kilbeggan, Abbeydorney, Boyle, Killeny, Jerpoint, Holycross, Aghamanister (later, Abbeymahon). Origins are obscure and debatable. For the most part I have followed Gwynn and Hadcock, *Medieval Religious Houses, Ireland*. See further H. G. Leask, 'Irish Cistercian monasteries: a pedigree and distribution map' *RSAIJn*. 78 (1948) 63–4; Conway, *Story of Mellifont*; G. Mac Niocaill, *Na Manaigh Liatha in Éirinn 1142–c. 1600* (1959).

[2] They were, with mother house in parentheses: Inch (Furness), Dunbrody (Dublin), Grey Abbey (Holmcultram), Comber (Whitland), Tintern (Tintern, Mon.), Graiguenamanagh (Stanley), Abington (Furness), Abbeylara (Dublin), Tracton (Whitland).

[3] Assaroe, Midleton, Corcumroe, Kilcooly, Abbeyleix, Killeny, Monasterevin, Abbeyknockmoy, Abbeyshrule, Macosquin. Only the last named was colonized from outside Ireland (Morimond).

Map 4. Cistercian houses at the time of Stephen of Lexington's visitation (1228).

vanced civilization which had given it birth, to other remote and rude areas of Britain. In Yorkshire and Wales, as well as Ireland, Cistercian advance was striking, but it was not without incidents of strife and violence to mar its record. Mellifont itself took root in an atmosphere of intense native distrust of outsiders. The original community sent from Clairvaux *c.* 1140, included a number, perhaps a predominance, of French monks. They were to return home very speedily. St Bernard explained to St Malachy that they had done so because of the ill-discipline of the Irish. Though some French monks were prevailed on to return, St Bernard found it difficult to find men willing to go to Ireland because of the first French experience of it.[1] Evidence concerning the domestic history of Mellifont in its earliest decades is sparse.[2] Such as it is, it points to two other sources of strife in addition to hostility to foreigners: family and political rivalries, reflected in disputes over the abbacy; the presence in the monastery of those who preferred to continue the traditions of Celtic monasticism, even in a house which had been Cistercian in origin. The evidence does not warrant the painting of any black picture. But all the indications suggest that in the twelfth century the Irish Cistercian family made its progress in the teeth of some formidable obstacles— involvement, through family and tribal connexions, in the violence so characteristic of secular society, the persistence in debased form of older monastic ways, the pertinacious particularism which was quick to make of the general chapter of the order an irrelevant foreign body. Here were problems enough, without the additional burden of coming to terms with a new, foreign ruling class and a new dimension added to the province, composed of foreign monks.

The first news of serious trouble among the Irish Cistercians comes in the *Statuta* of the general chapter held in 1216.[3] The abbot of

---

[1] St Bernard, Ep. 357 *PL* 182. 559. On the trouble between Irish and French monks, Conway, *Story of Mellifont* 9-11.

[2] See in general, C. Conway, 'Sources for the history of the Irish Cistercians' *Proc. ICHC* (1959) 16-23 and for the pre-Invasion history of Mellifont, *idem Story of Mellifont* 6-16, 35-7.

[3] 'Praecipitur abbati Claraevallis ut in domo Mellifontis in qua multa enormia succrevisse dicuntur, quae corrigenda invenerit tam in capite quam in membris sic emendet quatenus tot et tantarum enormitatum querelae ad Capitulum generale de cetero perveniant' J. M. Canivez, *Statuta Capitulorum Generalium ... t.1 Ab anno 1116 ad annum 1220* (1933) 456. (1216. 32). There seems to have been trouble earlier

Clairvaux was then instructed to investigate and amend as necessary the 'many enormities' which, it had been reported, flourished in Clairvaux's daughter house of Mellifont. The general chapter for the following year recorded that when its official Visitors arrived at Mellifont they found their entry barred by a great crowd of armed lay brothers and they were driven away. A similar rebellion had taken place when the Visitors arrived at Jerpoint, where the abbot enjoyed the support of the abbots of Baltinglass, Killeny, Kilbeggan and Bective.[1] Clearly this was a rebellion of very serious proportions. It cannot be a coincidence that these first houses to be named as participants in what came to be called the *conspiratio Mellifontis* were, by this date, well within the Anglo-French area.

The general chapter began to try to solve what was to prove one of its most obdurate problems. The abbots of Mellifont and Jerpoint were deposed *in instanti*; the remaining four abbots were disciplined, but not deposed. New Visitors were appointed, the abbots of La Trappe (Normandy) and Cwmhir. In 1220 and again in 1221, the general chapter took account of the need to correct Mellifont and other houses in Ireland, and sent Visitors there.[2]

It assigned responsibility for the correction of Mellifont to the abbot of Clairvaux, allowing him to appoint deputies if necessary. These were empowered in general to act with the full authority of the general chapter. Specifically, they were given authority to ask

in Maigue and her daughters, *ibid.* (1202.26) if the 'Maugia' of the statute, un-identified by Canivez, is to be read as 'Maigue'.

1 'Quattuor abbates, scilicet de Valle Salutis (Baltinglass), de Valle Dei (Killeny), de Benedictione (Kilbeggan) et de Beatitudine (Bective), qui perturbationi quae facta est in domo de Ieriponte (Jerpoint) contra visitatores interfuerunt et assensum prae-buerunt, infra hos quadraginta dies extra stallum abbatis maneant. De abbate tamen de Beatitudine qui dum prior esset Mellifontis hominem, ut dicitur, in cippo posuit qui et ibi mortuus est, abbati Claraevallis committitur qui omnem diligentiam adhibeat ut domus Mellifontis tam in spiritualibus quam in temporalibus corrigetur et ordinetur' Canivez, *Statuta* I. 470–1 (1217. 25). 'Abbas Mellifontis qui Visitatores irreverenter repulit, et qui multa enormia in domo sua sustinuit diutius et non correxit, et qui portas violenter clausas per multitudinem conversorum visitatoribus egressum prohibuit, et qui filium abbatem de quo multa turpia et enormia dicta sunt, cum correxisse debuisset, diu sustinuit, deponitur in instanti ... Abbas de Ieriponte qui, cum quattuor aliis abbatibus, tertia die visitationis a patre abbate vocatus ad omnimodam contumaciam, inobedientiam et turbationem contra visitatores et patrem abbatem devenit, et quia totum conventum concitavit, deponitur in instanti' *ibid.* 483 (1217. 78, 79).
2 Canivez, *Statuta* I (1219. 33), (1220. 12); 2 (1221. 21, 22).

help from the secular arm, which was in effect to empower them to put themselves under the protection of any lay ruler who would use force on their behalf. Pope Gregory IX was to be told by the abbot of Citeaux that the order deliberately chose Visitors of different nationalities—'Irish, Welsh, English, Flemish, French, Lombard and many from Clairvaux itself'—in order to avoid any suggestion that disciplinary action was being influenced by any national bias.[1]

Nothing is known of the actions of the Visitors except their repetition of the same story of the collapse of monastic discipline, of lack of care of monastic buildings and properties, of conspiracies and of frequent rebellions attended by plots to assassinate and their lack of success in achieving correction. The general chapter was still, in 1226, considering what steps should be taken to reform Mellifont and her *generatio*. Again the abbot of Clairvaux was given the full authority of the order to devise a solution.[2]

Of the visitation which followed in 1227 we have more knowledge. It was conducted by Bernard, abbot of the French house of Froid-mont[3] and the abbot of Buildwas in Shropshire. Their efforts brought drastic action.

---

[1] 'Ascendentibus undique clamoribus tam cleri quam populi a multis retroactis temporibus super multiplicibus exordinationibus et delictis enormibus Hibernie ordinis nostri ad audientiam nostram, non modicum contristati et graui merore sauciati visitatores viros idoneos annuatim ad partes Hibernie destinauimus, qui Deum habentes pre oculis super auditis excessibus diligenter inquirerent et eorum correctioni secundum formam ordinis manum apponerent. Ipsi vero officium uisitationis propter dictorum inobedientiam et rebellionem exequi non ualentes ad plenum maiora hiis, que ad nos prius delata fuerant, retulerunt. Unde, ne in processu nostro posset aliquid odio uel gratie seu precipitationi aut inprouidentie inputari, visitatores diuersarum linguarum, uidelicet de ipsa Hibernia, Wallia, Anglia, Flandria, Francia et Lumbardia et plures de Claravalle, temporibus diuersis in potestate maiori duximus destinandos, qui successiue inuenientes in eis ordinis dissipationem, dilapidationem temporalium, conspirationes, rebelliones et mortis machinationes frequentes, insuper excessus grauissimos et enormes in aliis literis annotatos quosdam de ipsis abbatis secundum formam ordinis deposuerunt; de monachis uero alios emiserunt a suis domibus ad domos alias ordinatas, alios secundum formam ordinis modis aliis punierunt pro posse nitentes, sed incassum, ordinem reformare.' Abbot Walter of Ochies's letter is in the *Registrum Epistolarum Stephani de Lexington* ed. B. Griesser, *Analecta s. o. Cisterciensis* 2 (1946) 1. 12–13. The editor's suggested date of 1227 is almost certainly too early.

[2] Canivez, *Statuta* 2 (1226. 15) His commission was continued the following year 'ut quod bene coeptum est, dante Domino, melius consummetur' (1227. 28).

[3] There is extant a letter of Abbot Bernard's written in Dublin, 22 July 1227 describing himself as sent by the general chapter 'ad abbatias Hybernie visitandas in plenitudine

The Visitors found that among the chief supporters of the *conspiratio Mellifontis* were the abbots of Assaroe, Boyle, Fermoy, Abbeydorney and Newry. The appearance of these names makes it clear that the whole of the Mellifont *generatio* was now affected. The general chapter of 1227 deposed these rebels *in instanti*.[1] The general chapter's next step, taken on the advice of the Visitors, marked an important and radical policy change. It was decided that the cause of reform would be promoted if certain houses had their filiation changed and were reallocated to the care of a different mother house. Since it was the mother house which took responsibility for the ordinary visitation and supervision of its daughters, the purpose of the change is obvious. The decision was that Maigue be removed from the parentage of Mellifont and be given to Margam (Monmouthshire), Baltinglass from Mellifont to Fountains (Yorkshire) and Inislounaght from Maigue to Furness (Lancashire). Further, it was decided that Killeny, a daughter of Jerpoint, was too small and too encumbered with debt for self-sufficiency; its union with Graiguenamanagh (an Anglo-French foundation) was decreed. Finally an investigation of the state of Holy Cross was ordered. If it were found to be too small, it was to be united to Abington (not to its mother house, Maigue, but to an Anglo-French foundation). These decisions were the start of a new policy, one which indeed had already at least in part been started by the Visitors themselves.[2] The general chapter

potestatis', 'The Charters of the Cistercian Abbey of Duiske in the county of Kilkenny' ed. C. M. Butler and J. H. Bernard *PRIA* 35 (1918) sect. C. 19. 44.

1 'De Samaria (Assaroe), de Buellio (Boyle), de Castro Dei (Fermoy), de Kyrie Eleison (Abbeydorney), de Viridi Ligno (Newry) abbates qui fuerunt de principalibus conspiratoribus in conspiratione Mellifontis, deponuntur in instanti. Abbates Sanctae Mariae Dublinensis et de Portu Sanctae Mariae (Dunbrody) hoc eis denuntient' Canivez, *Statuta* 2 (1227. 29).

2 'Abbatia de Maio (Maigue) huc usque filia Mellifontis datur in perpetuam filiam abbatiae de Margam ob ordinis reformationem. Abbatia Vallis Salutis (Baltinglass) datur eodem modo abbatiae de Fontanis (Fountains) in Anglia. Abbatia de Surio (Suir: Inislounaght) huc usque filia de Maio eodem modo datur abbatiae de Furnesio. Abbatia de Valle Dei (Killeny) huc usque filia Geripontis, quia per se non valet, unitur abbatiae S. Salvatoris (Graiguenamanagh) cum omnibus bonis suis. De abbatia vero S. Crucis (Holycross) huc usque filia de Maio, statuitur ut si visitatores Capituli generalis viderint quod per se subsistere non valeat, abbatiae de Vuquchin (Abington) uniatur.' Canivez, *Statuta* 2 (1227. 36). The union of Killeny to Graiguenamanagh had been ordered by the Visitor and was confirmed by the general chapter, Butler and Bernard, *Duiske Charters* 19–22. There is no record of his commanding the other changes whilst he was in Ireland.

renewed its commission to the abbot of Clairvaux, 'so that what had been well begun, might under God be the better brought to a successful conclusion'.

For the visitation of 1228, the abbot of Clairvaux's deputy was the abbot of the Wiltshire house of Stanley, which already had a daughter in Ireland, Graiguenamanagh founded by William Marshal in 1204.[1] Abbot Stephen of Lexington was of a Nottinghamshire family which was to make a name in the meritocracy of thirteenth century England. His eldest brother was to succeed Robert Grosseteste in the see of Lincoln (1254–8), another brother became a judge in the court of common pleas and a third became an official of Henry III's Household.[2] Stephen himself was destined for high position in his order. In 1227, he was a relatively recent entrant into the Cistercian ranks. He had studied at both Oxford and Paris and had his feet already on the rungs of the ladder to a successful career in the diocesan Church when, under the influence of his former teacher, the saintly Edmund Rich, now archbishop of Canterbury, he renounced the world for the cloister, *c.* 1221. Stephen was perhaps that type of high-minded university man who a decade or so later might well have chosen the friars rather than the white monks. The Cistercians quickly recognized his worth and he was soon appointed abbot of Stanley. In 1229 he became abbot of Savigny and in 1243 abbot of Clairvaux itself. He made a niche for himself in the intellectual history of medieval Europe through his responsibility for the establishment of the first Cistercian house of studies at Paris, despite the opposition of conservative elements in the order. This commission as Visitor-General of the Cistercians of Ireland was his first major work for the order as a whole.

He came to Ireland as bearer of the 'plenitude of power' of the

---

[1] Cf. Butler and Bernard, *Duiske Charters* 13–14 for the beginnings of the foundation which should be supplemented by Canivez, *Statuta* 1 (1201. 40), (1202. 32). (1204. 22) and Conway, *Story of Mellifont* 48–9.

[2] Cf. *The Rolls and Register of Bishop Oliver Sutton* 1280–99 ed. R. M. T. Hill 3. (*The Lincoln Record Soc.* 48. 1954) xiv. 'Lexington' is the present Laxton. There is a useful outline sketch in *DNB* 11 by William Hunt. See further, C. H. Lawrence, 'Stephen of Lexington and Cistercian University Studies in the Thirteenth Century' *Jn. Eccles. Hist.* 11 (1960) 164–78. B. W. O'Dwyer, 'The Problem of reform in the Irish Cistercian monasteries and the attempted solution of Stephen of Lexington in 1228' *ibid.* 15 (1964) 186–91.

general chapter and equipped therefore with a formidable panoply of powers.[1] He might depose or promote or transfer or discipline monks as seemed expedient; change the status of monasteries and granges or where they were situated, as he saw fit; suspend, interdict, excommunicate, expel (if necessary, with the help of the secular arm) as he thought appropriate. In all things he was authorized to act as if he were the general chapter itself; his commands were issued in the name of the order itself. There were few of these powers he was not to exercise in Ireland. But Abbot Stephen came not merely to root up and to destroy but especially to build and to plant. The Cistercian way of life made of the visitation a positive infusion of new life, not a merely negative punitive instrument and events were to show that the Visitor-General was far from unmindful of the spirit in which he was required to correct and reform.

In addition to his general authorization as Visitor-General and the guidance of the Rule concerning visitation, Stephen bore with him the outlines of the policy the general chapter required him to implement in Ireland. This was the policy adopted by the general chapter, certainly since the visitation of Bernard of Froidmont and just possibly even earlier, of which there were three aspects: reorganization of the routine visitation and disciplinary procedure by removing daughters from their mother houses and allocating them, so to say, to foster-mothers; suppressing houses that were not viable; in at least some cases, substituting abbots who were not Irish for those Irish deposed for rebellion.

Before leaving for Ireland, Stephen spent some time taking advice about his mission[2] and in particular in recruiting a visitation team. His mandate allowed him to command the services of any monks whom he thought would be useful.[3] The abbots of Buildwas[4] and

---

[1] They are set out in his letters of credence, Butler and Bernard, *Duiske Charters* 27. Cf. also Lexington, *Registrum* 91.
[2] 'Ad partes siquidem predictas consultum minime duximus aliquatenus transmeare, nisi prius communi tam abbatum Anglie quam Wallie communicato consilio de forma procedendi, impetratis etiam tam a domino rege quam episcopis, quam magnatibus regni patrocinio et tuitione, per quos credebatur in hoc negotio viam preparari posse uel aditum aperiri' *Registrum* 31. 35.
[3] *Registrum* 92.
[4] Buildwas had a daughter in Ireland, St Mary's, Dublin. The abbot was to be entrusted with a substantial part of the work of the visitation, *Registrum* 66.

Margam,[1] both with Irish experience, were his chief lieutenants. He selected also a number of experienced monks from different houses, who were earmarked for the key positions of the whole operation: the abbacies of the culprit communities. He also took the precaution of bringing a common lawyer with him, whose area of activity was to be monastic property.

Abbot Stephen had need of every bit of the authority, guidance and encouragement that could be given him by the general chapter and by the Rule, of the support he asked for from civil authorities, of the loyalty of his band of assistants. For there can be little doubt about the sheer physical danger into which he was about to put himself and even less about the gravity of the situation with which he had been called upon to grapple. He was to try to solve a vast problem of widespread and endemic rebellion against the order, where recourse to violence, within as well as without the monastic world, was almost the accepted method of airing and solving grievance. He was to report back to the general chapter that he found in Ireland (he was speaking specifically of the Mellifont *generatio*) that everything of the Cistercian life had gone, save only the wearing of the habit.[2] He reported too the failure of the visitation of the previous year when the authority of the deputy appointed by Bernard of Froidmont on his departure, the foreign-born abbot of Abington, was repudiated and the creation of new abbots had been hotly opposed.[3] He found too the Cistercian world engulfed in national hatreds: Mellifont situated in 'most dangerous march territory between English and Irish';[4] the Irish community of Baltinglass rejecting a foreign

---

[1] *Registrum* 13. Stephen was particularly anxious to have the abbot of Margam because of his experience on the visitation in the previous year and had gone to Margam personally to persuade him. Not surprisingly, the abbot responded 'tepide' but his reluctance was overcome.

[2] Gregory IX was told: 'Nam in abbaciis Hibernie censura et ordo noster excepto habitu uix in aliquo seruabatur, eo quod nec in choro seruitium debitum nec in claustro silentium nec in capitulo disciplina nec in refectorio cibus communis nec in dormitorio quies monachalis secundum formam ordinis ...' *Registrum* 3. 14. This is based on Stephen's reports to the abbot of Clairvaux, e.g. *Registrum* 31 or to the general chapter, 33.

[3] *Registrum* 38.

[4] 'In pessima namque marchia et periculosa inter Anglicos et Hibernicos. Quapropter etsi quando sit ibi pax horaria, nulla tamen constans, nulla secura' *Registrum* 34. 42.

replacement of their own deposed abbot by throwing him from his horse, taking his abbatial seal away from him and barring his entrance by force of arms;[1] the Irish abbot of Bective in fear of his life from Walter de Lacy;[2] the Cistercian archbishop of Cashel more interested (Stephen thought) in promoting the good of his own nation than of pure religion;[3] English monks ejected by the Irish monks of Maigue.[4]

How Stephen went about his daunting task[5] can be traced in some detail, because of the fortuitous survival of his *Register*.[6] Here are to be found copies of the letters he wrote to his Cistercian superiors, to all those, Cistercian abbots, prelates in England and Ireland, secular powers and so on, from whom he hoped to get help in his mission, to the various Cistercian communities in Ireland. Here also are copies of a number of official documents relevant to the visitation procedure employed: decrees; instructions to deputies; papal correspondence. In all, the *Register* is a quite unique document of Irish medieval ecclesiastical history, indeed of Cistercian history in general, throwing a flood of light, albeit often lurid, on the Irish Cistercian scene and on the response of Cistercian authority to the crisis. It also illustrates, as does no other document, just how painful, to both peoples, could be the impact of the Anglo-French on the Irish Church.

Almost none of the entries in the *Register* is dated, dating references in the texts themselves are few and so the actual chronology of the visitation remains somewhat indeterminate. There is no certain indication of when Abbot Stephen arrived in and departed from

---

1 *Registrum* 38.
2 'Abbas vero de Beatitudine similiter de alia lingua et natione per metum et terrorem domini W. de Lacy uix utcumque usque ad aduentum nostrum in domo sua habitauit' *Registrum* 38. 48–9.
3 'Timemus namque in parte domnum Cassellensem episcopum commorantem apud Cistercium, quem nostis [i.e. the abbot of Clairvaux] acceptorem nationis et non pure religionis, plus collaudatorem sue gentis quam bene composite mentis aliene' *Registrum* 34. 42. The archbishop was Mairin O Briain (1223–37).
4 'Nam abbatem proprium et monachos quosdam insimul et conuersos auctoritate ordinis illuc destinatos, ut ordinem docerent omnino ibidem adnichilatum et disciplinam reformarent, uiolenter excluserunt et ab abbatia penitus expulerunt' *Registrum* 4. 16.
5 He frequently expressed himself in great anguish: 'Quapropter labores et dolores nec non et mortis pericula, quibus incessanter exponimur, pro honore religionis et legibus paternis sub breuitate stili nemo posset transcurrere' *Registrum* 38. 49.
6 Now National Library, Turin MS D. VI. 25.

Ireland. It is clear, however, that the active period lay between early
May and early September of 1228. It was a summer of intense activity. Every house seems to have been visited. The most onerous and
often the most dangerous visits Stephen made himself; others he
entrusted to deputies, in particular to the abbot of Buildwas. At least
two meetings of abbots and others were held, both in June, a
colloquium at Graiguenamanagh[1] (which, as a daughter of his own
house of Stanley, was probably his headquarters), followed by a
capitulum at Dublin.[2] It was at this chapter that the major decisions of
the visitation were taken.

The *Register* includes detailed descriptions of the reception of the
Visitors at Maigue and at Mellifont and of the steps taken to reform
these houses. These seem to have been the most troublesome houses,
and in watching Stephen of Lexington at work in them, we may
form some impression of the conduct of his visitation as a whole and
acquire some of the background information essential for the understanding of the policy by which he sought to compose the strife.

Abbot Stephen and his *socii* gained entry into Mellifont shortly
before Mass on 27 July. The Dublin chapter had already decided to
take some of her daughters away from her. Her (Irish) abbot had
offered his resignation through the abbot of Citeaux which Stephen
had been reluctant to accept because he thought him suitable for the
post, both for his personal qualities and because he was acceptable to
the English. Stephen refrained from insisting that he stay on, however, lest thereby he was in effect signing his death warrant. Thus
Stephen had the worst forebodings of what was in store for him and
his party at Mellifont and they came anticipating and prepared for
martyrdom. Their fears were not confirmed. The hostility they
encountered was no more than verbal, entry was gained and for
seven days the community listened to Stephen whilst he harangued
them so vigorously that often 'he could scarcely speak or even
open his jaws'.[3]

He was effective. By the end of the first day he had persuaded the
monks to take an oath, submitting themselves to the prescribed legal

---

[1] *Registrum* 28.   [2] *Registrum* 32, 33.

[3] 'Nam, teste Deo, non cessantes contionari ad populum bestialem per VII dies
continuos sepius tanta affecti fuimus lassitudine, ut uix sermonem proferre aut fauces
possemus aperire' *Registrum* 37. 46.

processes of the order and renouncing conspiracy and rebellion. They were absolved and reconciled before the Blessed Sacrament. This major step accomplished, Stephen proceeded to have an abbot appointed. He did this 'suddenly', so that external interests, whether family or criminal, should have no opportunity of influencing the choice. Jocelyn, prior of Beaubec in France, was appointed.

The rest of the week in Mellifont, Stephen devoted to the visitation proper, following a visitation procedure apparently devised for use in Ireland by Bernard of Froidmont. There were sentences to be passed. He allowed twelve of the less guilty monks and sixteen brothers to remain in Mellifont. The remainder, to the number of about forty, who had deserted the order but were now reconciled, were sent in penance to monasteries abroad, under orders not to return without the special licence of the abbot of Clairvaux (their mother house). Stephen advised that dignitary not to be beguiled by fair promises into an injudicious clemency: to allow these men to return would spell the expulsion of the new abbot and thus make it correspondingly more difficult to get another to undertake the post, and so the second stage would be worse than the first. Rather should he build up the *religio* of Mellifont by sending monks of his own choice. Shortage of good monks was the greatest danger threatening the Cistercians of Ireland, in Stephen's opinion, and this could and should be remedied by assistance from outside. He protested that the order was not trying to exclude a nation from its ranks, but sought only to weed out the unsuitable and the dissolute.

Abbot Stephen had an educational programme to supplement his disciplinary efforts. No one should be professed who was unable to speak and read French and Latin: 'How can a man love the cloister and learning if he knows only Irish?'[1] He urged—foreshadowing of the policy he was later to generalize for the whole order—that Irish monks should seek higher education abroad, at Oxford or Paris, or other famous seats of learning.[2]

[1] 'Quomodo autem diliget claustrum aut librum, qui nichil nouit nisi Hibernicum? Nec aliud nisi turris Babel construi poterit, ubi nec discipulus magistrum intelligit nec e contra nec congrue dinoscitur, ut dum unus petit panem, alius pro pane porrigat lapidem seu pro pisce tribuat scorpionem' (cf. Matth. 7. 9–10) *Registrum* 37. 47.

[2] 'Quapropter Hiberniensibus iniunximus, quod si quem de suis in ordine de cetero recipi desiderent, Parisius uel Oxonium uel ad alias ciuitates famosas mittere stu-

There is most of Stephen's visitation policy to be seen in the account of his treatment of this one house of Mellifont: reallocation of daughter houses and concomitant encouragement of new mothers to become involved with their adopted daughters;[1] the exiling of guilty monks (not necessarily permanently);[2] clemency for the less guilty; revitalization of the community by the appointment of a new abbot and the introduction of fresh monks, all from outside Ireland; insistence on knowledge of Latin (for obvious reasons) and of French, in order to facilitate communication between Irish monks, their mothers outside, the general chapter and such Visitors as it might send; the encouragement of intellectual as well as of monastic formation. In all, a combination of administrative, coercive, pastoral and educational devices overcame what the abbot of Citeaux told Gregory IX was the 'unheard of disorderliness and extraordinarily poor quality' of Irish Cistercianism.

One other aspect of Stephen's policy, the use of the secular power for police work against rebellious monks, can be seen in especially clear light from what happened when visitation of Maigue was made.[3] Its abbot had been deposed and a new abbot, with accompanying monks and brothers, had been drafted in from outside to teach the monastic life as it ought to be led. This new, foreign contingent was not permitted to enter the monastery and the elderly and more discreet of the original community having withdrawn, the remainder converted it into a castle prepared for siege. They had enlisted two hundred mercenaries, built a fortified tower, ready victualled, above the high altar, stored salted meat under the dormitories, stocked thirty head of cattle in the cloister, turned the church into a provision store for them and the garrison and converted the dormitories into armouries.

Visitors, in the persons of the abbot of nearby Abington and the cantor of Graiguenamanagh, began to take action against them.

deant, ubi litteras et loquele peritiam addiscant morumque compositionem, manifestiusque ipsis ostendimus, quod nullam intendit ordo excludere nationem, sed solummodo ineptos et inutiles et moribus humanis dissidentes' *Registrum* 37. 47.
[1] Stephen was to upbraid for neglect of their Irish responsibilities particularly the abbots of Furness (*Registrum* 25) and Fountains (*Registrum* 26, 69).
[2] Irish monks were sent *causa disciplinae* to: Fountains (*Registrum* 17, 18, 23, 75), Margam (19), Loos (Tournai: 47), Holmcultram (50), Byland (80).
[3] *Registrum* 4.

Legal process began with reiterated monitions, which were ignored; continued with minor excommunications of the rebels, and these were spurned; was taken further with their major excommunication, and this sentence in turn had no effect. The rebels were then threatened with capture and imprisonment by the secular arm. This too went for nothing. What convinced the Cistercian judges that the drastic action of calling in the police was necessary was their witnessing the public celebration of Mass by the excommunicates and their eating publicly with their hired fighting men. Application was then made to the *officialis* of the appropriate metropolitan (Cashel), who was Hubert de Burgh, bishop of Limerick. He was unable to gain entry. A force was assembled. On the bishop's instructions, a rampart that had been erected by the rebels on the east side of the church was pulled down and the besiegers made their way in, with some loss of life by the defenders.

The captured monks were now in the jurisdiction of the Bishop, but he remitted them to the Cistercians as *fugitivi* from that order. Stephen of Lexington, who had been in another part of the country, hastened to Maigue to deal with them. Along with the dean of that region, sent by the Bishop, the church, defiled by the celebration of Mass by excommunicates, was reconciled. Some of the rebel monks and brothers had fled, but others remained and asked for mercy. They were absolved. A new abbot and fresh monks were introduced. The abbot of Abington was given power to act in the name of the general chapter with authority to absolve and reconcile all save the ringleaders who were referred to the judgment of the general chapter. Stephen was not averse to using force to break rebellion, but he was clement with individuals when resistance had been suppressed.

It was a cardinal point of his visitation strategy to enlist the permanent protection of secular rulers, Irish and foreign. He asked the king of Thomond to cooperate in securing the capture of excommunicate and schismatic monks and to protect Maigue and Abbeydorney.[1] He authorized the abbot of Maigue to spare no expense in securing the good offices of the justiciar and other authorities for the well-being of his house.[2]

---

[1] *Registrum* 9, 10.

[2] '... quod cum summa discretionis prudentia dictum negotium uiriliter prosequamini usque ad condignam consummationem nullatenus percentes pecunie uel

These two visitations allow us to see the particularities of Stephen's policy, as it impinged on individual houses and individual monks. The most significant general change was decreed by the Dublin chapter which met in late June.[1] The main figures of this meeting were Abbot Stephen himself and his aides, the abbots of Buildwas and Margam. There were fourteen abbots of houses in Ireland present, half of whom were from houses of Anglo-French foundation and, of the other half, it seems safe to presume that they were the new foreign appointees of the Visitor-General.[2] The main business of the chapter, at least as reported to the abbot of Clairvaux and for which ratification by the general chapter was sought and obtained, concerned the refiliation of monasteries. As has been seen, the policy of reallocating houses to other mothers in order to tighten discipline through efficient visitation had already been introduced by Bernard of Froidmont and approved by the general chapter. This was taken further by Stephen of Lexington and his advisers. The result was a drastic realignment of the parentage of the Irish houses. The earlier decision had affected only three houses. Twelve more were now to be changed. All the new foster-mothers were to be houses outside Ireland and the five concerned had all already an Irish dependency. The following dispositions were made:

Under	CLAIRVAUX	Mellifont (Clairvaux)
		Bective (Mellifont)
		Boyle (Mellifont)
		Abbeyknockmoy (Boyle)
	MARGAM	*Maigue* (Mellifont)
		Holycross (Maigue)
		Midleton (Maigue)
		Abbeydorney (Maigue)

alterius substantie erogationi domno Iusticiario et aliis, qui poterunt iuvare in hac causa, liberaliter faciende, si necesse fuerit, ita quod terra remaneat omnino nuda; maius est enim, ut res domus largiter expendantur pro causa Dei et ordinis, quam consumantur a scismaticis et excommunicatis et pro causa diaboli in ordinis perpetuam confusionem ...' *Registrum* 7.

[1] *Registrum* 32, 33, 87–9.
[2] They were Dublin, Graiguenamanagh, Dunbrody, Abington, Tracton, Tintern, Jerpoint, Bective, Maigue, Baltinglass, Holycross, Abbeylara, Monasterevin, Kilcooley. A fuller list than *Registrum* 88 is in Butler and Bernard, *Duiske Charters* 57.

FURNESS	Abington (Furness) *Inislounaght* (Maigue) Fermoy (Inislounaght) Corcumroe (Inislounaght)
FOUNTAINS	*Baltinglass* (Mellifont) Jerpoint (Baltinglass) Monasterevin (Baltinglass)

It was explained that there were many reasons for making these changes but chief among them was the intention of breaking the 'unitas perniciosa' of the Mellifont *filiatio* which had given strength and cohesion to the whole rebellion.[1] It was also explained that to each mother had been given at least two houses so that if one were to fall back into evil ways the existence of another would afford some chance of escape and refuge for obedient monks.

The chapter decided further that Glengragh (Inislounaght) having only eight monks, nine brothers and three carucates of land, was too small and too poor for autonomous existence. It was therefore united with Dunbrody, the nearest house (which also happened to be Anglo-French). The union of Kilbeggan (Mellifont) to Bective was also ordered. Bective, in close proximity to Trim, centre of the de Lacy lordship and now almost certainly anglicized, had come to have an important strategic function in planning the Cistercian reform. Visitors could be sure of safe access to it and security within it. Mellifont was but a short distance away and it was thought too that it would afford access to Boyle in the remote west.

This is another detail of Stephen's policy of using lay powers for protection of Visitors and general police duties on behalf of the order. He sought lay help diligently wherever it might be found: from Irish rulers such as the king of Thomond to help Maigue and the king of Oriel to help Mellifont;[2] from the seneschal of the

---

1 '. . . exitum alium nequaquam reperire ualuimus, quo uel horrendis conspirationibus uel inueteratis exordinationibus finis imponatur et respiret religio, nisi abbatie quedam domorum minus ordinatarum subiectioni subtracte aliquibus aliarum regionum abbaciis, que ruinas ordinis tam in spiritualibus quam temporalibus et uelint et ualeant maturius reparare, tanquam matribus iure perpetuo supponantur . . .' *Registrum* 32. 37.

2 *Registrum* 52 with the threat that if there were further rebellion, Mellifont would be suppressed and refounded in some safer place, England or Leinster.

Marshal lordship of Leinster,[1] where numerous houses were situated; from the justiciar for overall help and also especially in Munster.[2] He used his connexions in England (his brother Richard[3] and the bishop of Chester[4]) to alert the King to the need to prod the justiciar into action, for he had found the lands under direct royal jurisdiction to be less well policed, from the Cistercian point of view, than the lordships. It would, however, be quite wrong to deduce from this care to enlist the help of the secular arm that Stephen of Lexington thought that reform of the Cistercians was primarily a police operation. But a Cistercian Visitor was exposed to violence and personal danger—a member of his own party was severely wounded by robbers near Kilcooley[5]—and Stephen wanted to ensure above all that Visitors should have protection when moving about the country, and, if need be, have secular help in bringing fugitive monks to Cistercian justice.

The general chapter approved of Stephen's work, ratified his decisions and renewed his commission for a further year.[6] He was, however, not able to return to Ireland but delegated his office to the abbots of Dublin and Graiguenamanagh.[7] To each of these abbots-deputy he sent a schedule of instructions which they were to implement universally throughout Ireland.[8] These *articuli* constitute the next stage of his policy. They were the fruit of his own experience, and had presumably been drawn up by him, but having been ratified by the general chapter, they were promulgated in its name. They thus represented not only Stephen's own mind but the policy officially enjoined by the supreme authority of the order.

As the nature of these instructions speak for themselves, they can perhaps be given in full: .

Instructions to be kept generally throughout Ireland

1. No one shall be admitted to be a monk, no matter what his nationality,

---

[1] *Registrum* 85; identification of the addressee, Butler and Bernard, *Duiske Charters* 47.

[2] *Registrum* 76.   [3] *Registrum* 44.

[4] *Registrum* 79. Stephen was clearly surprised that Maigue, so near to Limerick, could be so unruly with English monks expelled. If William Marshal or Walter de Lacy were in charge such things could not happen. They happen only in Munster 'ubi dominus Rex singulariter et principaliter optinet dominationem'.

[5] *Registrum* 78. 79.

[6] Canivez, *Statuta* 2 (1228. 37. Stanley here misidentified as Stoneley). *Registrum* 91.

[7] *Registrum* 93.   [8] *Registrum* 95.

unless he can confess his faults in French or Latin, in order that when the visitors and correctors of the order come he can understand them and be understood by them.

2. The charters and all legal documents of houses shall be kept together in such safe keeping as shall make it impossible in the future for wicked men to steal them or use them for fraudulent purposes.

3. The rule shall in future be explained only in French and the monks' chapter conducted in either French or Latin so that in the future anyone who wishes to be received as a monk must first have attended such a school as would teach him to conduct himself less uncouthly.

4. As punishment for the conspiracies which have arisen generally throughout the Irish houses, it is strictly forbidden for any monk of that people to be appointed abbot, in order that obedience to the order be fully proved and that having first learned how to be pupils, they may in due time and place be the more capable masters.

5. It is forbidden under pain of anathema for any lands or holdings to be alienated without the prior consent and confirmation of the father abbot. This is commanded under pain of deposition from office and removal from the council.

6. No property shall be leased for a longer period than seven years so that there shall be recent memory of the transaction. It is forbidden to execute a lease without the appropriate safeguards of previously seeking serious and responsible advice and with appropriate consultation taken publicly and formally.

7. So that for the future the property of houses should not be wasted nor the crime of simony committed through lack of forethought, it is strictly commanded under the penalties already mentioned that monks in the future should not buy land nor accept patronage of churches unless correct and careful inquisition has first been made, so that any entry or possession shall be fully legal and secure in title.

8. All officials of monasteries and granges who have responsibility for possessions, are strictly commanded to render true and accurate account to their abbot and council or to those specially appointed for the purpose by the abbot. Whatever is kept back will be held against the concealer for theft or holding property and he will be liable to the established penalties for these crimes.

9. It is commanded under the same penalty that no brother shall sell anything without the consent or licence of his abbot or cellarer.

10. Monks and brothers who have been dismissed to other houses shall not be recalled without the special permission of the abbot of Clairvaux, properly obtained without falsehood or suppression of the truth. A

grace or dispensation obtained by lying or concealing the truth is *ipso iure* invalid.

11. On pain of anathema, deposition from office, removal from the council, it is strictly forbidden that ever for the future should any woman be received as a nun in the houses of Ireland, because of the shameful disorderliness and scandals to which this practice has given rise.

12. By authority of the order and of the general chapter, the abbots of Dublin and Graiguenamanagh are strictly commanded on their obedience to promulgate the above instructions, in their exact form, their seals attached, in all the houses in Ireland.

13. Every house shall keep carefully its own copy of these instructions. The said abbots shall order them to be read once a month for a year, under pain of serious and certain sentence.

With this schedule of instructions went a covering letter of admonition and advice to each of the abbots-deputy.[1] It is almost a gloss on the *articuli* and adds some additional interesting detail of information and emphasis.

His main advice was that there should be no more major changes until the results of the recent changes had had time to show, though of course visitation, correction and reform must be pressed hard. Most of his advice is about visitation. Visitations of abbeys in the more dangerous and remoter areas might be delegated to the abbots most proximate to them, but they should first be summoned and person- ally instructed about their mission. Special attention should be given to the daughters of Clairvaux and in particular to Mellifont, Baltin- glass and Maigue, formerly the chief trouble-spots. None of the expelled community of Baltinglass should in any circumstances be readmitted. They should not hesitate about calling in the help of the secular power at need. On the other hand, with reference to the remaining fugitives of the Maigue community, they might act mercifully, insisting first, however, on the return of the abbey's charters with which they had absconded.

There were special provisions in respect of the native Irish houses in Connacht and parts of Ulster, which were not mentioned in the schedule. Boyle and Fermoy should be visited by two of Irish nationality, preferably in association with the abbot of Abbeyshrule

---

[1] *Registrum* 94.

(an Irish house). These Visitors should be carefully selected and briefed on how to carry out their duties according to the accompanying schedule and the customary procedures of the order. Abbots of recent creation might be excused attendance at the general chapter, but the abbots of Inch and Grey Abbey, who have been absentees, should go.

One special provision is of great interest. Stephen specified that should the abbeys of Corcumroe, Newry or Abbeyshrule fall vacant, the abbots-deputy should take care to provide abbots of Irish nationality. This is a most significant qualification of the rule that no one of Irish race should be made abbot for three years. It may here be recalled that he had himself when in Ireland chosen an Irishman to be abbot of Boyle, only withdrawing his support on learning that his candidate had been one of the Mellifont rebels. Even so he had envisaged the possibility of a native Irishman being selected by the Visitors for Boyle.[1] It is clear that Stephen was quite prepared to have Irish abbots where expedient, just as he was prepared to support Irish Cistercians for bishoprics in Irish areas.[2]

Stephen's final words to his substitutes were about the spirit which should inform their work. They should immediately address themselves to the other abbots, speaking to them of love, of chastity and sobriety, of charity and of bearing one another's burdens. They must warn these abbots against unnecessary absence from their monasteries; they must lend themselves unceasingly to restoring and reforming their houses. If by mischance they find abbots who are unchaste or drunken they are to depose them for fear of greater scandals. Other faults, however, should be treated patiently and tolerantly. Benign paternalism was the watchword. Instruction rather than severity was to be the order of the day so that with patience and charitable forbearance the culpable and the backward might grow to knowledge and love of the Cistercian way of life.[3]

---

[1] *Registrum* 65.

[2] *Registrum* 67, to the bishop of Salisbury asking him to support the promotion of Nehemias, prior of Mellifont to the see of Clogher, a diocese for the most part 'inter Hibernos puros'.

[3] *Registrum* 94. 92. These instructions are in exact accord with the *monita salutaria* he had earlier addressed to the abbot-elect of Suir: 'Conuentum uestrum tractetis benigna instructione magis quam aliqua austeritate propter diuturnam dissuetudinem, studentes pro posse amari ab ipsis et ab hominibus prouintie, in hoc initio

Was Stephen of Lexington guilty of discriminating against the native Irish? He was sensitive about this accusation which was made in the course of his visitation.[1] It has been repeated in various degrees of strength—from the charge of a 'certain bias'[2] to that of imposing *apartheid*[3]—by modern historians.

It is not difficult to understand how such accusations came to be formulated. To some of his Irish contemporaries the policy of appointing only foreign abbots for Irish houses, in itself a very unpopular measure,[4] made Stephen an *acceptor nationis*, a discriminator. To modern historians his apparently disparaging comment on the Irish language ('Quomodo autem diliget claustrum aut librum qui nichil nouit nisi Hibernicum?') has suggested a similar conclusion.

It must be recalled that the policy of rebuilding the communities of Irish monks by putting them under the control of foreign houses and drafting in foreign abbots and monks was not of Stephen's making. It was of the general chapter's. Further, when Stephen implemented it more fully, his decisions were authorized by the general chapter. Thus if there is any charge of national discrimination it should be levelled at the order as a whole, not at Stephen personally. The policy must be judged in the context of a decade of persistent defiance of the order's authority; it was a radical response to a crisis situation. It was designed to re-establish that universality and uniformity which made the Cistercian way of life, by setting the internationalism of the order to break down that insularity of the Irish houses which was held to be the root cause of the trouble. The

dissimulantes aliqua peccata eorum ad tempus et exordinationes, quousque intelligibiliores sint et magis capaces ... patientia et benignitate semper armati uincatis in bono malum' *Registrum* 76.

1 'Nec mirari debetis [he is addressing the abbot of Furness] quod sicut quidam nos facturos credebant, ad exterminationem gentis non intendimus, quia omnino non expediret uobis aut ordini. Nam oportet eos paulatim et per partes delere, ne forte multiplicentur contra nos bestie agri, hoc est bestiales homines, qui in campestris et montanis super harenam multiplicati omnia indifferenter in ultionem gentis sue exterminarent et delerent.' *Registrum* 25.

2 Conway, *Story of Mellifont* 69.

3 See the comment of B. W. O'Dwyer against this description, *Journal of Religious Studies* (1968) 300. But this author considers 'the abbot's own grasp of the problem had subjective, emotional elements which militated against his ability of being completely spiritual or even fair to the Irish monks' *ibid.* 296.

4 He told the bishop of Salisbury: 'Abbates siquidem plures ibidem creauimus lingue alterius et nationis non sine magnis et crebris mortis periculis' *Registrum* 40. 51.

bias was against Irish particularism, not against the Irish as such. The order, as a universal institution, was operating within its universal framework to suppress what it saw as a rejection of its universalism. There was no place in the Cistercian order for national individualism of monastic practice.

About his insistence on knowledge of French and Latin, Stephen made it quite clear that his complaint was not against Irish as such. He would be equally hostile to a postulant who knew nothing but English or Scots or Welsh.[1] His point was that Latin was the language of the universal Church and that the order, born and bred in France, had French as its common vernacular. Without it there could not be effective communication between head and members.

Judgments of the overall conduct of the visitation by Stephen of Lexington will inevitably vary among historians. On the whole, opinion has tended to go against him, because of suspicions of his impartiality. Nevertheless his order seems to have been well pleased with his work for it confirmed it, reappointed him Visitor-General and apparently saw in it the mark of outstanding leadership quality for within a few months of leaving Ireland he had been made abbot of the major house of Savigny. Certainly his *Register* supplies evidence enough of his zeal for the order, energy, courage, firmness, common sense and basic humanity for one to understand how this man rose to a position of high authority in the order.

The visitation may have been a personal success for Stephen of Lexington. Was it a success for the Cistercians of Ireland?

In 1231 the general chapter found it necessary to appeal to Pope Gregory IX for help after renewed violence in Ireland. The abbot of Fermoy and a monk of Inislounaght had been killed and the communities of these two houses and of Corcumroe had refused admission to Visitors sent by their father abbot of Furness. The abbot of Monasterevin and a brother of Jerpoint had been blinded.

---

[1] 'Prohibemus insuper auctoritate supra memorata sub pena depositionis uel eiectionis, ne unquam recipiatis in monachum aliquem, nisi qui sciat culpam suam confiteri gallice uel latine. Nec intelligimus presenti statuto aliquas excludere nationes, Anglicas, Scotticas, Walenses aut Hibernicas, sed tantummodo personas ordini inutiles et omnino infructuosas. Quomodo namque ordinem diliget aut silencii seruabit grauitatem uel claustri disciplinam, qui omnino nullum in scriptura nouit inuenire solatium, non in lege Dei meditari saltim modicum quiddam die aut nocte?' *Registrum* 52 (To the abbot and community of Tracton).

Gregory IX vigorously denounced dissolute monks as 'beasts who have rotted in their own dung' (Joel 1. 17) and asked Henry III, the justiciar and other authorities to give every help in the bringing of the guilty to justice and in protecting Cistercian Visitors.[1] There were, too, complaints in the general chapters of 1232 and 1233 of widespread absenteeism by Irish abbots.[2] It is abundantly clear that Stephen of Lexington's many times expressed appreciation of the effort, time and skill needed to resolve Irish Cistercian problems was not over-cautious.

In the longer term, however, such indications of the health of the Irish province as are supplied by the *Statuta* of the general chapter, indicate improvement. At least there was no further report of repulsion of Visitors and of physical violence. Absenteeism from general chapter and inadequate visitation remained as problems, however.

In 1271 the general chapter spoke of the *quaestio taediosa* of the visitation of Irish houses which so frequently came to its ears. This entry in the *Statuta* almost certainly indicates that one of the dangers envisaged by Stephen of Lexington had not been avoided. He had found it necessary to urge the abbots of Fountains and Furness to take their new responsibilities more seriously and not neglect their daughters in Ireland. The policy of placing the burden of routine visitation on abbots of houses outside Ireland was not a success. In 1274 the general chapter decreed a return to the *status quo* and the Irish houses were restored to their former paternity and system of visitation.[3]

The presence in the university of Oxford in 1291 of one Thomas of Mellifont[4] may be the trace of an enduring contribution of Stephen of Lexington to Irish Cistercianism: his encouragement of the pursuit of education abroad.

The ultimate solution of Irish Cistercian problems lay in the achievement of the harmonious integration of Irish and foreign in Irish society as a whole. We shall see how, at the end of our period, the Cistercians in Ireland were still plagued with severe tensions between the peoples.

[1] *Registrum* 111; *Pont. hib.* 2. 205; Canivez, *Statuta* 2 (1230. 20; 1231. 27, 34).
[2] Canivez, *Statuta* 2 (1232. 50; 1233. 47; 1237. 47; 1239. 54; 1246. 55; 1253. 27).
[3] See below, p. 159.
[4] Emden, *Biographical Register, Oxford* 2. 1256.

Chapter 5

ECCLESIA HIBERNICANA

Another institution, closely connected with the twelfth-century reform and with the name of Malachy, which was to become a casualty in the thirteenth century, was the primacy of Armagh. With its undermining went the *de iure* unity of the Irish Church, in particular the possibility of all the bishops of Ireland meeting together for the good of the whole *ecclesia hibernicana*. This disunity, reflecting both the particularism of Ireland itself and the post-Invasion national divisions, must be given significance as a factor impeding further progress in reform of the Church.

Armagh of course owed its traditional seniority to its association with St Patrick.[1] As the pope was heir of St Peter, *comharba Peadair*, so the prelate of Armagh was heir to the founder of Christianity in Ireland and his established title, *comharba Padraig*. All the schemes of diocesan construction of the twelfth century envisaged the preservation of this seniority and planned an unquestionable primatial prerogative for the see of Patrick. At the council of Rathbreasail in 1111, as reported in the lost Clonenagh annals, Armagh signed as archbishop and as primate of all the bishops of Ireland.[2] At Kells in 1152, though four metropolitans were now constituted, Armagh was designated, according to one source 'in primatem'[3] and according to another, 'primas tocius Hibernie'.[4] There can be no doubt at all that it was intended, and intended by the pope whose legate presided at Kells, that Armagh should have the senior position and enjoy place as first of the bishops of Ireland.

There is no certitude, however, about what was intended as to the

---

[1] Cf. Kenney, *Sources* 319–54; Hughes, *The Church in early Irish society* ch. 11.
[2] Keating, *History of Ireland* 2. 306.
[3] 'Insuper Armachanum archiepiscopum in primatem super alios prout decuit ordinavit [i.e. Cardinal John Paparo]' *Clonenagh Annals* in Keating, *History of Ireland* 2. 314.
[4] Cf. Lawlor, 'A fresh authority for the synod of Kells' 18.

primatial content of this dignity. Was Armagh to be simply *primus inter pares* among the metropolitans? Was its position to be a primacy of honour only or was it a primacy of jurisdiction? Was it intended that Armagh should enjoy rights of visitation in other provinces and exact offerings as of right? These were not academic questions for, leaving aside all customs of an earlier period, there were abundant precedents in the twelfth century itself that Armagh did not construe its primacy as one of precedence only. The career of Celsus, with his activity in all the provinces and his visitation and exaction of dues from Cashel, for example, was evidence enough.[1] One question was of particular delicacy. Did the newly accomplished integration of Dublin in the structure of the Irish Church proper imply a jurisdictional subordination to Armagh?

These questions had still to be answered definitively when the Invasion began. There were no established norms to be discovered in the canons of the universal Church about the relationship of metropolitans to a primate. In such matters, approved custom or specific papal decision was all. No such specific ruling had been given at Kells and thus it seems likely that some dispute would inevitably have arisen had there been no Invasion. When Dublin became the centre of colonial government while Armagh, diocese and province, remained strongly native Irish, and the other two provinces were also considerably affected, some clarification of the relationship was inescapable.

This came with the appointment of John Cumin, the first foreigner to become archbishop of Dublin. In April 1182, he asked Pope Lucius III to take his new see under papal protection and to confirm all the rights of jurisdiction and property which pertained to it. This was a wise precaution in the prevailing uncertain political situation and it was to follow a precedent already set three years earlier by Archbishop Laurence O'Toole. The papal constitution for Cumin, however, contained one significant novelty. It included this provision:

In accordance with the authority of the holy canons, no archbishop or bishop if he be in the bishopric should without the consent of the archbishop of Dublin presume to hold any assembly or treat of any causes or

[1] Cf. the numerous entries *ALC* 95–127.

ecclesiastical business of the same diocese unless he has been instructed to do so by the pope or by his legate.[1]

This was to grant the autonomy of the Dublin diocese from any assertion of superior, primatial right. In the long perspective of history this papal decision now appears as the first step in a progress towards the establishment of a primacy for Dublin.[2] Its immediate significance, however, was much less dramatic. Even in the limited context of granting autonomy, the definition was a restricted one for its reference was only to the Dublin diocese, not to the province. It did not mark a breaking-off of relations with Armagh, for the primate presided in 1192 at the consecration of Cumin's new collegiate church of St Patrick's in Dublin.[3] It did not mark a rejection of the primacy of Armagh in principle by the new authorities for there is incontrovertible evidence that King John recognized that Armagh held the primacy.[4] Its significance lay in its formal, if implicit, ruling that in Dublin at least, the primacy was one of honour, not of jurisdiction.

Some historians have considered that the stirrings of a Dublin rivalry towards Armagh's primacy had shown themselves even before Lucius III's ruling. In 1177 John de Courcy on the second of his highly successful raids into Ulster in that year captured a number of relics, including the so-called Staff of Jesus, traditionally cherished as the very crozier used by St Patrick himself. Most of these relics were to be restored but the Staff was retained in Dublin where it remained until it was publicly burned at the Reformation as a superstitious object. The significance of this retention has been seen by Orpen and others as marking Dublin's attempt to give itself Patrician standing and thus to assist it in a claim to supremacy.[5] There is, however, no evidence to suggest that Cumin sought to make himself primate. John de Courcy himself, as might be expected of an earl of Ulster, was a champion of Armagh. At least this seems the correct deduction

---

[1] *Pont. hib.* I. 11. at p. 37. [2] Cf. Gwynn, 'Archbishop John Cumin' 296.
[3] Cf. Hand, 'Rivalry of the Cathedral Chapters' 195.
[4] Cf. *Cal. Docs. Irel. 1171–1257* 177; *Rotuli Litterarum Patentium* I. 29a using the term *primacia Hibernie* in connexion with Armagh. See also *Cal. cit.* 331 and *Rot. Litt. Claus.* 88a for a description of Archbishop Eugenius as primate of Ireland.
[5] Orpen, *Normans* 2. 30; Gwynn, 'St. Lawrence O'Toole' 234; J Szoverffy, 'The Anglo-Norman Conquest of Ireland and St. Patrick' *Rep. novum* 2 (1958) 6–16 at 13.

from the *Life of St Patrick* written in 1185–6 by Jocelin, monk of
Downpatrick, formerly of Furness. The work was written with the
encouragement of de Courcy, Malachy, bishop of Down and Tomaltach Ua Conchobair, archbishop of Armagh.[1] The *Life* included a
highly coloured and clearly fictitious account of the conversion of
the king and citizens of Dublin by St Patrick. In exchange for their
Christianity, Jocelin reported, all the Dubliners 'by oath bound
themselves and all their posterity to the service of St Patrick and the
primacy of the archbishops of Armagh'. This *servitium* included
tribute and a list of its *reditus* was included. The moral of this story
was not difficult to read. But the future of the primacy of Armagh
was not to lie in Irish prelates and foreign barons agreeing that
Dublin was subject to Armagh.

Archbishop Henry of London (1213–28), like his two predecessors,
sought confirmation of the position of his archbishopric from the
pope. Innocent III issued such a confirmation in May 1216 and it
contained the prohibition about external intervention in Dublin in
the words used by Lucius III. This time, however, there was added a
permission to have his cross borne before him in his own diocese and
those of his suffragans.[2] Innocent III died some months later and
Henry of London prudently secured a reissue in the same form from
Honorius III (October 1216).[3] In December 1221, however, he
secured a more clear cut and ampler restatement of the principle of
Dublin's autonomy:

Since according to the precept of divine law, no one should put his sickle
into another's harvest lest one should seem to do to another what one
does not wish to have done to one's self by another, we listen with favour
to your entreaties and by authority of this document, forbid any archbishop or any other Irish prelate other than your own suffragans or a legate
of the apostolic see to have a cross borne before him, to summon assemblies, excepting religious orders, or deal with ecclesiastical causes unless
delegated by the apostolic see, in the province of Dublin.[4]

So far there is nothing in principle in Henry of London's attitude
substantially different from John Cumin's, though he did go to
greater lengths to have the autonomy of Dublin defined beyond

[1] *Acta Sanctorum* (March t. 2) 536–77 at 536.
[2] *Pont. hib.* 1. 97.　　　[3] *Ibid.* 104.　　　[4] *Ibid.* 148.

dispute. There is, however, one piece of evidence to suggest that his sights were set much higher. There is a seal matrix still existing, of thirteenth century origin.[1] On one side is inscribed: SIGILLVM SANCTI SEPULCHRI. St Sepulchre's was a manor of the archbishopric of Dublin. The other side bears the words: PRIMAS: IBERNIE: AC: SEDIS: LEGATUS. AC should presumably read AP. The only lord of St Sepulchre's who was legate of the apostolic see was Henry of London who held that office from 1217 to 1220. Henry of London, then, claimed to be primate.

Still, this claim by this particular archbishop does not seem to have matured into anything very significant. No papal recognition of it, if sought, was forthcoming. Honorius III's inhibition of external intervention in the Dublin province (1221) was later than the date of this seal and is a long way short of a recognition of primacy. No royal recognition, if sought, was forthcoming. There is no further evidence that Henry of London made a practice of calling himself primate. At least one prominent Dublin ecclesiastical source of the 1220's acknowledges contemporary papal recognition of the primacy of Armagh.[2] It is almost certain that no thirteenth century archbishop of Dublin laid claim to primacy. That was to be a development of the early fourteenth century.

Dublin was not the only province to seek freedom of Armagh. Both Cashel and Tuam sought to tread a comparable path.

Cashel's attempt was made apparently in solid alliance with Dublin. The two archbishops and their suffragans made a solemn compact to oppose Armagh *maxime in causa primatie*.[3] Details of this arrangement and the circumstances of its negotiations are not available. In 1244 Innocent IV received a complaint from Albert Suerbeer, archbishop of Armagh, of how his primatial rights were resisted in the Cashel province. The Pope's response was to appoint a commission to investigate Armagh's right to visit Cashel (and Tuam also) and levy customary dues.[4] No decision about Cashel has been recorded in the papal registers. However, in the absence of any

---

[1] Cf. C. F. R. Armstrong, *Irish seal-matrices and seals* (1913) 51–2. It is now National Museum, Dublin, Reg. no. 1894. 5. I am very grateful to Rev. Professor A. Gwynn, s. J. who drew my attention to this evidence. Cf. also *Pont. hib.* 1. 235.

[2] *Ann. St. Mary's Dublin s.a.* 1220. 280.

[3] Cf. *Crede mihi* ed. J. T. Gilbert (1897) 67.   [4] *Pont. hib.* 2. 255.

record of any future primatial activity in the Cashel province, it is a fair assumption that Cashel achieved its exemption at least *de facto*.

Tuam, on the other hand, lost its case and its subjection to the primatial jurisdiction of Armagh was emphatically stated by Alexander IV in 1255.[1]

A short account of this failure might well be prefaced with the comment that these primatial disputes are far from being a simple story of native Irish and Anglo-French rivalry. Henry of London secured his autonomy and claimed a primacy when the archbishop of Armagh was Luke Netterville, of his own nationality. Cashel, whose archbishops were all native Irish in this period, allied with Dublin whose prelates were invariably Anglo-French. Tuam, a native Irish province to a man at this time, in resisting Armagh was challenging one of the oldest traditions of the Irish Church. Finally, the battle for the reassertion of the primatial rights of Armagh was first joined by a prelate foreign to all the peoples of Ireland, Albert Suerbeer of Cologne.

Albert was papally provided to Armagh in 1240, owing his appointment to his connexion with Cardinal Otto, in England as papal legate at the time of the Armagh vacancy. Though his appointment was fortuitous and he was a stranger to British conditions, he came prepared to stand up for the rights of his see. He arrived in Ireland in 1241 armed with ambitions and papal authorizations to secure his authority over what the Irish annalists called 'the churches of Patrick' and 'Patrick's land' in provinces other than Armagh.[2] It was the implementation of these allegedly traditional claims that aroused the opposition of Cashel and Tuam and led to the investigation of the primatial position set on foot by Innocent IV in 1244.

As has been indicated, nothing is known of the papal mind after this inquiry. But Albert's successor Abraham O'Connellan kept up the pressure at least as far as Tuam was concerned and in October 1255 was rewarded with a papal ruling that Armagh did possess a *ius primatie* of long standing in the western province and a specific definition of what its rights were:

... the archbishop of Armagh and each of his successors are allowed to call themselves if they wish primates of the province of Tuam and to

[1] *Ibid.* 412.   [2] Cf. *ALC* I. 353, 355–7; *Annals of Connacht* 72, 74.

cause their cross to be carried before them throughout the whole of that province whenever and as often as they pass through it, and they may also make visitation of twenty seven days duration in the province once each quinquennium ...[1]

It is difficult to know how effectively the primates exercised this right. The indications are, however, that the settlement was accepted.

No doubt the documentary evidence of the historical foundations of his primacy which had been put forward by Archbishop Abraham O'Connellan was responsible for the change in the way the papal curia addressed archbishops of Armagh. In 1256, Alexander IV addressed the Archbishop as *primas*,[2] the first use of the term in an extant papal letter, and in later letters, *totius Hibernie primas*.[3] The papacy continued to use both terms indiscriminately. As far as the papacy was concerned, Armagh was the only primate. The distinction between *totius Hiberniae primas* (Armagh) and *primas Hiberniae* (Dublin) lay in the distant future.

There is one more episode to be considered to complete the story of the first century or so of the primacy after the council of Kells. It was not only the three other metropolitans which sought exemption from Armagh's jurisdiction. One of its own suffragan sees also made a bid for independence. Meath, an area heavily settled by the earliest invaders, was one of the first dioceses to become anglicized. The attempt of Bishop Hugh of Taghmon to persuade the pope to grant his diocese exemption from archiepiscopal visitation is doubtless due at least in part to unwillingness to subject an Anglo-French diocese to an Irish metropolitan. The Bishop pursued his cause vigorously at the papal curia. His efforts left no impression on the papal registers, however, but it is known that the decision went against him.[4] This decision Archbishop Patrick O'Scannell O.P. promulgated in a

---

[1] *Pont. hib.* 2. 412 at p. 241.

[2] *Ibid.* 425, 449.   [3] *Ibid.* 458, 459.

[4] The Register of Archbishop Octavian (1478–1513) records of a provincial council held at Drogheda in January 1262: 'Item in eodem concilio contencio que orta fuerat inter predictum dominum Armachanum et Episcopum et clerum Midenses fuerat sedata post multas appellationes magnas expensas Midensium ad curiam Romanam, licet in fine nichil obtinuissent' *Reg. Octavian* (Reeves TSS (Trinity College, Dublin) 2. 915–16). There is a formal document of *composicio* dated 9 April 1265 in *Reg. St. Thomas, Dublin* RS 71–3, wherein Armagh is described as *primas Hibernie*.

provincial council held in Drogheda in January 1262. The Primate made of this council an occasion to assert his primatial claims. To an audience that in addition to his own suffragans (who included Meath) was composed of the suffragans of Tuam province (present as acknowledgment of primatial right), some Dublin canons, officials of the civil administration and barons of the colony,[1] he promulgated an alleged bull of Urban IV which gave formal recognition of Armagh's primacy:

Following the example of our predecessor Celestine, we confirm by apostolic authority for you and your successors the primacy of all Ireland which your predecessors are known to have held unshakenly down to the present time and we command that the archbishops, bishops and other prelates of Ireland should at all times show you and your successors that obedience and reverence as is owed to a primate. We grant you licence to have borne before you the cross, standard of the lord, through the provinces and through the bishoprics subject to you by metropolitan right, just as it is known to have been granted to your predecessors.[2]

The privilege of Pope Celestine remains unknown to modern readers. There is no extant authentic version of Pope Urban's letter. Confirmed by Henry IV, however, in 1401, it was a weighty shot in the Armagh locker in later controversies.

Perhaps connected with this council and the presence of Crown officials at it, but certainly connected with this archbishop, was another development in Armagh–Dublin rivalry. Not permitted to have his primatial cross carried before him in the Dublin province, Armagh understandably refused to enter it. This was highly inconvenient for the Crown which might want his presence, for legal proceedings, for example, or at a slightly later period, at parliament.

[1] *Reg. Octavian*: '... frater Patricius O'Scanlain, archiepiscopus Ardmachanus, Hibernie primas concilium celebrauit apud pontem cum suffraganeis prouincie sue et quibusdam suffraganeis prouincie Tuamensis sibi iure primatico subiectis et quibusdam canonicis cathedralibus et consilio domini Dublinensis cui interfuerunt iustitiarius et quidam magnates Hibernie, et ibidem priuilegia ecclesie Ardmachane de iure primatie post renouationem in curia Romana publicata fuerunt.' Cf. J. Ussher, 'Controversy betwixt the archbishops of Armagh and Dublin' in Wilkins, *Concilia* 4. 80–6 at 80. The cooperation of Dublin seems even more dubious than the alleged letter of Urban IV.

[2] T. Rymer, ed. *Foedera, Conventiones et Litterae* 8. 208–9, an *inspeximus* of the alleged letter of Urban by Henry IV, 5 July 1401 on behalf of the then archbishop, John Colton (1381–1404).

Absence would render the primate liable to civil penalty. Hence an accommodation was made. It was recognized by the Crown that the archbishop of Armagh should not be required to attend personally at any court outside his own province but was allowed to be represented by proxy.[1] This became standard procedure and applied for participation in parliament also.[2]

The *ecclesia hibernicana* then had ceased to have constitutional unity. It had in effect broken up into three parts. These divisions corresponded in a general way to the broad effects of colonial settlement. The dioceses of the Armagh and Tuam provinces, with a few exceptions of which Meath was the most important, were ruled by native Irish bishops and for the most part remote from the Dublin administration, were the least affected by anglicization processes. They presented a sharp contrast to the highly anglicized dioceses of the Dublin province. Cashel stood about midway between these two positions, with both Irish and Anglo-French bishops, mixed chapters in some dioceses and most dioceses inevitably closely involved with colonial authorities. What had emerged by mid-thirteenth century was an entity which men came to call the *terre Engleis*. This common law area was substantially that part of the country which lay broadly speaking south of a line joining Carlingford Lough, Athlone and Limerick. The bulk of it was therefore in ecclesiastical terms, the Dublin and Cashel provinces. But Armagh was significantly affected through the southern part of the diocese being the county of Louth since 1233 and through Meath, Down and Connor in areas held as liberties by powerful barons. Tuam was also affected for there was a Connacht county by 1247 and a county of Roscommon had made its appearance by 1292.[3]

In the second half of the thirteenth century there may perhaps be discerned a certain trend towards some form of unity manifesting itself within this *terre Engleis*. What prompted bishops to think about collective action in a form of association wider than that constituted by individual provinces was the growing resentment at what was

---

Cf. A. Gwynn, 'Documents relating to the medieval province of Armagh' *Arch. hib.* 13 (1947) 2, 7. These letters of Edward (1262–5; *c.* 1300) refer to the archbishop as *primas*.

[2] Richardson and Sayles, *Medieval Irish Parliament* 123.

[3] J. Otway-Ruthven, 'Anglo-Irish shire government in the thirteenth century' *IHS* 5 (1946) 1–28; *idem Medieval Ireland* 174.

held to be the violation of the liberty of the Church by the attempts of royal officials and judges to impose those principles and procedures of the common law by which the jurisdiction of the spiritual power was to be regulated.

Protests against this pressure by the Crown to limit what prelates considered their proper authority were formulated initially on the provincial level—by Tuam in 1255, by Dublin in 1260, by Armagh probably shortly afterwards. They were addressed, in the form of petitions, either to the pope or to the king and sometimes to both. The term *ecclesia hibernicana* was used not uncommonly in protests of this kind. In this context it did not refer to all the bishops and dioceses of Ireland though the complainants might, as in the Tuam instance, claim to speak on behalf of all. Rather it meant those bishops whether native Irish, Anglo-Irish or English born who were affected by the attempts of royal officials to restrict ecclesiastical jurisdiction. Its use denoted the Church in the *terre Engleis* becoming conscious of a common threat.[1]

It was in 1291 that the most noteworthy attempts for action on a scale wider than the provincial were made. An attempt by Edward I to tax the Irish Church made bishops more alert to the need to join together to resist the King's demands and to bargain with him.[2] In that year, the King, in need of money to ransom his cousin, now king of Sicily, from the king of Aragon, sought to exploit his Irish re- sources. Thomas Quantok, later to be bishop of Emly and chancellor of Ireland, was entrusted with the task of raising the wind from both baronage and clergy in Ireland. A parliament had been summoned for 6 May to receive him and hear the nature of the King's proposals. A parallel assembly, 'of the prelates of the whole of Ireland' according to Bishop Nicholas Cusack of Kildare who was there, met on 13 May.[3] The prelates came prepared. They reacted to the demand for money by presenting articles of grievance for redress.[4]

In the event, despite (or perhaps because of) numerous meetings of

1 These *gravamina* of the *ecclesia hibernicana* are analysed in detail in the next chapter.
2 Cf. *Parliaments and Councils of Medieval Ireland* ed. H. G. Richardson and G. O. Sayles 193–9 (with documents); Watt, 'English Law and the Irish Church' *Gwynn Studies* 157–9.
3 Cf. W. Prynne, *Exact Chronological Vindication of our King's Supreme Jurisdiction* 3. 442 for Nicholas's letter to Edward I.
4 *Stat. Irel. John–Henry V* 178–91, discussed below pp. 132–34.

provincial and diocesan assemblies all over Ireland to discuss this demand, Edward got very little money and the *ecclesia hibernicana* rather less redress of grievance than it had asked for. But the point of significance for the future was that an important precedent had been set. It had been demonstrated that the bishops of the Irish Church could surmount their national and constitutional divisions in the service of a common ecclesiastical ideal.

To at least one metropolitan and his suffragans there seemed a pressing need to establish a permanent framework of joint ecclesiastical action to uphold *libertas ecclesie*. In this same year of 1291, the archbishop of Armagh, Nicholas Mac Maol Íosa, and the bishops of his province, meeting in September in the Dominican house at Trim, devised a scheme which was meant to close the ranks of the Irish bishops to present a solid front against secular encroachment on ecclesiastical rights.[1] The archbishop had obviously not forgotten that he had received some discouraging replies from Edward I in parliament at Westminster the previous year to his complaints that his Church had been 'dishonoured' in its liberties.[2]

The Armagh prelates bound themselves by oath that should the rights or liberties of their Churches be injured by any lay power they would at their common charge support each other in any court to which resistance to the aggression should take them. Sentences of excommunication should be promulgated in all dioceses so that a culprit could not escape penalty by leaving the diocese in which he had been excommunicated. The sanction for negligence or half-heartedness in honouring these obligations lay in payment of fine to the pope and to prelates who were keeping the agreement, money pledges having been previously lodged with the papacy. Every bishop, dean and chapter in Ireland was expected to become a party to this compact. Should anyone refuse he was to be proceeded against in the papal curia and boycotted by his ecclesiastical fellows in Ireland.

In the upshot, neither of these assemblies of the year 1291 was to

---

1 *Reg. Swayne* 2. 191-5v (Reeves TSS., T.C.D.); *The register of John Swayne* ed. D. A. Chart (1935); J. Ware, *Works* ed. W. Harris 1. 70; A. Gwynn, 'Nicholas Mac Maol Íosa, archbishop of Armagh (1272-1303)' *Féilsgríbhínn Mhic Néill* (1940) 394-405; Watt, 'English Law and the Irish Church' 158.
2 *Cal. Docs. Irel. 1285-92* 251-2; Gwynn, 'Armagh docs.' no. 6.

have any institutional consequence. The medieval Irish Church did not develop a convocation. The evidence of episcopal participation in parliament makes it highly improbable that any further general assemblies of bishops meeting in association with a session of parliament were held in our period. There is no evidence that the bishops of any other province agreed to the Trim compact, and it was not therefore destined to be the beginnings of any new found unity for the *ecclesia hibernicana*.

Chapter 6

THE CLERGY AND THE COMMON LAW
1255'91

The prelates of the *ecclesia hibernicana* had come to formulate their *gravamina* because they considered they were being denied justice. Men of the thirteenth century understood the concept of justice in the Roman definition adopted by canon and common lawyers alike, as a *ius suum cuique tribuens*.[1] Prelates might be deprived of their own right in different ways. It might be because judges and officials were inefficient or corrupt, serving their own ends and not those of justice or because of the illegal actions of others or because in particular cases the operation of the law bore hardly on individuals or because the law was obscure or made no provision for the particular eventuality. It might be because the law had been changed in ways that took from the clergy what they had hitherto enjoyed unchallenged. Denial of justice, deprivation of *ius suum* in all these ways, was alleged in the petitions addressed to king and pope by Irish prelates in the second half of the thirteenth century. Close study of these allegations throws much light on the way the common law system affected the Irish Church.

It must be observed by way of preliminary that neither king nor pope was any stranger to complaints from the clergy about the operation of the common law. The *ecclesia anglicana*, thanks to the energetic leadership of Robert Grosseteste, had made its first formulation of *gravamina* nearly two decades before anything at all comparable appeared from the *ecclesia hibernicana*. The clergy in England continued to protest vigorously and frequently against alleged violations of ecclesiastical liberty and usurpations of ecclesiastical jurisdiction by the Crown.[2] The clergy in Ireland fought the same

---

[1] *Decretales*, Proemium; Bracton, *De legibus* (ed. G. E. Woodbine) 2. 23. The definition was taken from Roman law, Digest 1. 1. 10.

[2] Cf. F. M. Powicke, *The Thirteenth Century* (1962) 453-8, 478-84; W. R. Jones, 'Bishops, Politics and the Two Laws: the *gravamina* of the English clergy 1237-1399' *Speculum* 41 (1966) 209-45.

battle in miniature; sometimes, it must be said, after the issue had already been settled in England. The historian who investigates the relationship which prevailed in Ireland between the clergy and the central government must keep perspective by remembering that the larger part of that controversy between canon and common law, of which lists of clerical *gravamina* were the expression, took place in England. Nevertheless the experience of the *ecclesia anglicana* was not the only conditioning element operative in the Irish part of the story. Right perspective demands, too, attention to specifically Irish circumstances, not least to conflict engendered by the confrontation of the common law with the traditions and customs of the Church as they had been understood before the Invasion.

There are abundant sources for the study of the problem in England, for full lists of English *gravamina* have been faithfully preserved in chronicles and parliamentary records, in a wealth of detail far beyond anything available for Ireland. Here the documentation is sparse in quantity and uncertain in textual quality, for much of it must be read in fragmentary or mutilated manuscripts. The value of some of it, too, is restricted through absence of indications of date, authorship and circumstantial background. It has also to be borne in mind that there is little surviving record before 1295 of the actual functioning of the justiciar's court in the light of whose records the prelates' accusations might be tested, clarified or illustrated. Nevertheless there is enough material to form some impression of the movement of legal theory and practice in this most significant of controversies.

It is more than likely that further lists of Irish *gravamina* will be recovered by future research. At present, however, the following documents make up the dossier:

1. Florence MacFlynn, archbishop of Tuam and suffragans to Henry III and Alexander IV (1255)[1]
2. Unknown provenance ('ecclesia Hybernicana') and destination: in Lambeth MS 619 (post 1256)[2]

---

[1] *Calendar of Close Rolls 1254–56* 412–14.
[2] Ed. M. P. Sheehy, 'English law in medieval Ireland. Two illustrative documents' *Arch. hib.* 23 (1960) 167–75 at 174–5. The only dating indication is the reference to John fitz Geoffrey as 'quondam iusticiarius', an office he held from 1245 to 1256.

3. Fulk of Sandford, archbishop of Dublin and suffragans to Alexander IV and Urban IV (1260, 1261)[1]
4. Unnamed archbishop of Armagh (Patrick O'Scannell) to Prince Edward (probably 1261–70)[2]
5. Nicholas Mac Maol Íosa, archbishop of Armagh to Edward I (1278)[3]
6. David MacCarwill, archbishop of Cashel and suffragans to Edward I (c. 1280)[4]
7. Unknown provenance ('prelati Hybernie') to Edward I: in BM MS Aug. II[5]
8. Articuli Cleri ('ecclesia Hybernicana'): (May 1291)[6]
[9. Ecclesia hibernicana to general council of Vienne (1311–13)][7]

The analysis of these texts may begin with a short narrative survey of them.

Not all Archbishop Florence MacFlynn's contacts with the English legal system had worked to his disadvantage. Successive archbishops of Tuam had looked with disfavour on the existence of the neighbouring diocese of Annaghdown and had sought, not unsuccessfully, to absorb it.[8] In 1253, Henry III recognized the right of the archbishop to the temporalities of the diocese and to the town of Annaghdown itself.[9] At the same time as he secured this success, however, the Archbishop made a complaint about molestation of his clergy and tenants by royal officials, mentioning in particular the seizure of the ecclesiastical property of convicted criminous clergy.[10] This first complaint proved to be but the prelude to a more thorough

1 J. T. Gilbert, Historic and municipal documents of Ireland, 1172–1320 RS 170–8.
2 BM Cleop. E. 1 fo. 186. The text is a fragment: there were originally twenty-three articles; eight only survive here. The articles themselves are not given; the text records only the replies by 'dominus' i.e. Prince Edward, who held the lordship of Ireland from 1254.
3 Gwynn, 'Armagh docs.' 2.
4 J. Otway-Ruthven, 'The request of the Irish for English Law, 1277–80' IHS 6 (1949) 261–70 at 267–70 (with English translation).
5 Sheehy, 'Two illustrative documents' 171–4.
6 Stat. Irel. John–Henry V 178–91 (with English translation).
7 F. Ehrle, 'Ein Bruchstück der Akten des Konzils von Vienne' Archiv für Literatur und Kirchengeschichte 4 (1888) 361–470 at 369–99 passim.
8 For a short summary of Tuam–Annaghdown relations, Gwynn, Hbk Brit. Chron. 345.
9 Cal. Cl. Rolls 1251–53 497.
10 Ibid.

ventilation of grievances. In July 1255 Florence and Sean O'Laidig
O.P., bishop of Killala, went personally to Henry III on behalf of their
province and as spokesmen, they claimed, of all the Irish clergy, and
presented six articles of complaint.[1] At the same time they sent
representatives to the curia to solicit support from Pope Alexander
IV.[2]

Both King and Pope gave the prelates a sympathetic hearing.
Henry III answered their complaints in detail; instructions were sent
to the justiciar that he should give remedy and some legal ambigui-
ties were clarified.[3] The main complaint was about the way the law
was being enforced: clergy and tenants, summoned to answer at
distant courts, found the labour and expense too much and were often
forced to make prejudicial compositions. Judges were corrupt, it was
complained, and negotiated with litigants for personal gain.

The *gravamina* were presented rather differently to the Pope.[4]
Royal judges, it was said, prevented the faithful from making
bequests for such pious purposes as the crusade; they prohibited cases
of *ius patronatus* from being heard in ecclesiastical courts; they would
not allow ecclesiastical judges to hear any property cases except such
as were testamentary or matrimonial. The Pope appointed judge-
delegates to restrain the justiciar and his ministers from such violations of ecclesiastical liberty. But it seems improbable that the bishop,
dean and archdeacons of Killaloe and Kilfenora, all native Irishmen,
would'make much impression on English officialdom, some of whom
Henry III had in any case already successfully preserved from excommunication through his proctor at the curia. Certainly there is
nothing in the evidence to suggest that the Pope made any headway
towards changing these established principles of the common law of
which Tuam was complaining.

The same justiciar, John fitz Geoffrey, who was the subject of
Tuam's complaints, was also under attack in the second of the documents listed above. He was charged with responsibility for depriving
the Church of liberties it had possessed before the coming of Henry
II. This is a very interesting text, though its fragmentary and
mutilated nature leaves certain facets ambiguous. Its leading feature
is an appeal to the logic of Adrian IV's *Laudabiliter*, a copy of which

[1] *Cal. Cl. Rolls 1254–56* 213–14.   [2] *Cal. Docs. Irel. 1252–84* 475.
[3] *Cal. Cl. Rolls 1254–56* 412–14.   [4] *Pont. hib.* 2. 413–15.

was sent with the petition to the authority to whom it was directed. It is impossible to say whether this was pope or king. The style in which it refers to the king and his ministers suggests that it was not he who was being addressed and the use of *Laudabiliter* might be thought to be more apposite in a papal context. If this surmise is correct, the argument was apparently to impress on the pope that Adrian IV had permitted Henry II to subjugate Ireland explicitly for the purpose, among others, of enlarging the boundaries of the Church whereas, in practice, his successors had restricted its boundaries by depriving it of liberties it had for long previously enjoyed. Chief of these liberties as conceded by the 'catholic princes of Ireland' was that of holding all ecclesiastical property in 'free, pure and perpetual free alms'. Nothing of merely human law remained in this context. Thus, it was claimed, not merely did prelates have jurisdiction over all spiritual cases, they had jurisdiction over all the criminal and civil cases of the tenants of their lands, whatever their legal status. Though laymen acted as judges in these cases they acted for the bishops and any fines inflicted belonged to them. But in these days, it was charged, the only suits touching property and money permitted to remain within the jurisdiction of ecclesiastical courts without incurring royal prohibition, were those of a matrimonial or testamentary nature. Further, should they seek to inflict money fines even in spiritual cases, they were prohibited and were punished for ignoring the prohibition, fines being levied on their *spiritualia* if they had no *temporalia*.

After the Tuam dispute of 1255, Pope Alexander IV again intervened in a comparable Irish situation in 1260. Fulk of Sandford as a sometime chancellor and treasurer of St Paul's, London was already an experienced lawyer and administrator when he was papally provided to Dublin in 1256.[1] He proved a diligent defender of the rights and liberties of his new see in a number of directions. An important part of his energetic zeal went into defending his jurisdiction against the Dublin administration and the city government, both of which were supported by the home government. Fulk went himself to the curia in 1260 and obtained from Alexander IV the appointment of judges-delegate to restrain those judges and officials

---

[1] Cf. T. F. Tout, *DNB s.n.* Sandford, Fulk de, for a summary of his career.

who were molesting the archbishop and his suffragans.[1] On the death of Alexander IV, Fulk persuaded Urban IV to appoint new judges, and himself to address Henry III on the specific issues touching ecclesiastical liberty. It is from the relevant papal letters that our knowledge of the Dublin *gravamina* comes.

The Dublin prelates spoke of 'new usurpations' and placed responsibility for them on the justiciar, William Dean.[2] Their complaints concerned alleged loss of jurisdictional rights previously enjoyed, 'by ancient approved and hitherto uncontested custom'. They complained of being deprived of jurisdiction over their lay subjects in cases of breach of faith or oath where money and possessions were involved; likewise in cases of defamation. Prosecution of laity who had injured clergy, which had customarily been of ecclesiastical competence, was now withdrawn from it. Worse, money suits even between clerical parties were prohibited, and so was litigation touching the rights of rectors over chapels belonging to their churches and over tithe rights in other churches. The redemption of ecclesiastical punishments by money fines for those offences like disobedience, usury, adultery and so on where the sacred canons order that prelates should make inquisition, was forbidden. When an ecclesiastical judge dissolved a marriage he was not allowed cognizance of the dowry, as previous laws and custom had permitted. If a citizen bequeathed any sort of burgage tenement (*burgasia*) to a church or religious house, the justiciar forbade ecclesiastical judges to compel the executors to fulfil the testator's wishes. Likewise ecclesiastical judges were no longer allowed jurisdiction over bequests for pious purposes from those tied to the soil (*betagii*).[3] Finally there were complaints about prohibitions. Clergy were arrested and punished by fines should they proceed in despite of a writ of prohibition. If a

---

[1] *Pont. hib.* 2. 489.

[2] The fullest account is in the Pope's letter to Henry III, Gilbert, *Historic and municipal documents* 172–5.

[3] 'Ceterum, si aliqui laici ascripti glebe, qui betagii vulgariter appellantur, aliqua de bonis suis ecclesiasticis vel religiosis, aut piis locis legant, pietatis intuitu, in ultima voluntate, sepedicti iusticiarii et ballivi impediunt ne per ipsos archiepiscopum, suffraganeos et iudices, sicut de prefata consuetudine obtentum est, in hoc voluntas testatoris execucioni mandatur' *ibid.* 174. On the legal status of *betagius* cf. G. J. Hand, *English Law in Ireland 1290–1324* (1967) ch. 10 and on the origin of the word, G. Mac Niocaill, 'The origins of the betagh' *Irish Jurist* 1 (1966) 292–8.

prelate lost a plea of prohibition he was fined. If someone had been excommunicated in the ecclesiastical court he could seek a writ of prohibition and whilst the case was pending, he did not lose his right to plead in the secular court, as an excommunicate should.

There is no evidence here any more than in the earlier Tuam case that papal intervention had the slightest effect. Archbishop Fulk, however, again sought papal support or at least the support of the papal legate then in England, Cardinal Ottobuono, in the second of his disputes about his ecclesiastical jurisdiction. This was in 1268, some four years after a searching *quo warranto* investigation into his secular jurisdiction,[1] when he came into conflict with the citizens of Dublin. The city was placed under interdict for persistent violation of ecclesiastical liberty. There were five main issues of contention: the municipality had sought to regulate the occasions and manner in which offerings should be made in the Dublin churches; it sought to regulate the administration of public penances; it forbade any ecclesiastical judge to have cognizance 'of usury or any other crime or any cause whatsoever save only testamentary and matrimonial ones'; it claimed jurisdiction over the goods of intestates; it decided that no citizen should be compelled to appear in an ecclesiastical court outside the city boundary. The Cardinal called on the bishops of Lismore and Waterford to reiterate sentences of solemn excommunication on Sunday and feast days for these and many other *enormia* until the guilty should make satisfaction.[2]

It proved to be the justiciar, Robert of Ufford, who was the peacemaker between the mayor and the archbishop. The composition made between the contending parties constituted an important clarification of basic principles:

Should anyone be guilty of public sin he may first make satisfaction with a money fine. If he persists in public sin and the matter is grave, he shall then be flogged round the church. Should he still persist he should be flogged at procession on some solemn day at Holy Trinity or St Patrick's. If he still fails to desist from his sin, the archbishop's official will denounce him to the mayor and corporation, so that he might be expelled from the city or flogged through it. Agreement was also reached about making

---

[1] Texts in Gilbert, *Historic and municipal documents* 141–66; C. McNeill, 'The secular jurisdiction of the early archbishops of Dublin' *RSAIJn* 45 (1915) 81–108.

[2] Gilbert, *Historic and municipal documents* 180–2.

inquisitions, namely that general inquisition might be made through the city once each year, that it should concern itself both with public and manifest and not secret sins and that in circumstances of great necessity the inquisition might be repeated, but not more than once. Thirdly it was provided and ordained that no citizen should be drawn out of the deanery of the city by any of the archbishop's officials. He should answer within the city and do before his ordinary judges whatever the law requires him to do.[1]

The first Armagh document in our series comes to us in very fragmented form. There survive only the replies made to articles 17 to 23 of the list which the archbishop had submitted. The document is undated but as the replies stand in the name of the *dominus terre* and not of the *rex* it must be dated within the period when Prince Edward held the lordship of Ireland. Thus the most likely petitioner was Archbishop Patrick O'Scannell (1261–70).

Even in the truncated form in which it comes to us, Edward's response to the Archbishop is full of interest. There is clarification about the jurisdiction of ecclesiastical courts concerning sins and about the use of the sanction of excommunication. For one guilty of usury, it was ruled, it is fitting that he should go to the bishop's court for sentence of salutary penance. But the bishop does not thereby have jurisdiction over his chattels or real property. A usurer has been guilty of theft, an offence punishable in the royal courts and the disposition of his chattels and property must therefore be the same as for a thief.[2] In comparable fashion, those accused of sexual sins must go before their bishop, there to make purgation if they can. If they fail to attend, the bishop may punish them. Similarly he may compel the attendance of witnesses in matrimonial and testamentary cases. But because he has the power of compulsion (through excommunication), he is not thereby permitted to hold assemblies of laymen for the denunciation of sinners, for by such assemblies lords might suffer hurt through loss of labour.[3] About the shunning of an excommuni-

---

[1] *Ibid.* 182–3.

[2] 'Ad sextum decimum articulum de usuris, respondetur quod licet episcopis pro peccato illo penitenciam usurario iniungere salutarem, set quia committendo usuram usurarius furtum committit et super hoc est conuictus, catalla et terre usurarii sicut catalla furis sunt. Et si qui sequi voluerint contra huiusmodi usurarium, restituantur eis bona sua que ipsi usurarii per usuram extorquerunt.'

[3] 'Ad septimum decimum articulum, respondetur quod si aliquis diffamatus uel

cate it was ruled that if he complained that he had been wrongfully excommunicated in that he should not have been brought before an ecclesiastical court because the matter was temporal, he is permitted to bring this to the proof, but he remains legally disqualified for bringing actions of any other kind.[1]

Two entries relate to specifically Irish conditions and give us a glimpse of pre-Invasion Armagh custom. The Archbishop claimed that it was Armagh custom that during vacancies of his suffragan sees, he had custody of temporalities. To this, answer was made that such custody, in Armagh as throughout Ireland, belonged exclusively to the king, and the Archbishop had no right to temporalities of whatever kind they might be. Edward did promise an enquiry as to whether the archbishop of Armagh did hold any special privilege in this connexion.[2] An investigation did in fact take place and the sequel, in the pontificate of Patrick's successor, will be told later.

Archbishop Patrick pleaded custom of the province in another

accusatus fuerit de peccatis ut de fornicacione, adulterio et aliis, prelatus ipsum uocari faciat ut si ipsum de crimine uel peccato sibi imposito purgare possit, purgetur. Si autem purgare se nequeat, puniatur prout ad iurisdicionem ordinariam pertinet. Si autem certe persone nominate fuerint per quas ueritas melius sciri poterit, nominentur ad probandum matrimonium uel testamentum aliquod, et similiter in acusacionibus ubi instat actor, tales persone inpediende non sunt quin testimonium perhibeant ueritati. Set propter hoc non est congregacio laicorum facienda, quia per congregacionem huiusmodi debita seruicia dominis possent deperire.'

1 The full reply is perhaps a little obscure. Edward appears to be confirming the practice of caption by the civil power of properly sentenced excommunicates, 'nisi forsan excommunicatus conqueratur se esse excommunicatum pro aliqua re temporali de qua non debeat coram ordinario respondere, ad cuius probacionem debebit admitti, set in ceteris que proponit ut actor est interim euitandus'.

2 'Ad xix respondetur quod archiepiscopus de episcopatu vacante non se intromittat quantum ad temporalia set tantum se de spiritualibus intromittat, unde si prouentus episcopatus consistant in alimentis et archiepiscopus Armachanus ulla alimenta perceperit ab episcopatu qui uacuit, iustum est quod de perceptis regi respondet in ualore. Et nichilominus pro tanta presumpcione quod inuasit temporalia episcopatus uacantis et ad regem spectantis tenetur regi ad magnam emendam. Nec supponatur quod aliqua custodia episcopatus uacantis in Hibernia spectat ad Armacanum, quia compertum est pro constanti quod custodia omnium episcopatuum uacancium in Hiberniam spectant ad regem, et hactenus extitit in possessione earundem, et compotus de omnibus exitibus earundem regi debetur. Et tamen si ius speciale habeat, exhibeat illud, et iuri speciali reuerenter deferetur. Item tamen locum tenens domini super hoc inquirat et faciat de consilio fidelium domini terre iusticiam.'

matter. The entry, existing as it does only in the reply, is ambiguous.[1] The Archbishop had obviously raised the question of clergy who had been killed. Edward replied that justice should be 'according to the law and custom of the land' and that his representative in Ireland with his council of magnates would promulgate a decree to this effect. The significance of the reply lies in what was meant by custom of the land in the context for the position about murder of clergy in common law presents no problem. An addition to the text seems to hold the clue. It reads: *Fiat super hoc heru, si voluerint.* The custom involved would seem to be designated in the curious word *heru.* What does it mean? It is suggested very tentatively that it is a latinization of the Irish *eiríc* or some variant of that word. If this is so, the Archbishop seems to be asking that the practice known to native Irish law of exacting honour price for a killing should be payable for murder of clergy and it seems that Prince Edward was prepared to concede the request.

The second Armagh list of *gravamina,* those presented to Edward I in 1278 by Archbishop Nicholas Mac Maol Íosa are not of such general interest. But this prelate too argued that, since before the Invasion, archbishops of Armagh had enjoyed custody of temporalities of suffragan sees during vacancy and sought to preserve at least what remained of that right.[2]

[1] 'Ad vicesimum articulum, respondetur quod de clericis occisis, et de hiis quos forsan occidi contigerit in futurum, fiat iusticia secundum legem et consuetudinem terre, et super hoc per consilium magnatum Hibernie statuat locum tenens domini. Fiat super hoc heru, si voluerint.'

[2] 'Item cum ante introitum Anglicorum in Hiberniam ecclesia Ardmachana fuerit in possessione recipiendi temporalia tempore vacationis omnium episcopatuum provincie Ardmachane, et licet processu temporis per incuriam et negligentiam quorundam archiepiscoporum ballivi vestri possessionem temporalium quorundam episcopatuum sic vacantium in preiudicium ecclesie nostre sint ingressi: adhuc tamen ecclesia nostra Ardmachana est in possessione temporalium quorundam episcopatuum vacantium, in quorum possessione fuit dicta ecclesia, non solum ante ingressum Anglicorum, sed post ingressum ipsorum usque in hunc diem. Quare excellentie vestre supplicamus quatenus mandetur iusticiariis vestris ne nos seu ecclesiam nostram saltem super possessione nostra in predictis ecclesiis, in quarum possessione fuerunt hactenus predecessores nostri et hodie sumus, molestent. Et sciatis, domine reverende, quod nos peteremus possessionem nostram nobis reformari, ecclesiarum videlicet quas nunc tempore vacationis quoad temporalia possidetis, si speraremus apud excellentiam vestram exaudiri' Gwynn, 'Armagh docs.' 9. 10.

So far, it has been possible to examine *gravamina* from Tuam, Dublin and Armagh. For Cashel there is nothing extant of comparable nature, as far as is known, though of course it is not improbable that one or other of the two anonymous texts came from that province. Yet there is some striking evidence of the attitude of the archbishop of Cashel and his suffragans to the common law which though not of a *gravamina* type at all, is of quite crucial importance when any examination of the reaction of the Irish Church to the common law is in process. The Cashel prelates presented themselves as the champions of the extension among the Irish 'of the community of the Irish tongue' of the common law 'in order to put an end to evil law'.[1] The leaders of this movement, the men in whose name the native Irish made their request for English law, were David MacCarwill, the archbishop of Cashel, Bishop Matthew O Hogain of Killaloe, Bishop David O Cusby of Emly and the Cistercian abbot of Holycross, Peter O Conaing. They claimed the support of the five other Cashel bishops. The scheme was to purchase a general grant of English law, for which 10,000 marks had come to be the suggested selling price, the prelates to guarantee the sum, to use the full resources of ecclesiastical coercion on any Irish who would not receive and hold this law and to ensure that all other ecclesiastical authorities from the pope down should cooperate in implementing the reception of English law. As is well known, this scheme foundered, probably largely because of Anglo-Irish hostility.[2] An opportunity to integrate the two peoples was lost. Historians from Sir John Davies onward have not failed to 'note as a great defect in the civil policy of this kingdom ... the English laws were not communicated to the Irish'.[3] It was remarkable for a group of Irish prelates to view the adoption of the common law throughout Ireland as a means to ensure that 'loyalty peace and truth should be in the land'[4] at a time when the generality of the episcopate, Irish and

[1] 'Pur oster la mauueise ley e la desauenance ke est en la terre de Irlande endreit de Iresche lange' Otway-Ruthven, 'Request of the Irish' 267.
[2] Cf. J. Otway-Ruthven, 'The native Irish and English law in Ireland' *IHS* 7 (1950) 1–16 and *Medieval Ireland* 188–90; Hand, *English Law in Ireland* (1967) 189–93.
[3] *A discovery of the true causes why Ireland was never entirely subdued ...* (1612) in *Ireland under Elizabeth and James I* ed. H. Morley (1890) 268.
[4] '... lur voluntee est ke leautee pees e veritee pussent en la terre e sur ceo front

English, apparently looked on the common law with a somewhat jaundiced eye as an instrument by which they were treated unjustly.

The minds of many prelates were inclined to dwell more on the allegedly lost past merits of the common law than on any future benefits it might bestow. The *gravamina* of BM. Aug. II were introduced by recalling the council of Cashel. There is by now a familiar ring about the argument. It was claimed that up to the coming of Henry II, prelates enjoyed unchallenged jurisdiction over all criminal civil and pecuniary cases arising from ecclesiastical property and clergy, freemen and the unfree (*nativi*) were exempt from any secular exaction. The council of Cashel confirmed this position and it continued to be upheld inviolably for long thereafter. Now, however, the position had changed. There is complaint of being deprived of jurisdiction in cases concerning perjury, breach of faith and sacrilege, of excesses by officials; that criminous clergy are not allowed trial in the ecclesiastical court. It is declared comprehensively that it seemed contrary to all law if clergy whom the Lord has chosen *in sortem Dei* should be tried apparently in any matter by judges other than those who hold the place of Christ among them.[1] The prelates ask that robbers and despoilers of clerical property, being thereby sacrilegious, should be tried in the ecclesiastical court.

Two articles are noteworthy as relating to distinctively Irish conditions. The prelates claim that by pre-Invasion custom they had jurisdiction in cases concerning *miserabiles personae* (widows, orphans and so on), as the canons prescribed. We have Maitland's word for it that in the common law there was 'little or nothing to be heard in England about *miserabiles personae*'.[2] There is possibly here some confirmatory evidence that it was the custom of the Irish Church. The other article cannot be satisfactorily explained because the manuscript is severely defective at this point. But it would seem to be saying that clergy of Irish birth suffered the same disabilities at

escomeger toz icels de quele nacion ke il seient ke la pees nostre seignor le rey et lauantdite ley disturberont, e purchaceront del apostoil [i.e. the pope] sur ceo confermement' *ibid*. 268. There is apparently no evidence of any papal involvement.

[1] '... et omni iuri contrarium videretur existere si clerici quos in sortem Dei dominus ele(xit) ab aliis quam ab hiis qui Christi locum inter (ipso)s optinent debeant iudicari.' Sheehy, 'Two illustrative documents' 173 gives a different rendering.

[2] F. Pollock and F. W. Maitland, *History of English Law* (1898) I. 131.

common law as any other Irishmen, at least in some contexts. The King's reply to this entry is missing.[1]

There is no doubt, however, about the general tenor of the King's response to these *peticiones*. He made it clear that he read the dispositions of the council of Cashel rather differently. The council had ordained, he adjudged, precisely the *libertates* which the prelates now have. In other words the council of Cashel ruled, in this respect, what the King said it had ruled.[2] For the rest there was also no ambiguity about his thought. Whatever about the past, he meant the Irish position in the future to be the same as the English one. These laconic replies to individual complaints convey that message very adequately:

> Ecclesia anglicana non habet
> Faciant sicut ecclesia anglicana
> Fiat eis secundum quod fit prelatis in anglia
> In anglia de omnibus transgressionibus et
> tenementis respondent
> Istud non fit in anglia quia esset contra coronam

Something has already been said about the circumstances in which the so-called *Articuli Cleri* were presented in 1291. Of all the sets of *gravamina* with the king's rulings thereon this list would seem to have been the most authoritative. That it found a place in the *Red Book of the Exchequer of Ireland* suggests that it had achieved some quasi-statutory significance. For once, the text mentions names and cases: in Cashel diocese, Clonfert, Kildare, Ossory and Ferns. If the fact that this latter diocese figures more conspicuously than the others is an indication that the bishop of Ferns played a major part in drafting these *gravamina* then there is irony here, for Bishop Richard of Northampton was formerly a royal judge.[3]

The *Articuli Cleri* number thirteen. Each article carries two replies the first by the justiciar (William de Vescy) and the second by the King. The Justiciar made no rulings on principle. His attitude was

---

1 Sheehy, 'Two illustrative documents' 173.
2 'Rex intendit quod in concilio allegato fuit ordinatum quod haberent libertates quas nunc habent' *ibid*. 172.
3 Richardson and Sayles, *Administration of Ireland* 140–1 (justice itinerant: 1275, 1278, *c*. 1281, justice of common bench: 1278–82). He was bishop of Ferns from 1282 to 1304.

rather defensive—pleading war conditions at one point as a reason for the law being broken (art. 2),[1] emphasizing at another that the secular arm was frequently in action at the request of prelates (art. 5)—and placatory—affirming that there was no intention of prejudicing the Church (art. 8)[2] and insisting throughout that the courts and the person of the King were accessible to any prelate who felt himself denied justice.

The King reinforced this latter insistence. He had a word to say on behalf of his justiciar, reminding the prelates that they could not expect him to disseise his lord (art. 13). He advised the prelates who had suffered injury to make complaint to the justiciar. Should the denial of justice be because the law was defective, they should present their *gravamina* to the king and his council and the justiciar being summoned, justice would be done to them (art. 4).[3]

Most of the King's replies, however, took the form of reiterating the common law principle on the point at issue and promising justice in the particular case. There were rulings that clergy because of their privilege were not obliged to raise hue and cry (art. 1), that the law of sanctuary be observed (art. 2), that clergy should be delivered to the appropriate ecclesiastical judge on any charge of felony, but for misdemeanour he might be tried under sanction of fine in the temporal court (art. 3), that litigation about what was named in a will and specially bequeathed belonged to the ecclesiastical court whilst what was not mentioned belonged to the king (art. 9), that prelates be allowed to examine priests presented by laymen to benefices (art. 10), that dowry was of royal cognizance (art. 13). Somewhat surprisingly, on two major issues raised by the clergy where a ruling on principle would have been very appropriate, the King refrained from any general pronouncement, contenting himself for the most part with saying that those who felt themselves unjustly treated would receive justice if their complaint were substantiated.

---

1 'Multa pro inmunitate ecclesie Regis et Regni tempore et loco guerrinis permittenda sunt que alias permitti non debent' *Stat. Irel. John–Henry V* 178.

2 'Dominus rex non intendit prelatis ecclesie sue preiudicari set conquerentibus in hiis et aliis iusticiam in sua curia exhibere' *ibid.* 184.

3 The complaint was: 'Preterea hodie nituntur judices seculares et maxime ministri domini Regis quod clerici licet laicum feodum non habeant de omnibus accionibus personalibus et transgressionibus seu delictis respondere debeant coram eis omisso suo Episcopo contra omnia iura cum actor forum rei sequi debeat' *ibid.* 180.

The first of these was the full canonical claim of virtually complete exemption of clergy from secular jurisdiction (art. 4), still requested often in thirteenth century England, but never recognized in common law. The other was the complaint, like the first, already encountered among earlier *gravamina*, that ecclesiastical courts had lost their pristine jurisdiction over ecclesiastical crime (art. 8). This issue had been considerably clarified in England some years earlier in the 'statute' *Circumspecte agatis*.[1] No answer along the lines of that ruling was made, however, though the King did point out that jurisdiction concerning property stolen from churches and trespasses against the peace were his.

The remaining articles are of interest as relating to specifically Irish circumstances. Two of them (art. 6, 7) remind us that the Crown could be approached as a protector of the clergy, not merely as an oppressor. In Ireland, church lands within liberties, *crocea*, crosslands, were not administratively part of the liberty, but were reserved to the Crown's direct jurisdiction. In 1291 the prelates could appeal to the King's own self-interest in asking that seneschals of liberties should be restrained from summoning lay tenants and clergy of crosslands to their courts, as also from issuing writs of prohibition on their own authority.

Finally a provision was made which was to figure in future statutes regulating the relationship of the two peoples. The clergy claimed that when, in march areas, they exercised their pastoral ministry to men who were thieves and violent, whose need of spiritual aid was great, they were arrested as accessories (art. 5). To this the King replied that certain Irish prelates frequently made their ministry a cloak for evil deeds. It was ordered therefore that no such communications be made without reference to the justiciar.

How accurate a picture of the prevailing relationship between the canon and common laws is provided by this collection of *gravamina* and *peticiones*? Was the clergy as ill-used by the common law as these texts (the Cashel evidence apart) suggest?

These questions could only be answered satisfactorily if there were

---

[1] On which see Powicke, *The Thirteenth Century* 482–3. The only specific reference to this important clarificatory statement in Ireland I have come across is its inclusion in the *Red Book of Ossory* 44, catalogued by J. T. Gilbert, 'Archives of the see of Ossory' Hist. MSS Comm. 10 Rep. App. pt 5 (1885) 226.

in existence, accounts of proceedings in all types of court, contemporaneous with the episcopal criticisms we have been considering. Unfortunately no close comparison can be attempted between what was happening in the courts and what bishops were saying was happening or not happening. There are no records at all of proceedings in ecclesiastical courts and the first substantial evidence from the justiciar's court begins in 1295, some four years later than the last of the *gravamina* extant from Edward I's reign. Nevertheless the study of cases coming before the justiciar and his associates in 1295 and the years shortly thereafter allow some general observations to be made which will redress the balance of the discussion somewhat in allowing something to be said from the other side.

The first observation is very simply made. It had long been a first principle of the royal policy towards Ireland that the law of Ireland should be that of England. As has been seen, this was no less applicable to the Church than to other sections of society. It was the doctrine reaffirmed by Edward I in his replies to episcopal *gravamina*. It was the principle implemented in the practice of the courts. They were consistently and persistently hostile to anything which by the principles of common law established in England was usurpation of jurisdiction by ecclesiastics, whether this were in their capacity as ecclesiastical judges or in their lay capacity as holders of property and exercisers of the jurisdiction that went with it. When the clergy in Ireland, like their brethren in England, continued to ask in the name of the sacred canons that every personal action and every criminal charge against a cleric should be an exclusively ecclesiastical matter, it was asking for more than English law had ever conceded and it was wildly unrealistic to expect that the Crown would start making over such tracts of jurisdiction at this stage in its history. The trend was in the exactly contrary direction.

Further general observations must await more detailed examination of the practice of the justiciar's court.

Chapter 7

THE CLERGY AND THE COMMON LAW
1295-1314

The common law principle of the status of the clergy has been given classic formulation by Maitland: 'with one great and a few petty exceptions the clerk was protected by and subject to the same rules of temporal law which guarded and governed the layman'.[1] That the royal courts in Ireland maintained the same principle is amply borne out by the records of the justiciar's court. It is clear that in the preservation of the rights of the king and of the king's peace, the judges were not prepared to concede anything to clerical privilege beyond the established English practice. On the other hand, the clergy used the king's courts freely for their own purposes—in all civil actions against other clerics and laymen, in securing protection, even against ecclesiastical oppression, in demanding the help of the secular arm in the caption of excommunicates. And they enjoyed that *privilegium fori* which was the 'great exception' allowed to clerics from the normal operation of the law of felony.

The clergy in the common law area of Ireland had their 'benefit' in the same way as the clergy in England. A clerk accused of any felony, having proved his clergy, would be delivered to the ecclesiastical court for trial and punishment, if need be. The procedure was the usual English one.[2] The genuineness of the claim to be a clerk was strictly examined; the prisoner was required to show when and from whom he had received his orders.[3] If he was *bigamus*[4] or *degradatus*,[5] the privilege was forfeit, as it also was if at the time of his arrest, he was not in clerical dress.[6] If a clerk continued to demand 'benefit of clergy' when privilege was not allowed, he suffered the

---

[1] Maitland, *History of English Law* I. 422.
[2] On this procedure, see especially C. R. Cheney, 'The Punishment of Felonious Clerks,' *EHR* (1936) 215–36.
[3] Cf. *Calendar of the Justiciary Rolls, Ireland 1305–07* 493, 513.
[4] *Idem 1295–1303* 20, 21–2, 46; *idem 1305–07* 499.
[5] *Idem 1295–1303* 33.   [6] *Idem 1308–14* 217.

customary penalty for refusing the common law—committal 'to the diet' until he should change his mind and recognize the court.[1] On the other hand, should a cleric wish to renounce voluntarily his privilege, if ecclesiastical authority represented that such a renunciation was canonically invalid, the renunciation was discounted by the secular court, and he was delivered to the ecclesiastical one.[2] The courts were also strict about establishing the status of the bishops' commissaries to whom the accused were handed over, and an accused clerk might find himself recommitted if there was some flaw in the official's credentials.[3] If no commissary came to demand an accused and there was a *prima facie* case for recognizing his clerical status—which might be established by a literacy or singing test[4]—he was recommitted until claimed or 'to await grace'.[5]

These various authentification preliminaries completed, the jury, which was often called upon to take some part in them, addressed itself to its main business of assessing the truth of the charge. Its work was strictly an *inquisitio*; the clerk, not having recognized the jurisdiction of the court, did not plead. The jury's decision as to the veracity of the charge determined the next stage in the proceedings. If it declared an opinion favourable to the accused, he was released, free,[6] but not quite unscathed. For his chattels, confiscated on arrest, were not restored automatically. These were held to be forfeit on the technicality that by pleading his clergy, he had refused the common law. Normally, however, he would be allowed to make fine and recover them.[7] He would not regain them even if declared innocent, if he had attempted to evade arrest by flight.[8]

If the jury declared a clerk to be guilty, he was delivered by the

[1] *Idem 1305–07* 487; *idem 1308–14* 217.
[2] It was apparently forfeited if the crime was also sacrilege, cf. *idem 1308–14* 222 (a case of robbery from a church), though on payment of a fine the privilege might be allowed 'of grace', *ibid.* 220.
[3] *Cal. Justic. Rolls 1305–07* 478, 511.
[4] *Idem 1308–14* 208.
[5] *Idem 1305–07* 235, 498; *idem 1308–14* 253.
[6] *Idem 1295–1303* 46, 63.
[7] *Ibid.* 95 ('That it may be known for what he should be delivered to the bishop, let the truth be enquired by the country. The Jurors of Offolan say that he is not guilty. Therefore he is quit. But because he refused the common law, therefore to judgment as to his chattels. Afterwards he made fine by 5s to have his chattels ... His chattels were valued at 10s.') Similarly, *idem 1305–07* 235, 493; *idem 1308–14* 288.
[8] *Ibid.* 304.

bishop's commissary to await trial in the ecclesiastical court.[1] An occasional instance is to be found of a guilty clerk not being allowed delivery to the ecclesiastical judge, but generally speaking, the procedure was observed with all regularity. There is little evidence surviving of proceedings in the ecclesiastical court. The accused followed the normal canonical procedure of attempting his purgation, and public proclamation was made inviting anyone to present himself at stated times to make objections to the purgation of the accused. Apparently the royal justices were on their guard against the failure of ecclesiastical judges to try properly those whom their own courts had found to be guilty.[2] The verdict of the ecclesiastical court was certified to the king's court. If the accused had been found not guilty, he might sue for a writ of restitution of his chattels. The order of restitution, if granted, made a point of insisting that it was royal grace alone that allowed such restitution. The Church, as was being emphasized, might have jurisdiction over the person of the clerk; the State asserted its right over his property,[3] even, as has been seen, when it had itself found the accused innocent. It is hardly necessary to add that if the accused had not succeeded in purging himself, when the ecclesiastical judge certified this fact to the royal court, forfeiture of chattels was final.

All this amounts to the conclusion that Irish conditions had caused no change to be made in the principles and procedures in force in the king's courts against felonious clerks. Such information as the justiciary rolls record about regular proceedings in ecclesiastical courts indicates that the relationship between canon and common law as evolved in England applied likewise in Ireland. The right of sanctuary was upheld by the king's courts;[4] the courts of archdeacons and bishops judged moral offences and took money fines as redemp-

---

[1] A convenient place to study the usual procedure is *Cal. Justic. Rolls 1295–1303* 33–6 where the delivery of seven clerks including some of Irish nationality to the official of the bishop of Cork is recorded. The indices of this volume and *Cal. Justic. Rolls 1305–7 s.v.* clerks, Ecclesiastical, are an especially helpful guide to tracing the practices of the royal courts in this respect.

[2] See the investigation into the conducting of a purgation by the vicar-general of the Dublin diocese, *idem 1295–1303* 445–6.

[3] Cf. Cheney, 'Punishment of Felonious Clerks' 231–2.

[4] For examples see the indices of the *Cals. Justic. Rolls, s.v.* sanctuary.

tion of penances;[1] judgment of chattels in marital and testamentary cases was a recognized ecclesiastical matter,[2] as was tithe of less than a fourth of the annual value of the church concerned,[3] and the cooperation of the temporal power was available for the seizure of those who defied ecclesiastical penalties.[4] There seems no evidence that *Circumspecte agatis* and its *additio*, which together supply the norm of Edwardian principles on the extent of ecclesiastical jurisdiction permitted under the common law,[5] ever held the same position in Ireland as it did in England. But there seems no reason why it should be supposed that the theory behind the practice of the king's justices in Ireland was substantially different. Ecclesiastical criminals apart, clergy came to the king's courts by a variety of routes.

One well-trodden way was when the Crown was preserving its own rights—for example, if pleas of the Crown were being heard without warrant in the secular court of an ecclesiastic[6] or where

---

[1] See the cases concerning fornication, adultery and perjury, *Cal. Justic. Rolls 1295–1303* 96; *idem 1305–07* 451.

[2] As proceedings on prohibition on the hearing of cases touching lay chattels in courts christian makes clear. See, for example, the successful petition of Michael of Exeter, bishop of Ossory against a writ of prohibition in a disputed will case, *Cal. Justic. Rolls 1295–1303* 269.

[3] *Idem 1308–14* 95.

[4] Numerous examples are listed in the indices of the *Cals. Justic. Rolls*, *s.v.* excommunication (see *idem 1295–1303* 338 for the principle that an excommunicate cannot sue in the king's court). But the system had its drawbacks for episcopal justice in that proceedings might be slow and cumbersome, and also that it might allow a certain power of review over the case heard by the bishop to the royal court. In 1299, Richard of Northampton, bishop of Ferns, petitioned the king that two years earlier he had asked the sheriff of Waterford to proceed against five persons whom he had excommunicated. They had successfully petitioned the king for a stay of execution by the sheriff on the grounds of an impending appeal to Rome against the bishop's sentence. No appeal was in fact made and the bishop had to ask the king to reinstruct the sheriff to act. The king did so, ordering the sheriff to summon the guilty 'to show wherefore he should not proceed to the taking of them' *Cal. Justic. Rolls 1295–1303* 269–70.

[5] Cf. E. B. Graves, 'Circumspecte Agatis' *EHR* 43 (1928) 1–20; H. G. Richardson and G. O. Sayles, 'The Clergy in the Easter Parliament, 1285' *ibid.* 52 (1937) 220–34; G. B. Flahiff, 'The Writ of Prohibition to Courts Christian in the Thirteenth Century' *Mediaeval Studies* 6 (1944) at 302–13; F. M. Powicke, *The Thirteenth Century* 480–3.

[6] Reference has been made above to the *quo warranto* investigation into the secular jurisdiction of the archbishop of Dublin in 1264. Cf. for further *quo warranto* proceedings *Cal. Justic. Rolls 1295–1303* 103 (Armagh: Down); 149 (Prior of St Patrick's, Down); 316–17 (Tuam).

rights of advowson were thought to have been lost to a bishop[1] or where bishops stood accused of impeding the king's officials[2] or where cathedral chapters failed to observe the required procedure in the conduct of an episcopal election.[3]

Another was when laymen thought they had been injured by an ecclesiastical judge. It was not only royal courts which could abuse their jurisdiction. If it was against clerical principles, as the *gravamina* show, that a layman might bring a cleric into a secular court, it was no doubt in the interests of justice that an ecclesiastical judge could be brought to account for such abuse. The royal courts stood open to any layman who thought he had been ill-used by a cleric. He might complain, for example, of the use of spiritual sanctions to compel him to appear in an ecclesiastical court in a lay plea.[4] He could complain if he considered he had been wrongfully imprisoned by a bishop.[5] If he had been excommunicated and his bishop had had recourse to the sheriff for his caption, there was an opportunity to show cause why the sheriff should not proceed to arrest him and deliver him to the ecclesiastical judge.[6]

Conversely, the royal courts stood open to ecclesiastics who considered they had been oppressed by laymen, not least by royal officials. It has already been noticed that a common reply to clerical *gravamina* was a promise that remedy would be given if the complaint were justified and that the royal courts were in many cases the appropriate place of resort for such remedy. That *gravamina* were frequently presented to the king himself demonstrates that direct appeal was a favoured method of seeking redress and there is evidence enough that prelates from Ireland continued to consider it

---

[1] *Cal. Justic. Rolls 1295–1303* III.

[2] E.g. the bishops of Cork and Cloyne who threatened excommunication of any royal official who in execution of his mandate to collect corn for the provisioning of Gascony took it against the will of the clergy, *ibid.* 95–6.

[3] The chapter of Clonmacnois was fined in 1280 for electing without a licence, *Cal. Docs. Irel.* 1772, Killaloe likewise in 1299, *Cal. Justic. Rolls* 243; Ossory (and the bishop-elect) in 1302, *ibid.* 450–1; Killala in 1306 (and Tuam for confirming without royal assent), *Cal. Justic. Rolls* 275–6.

[4] E.g. *Cal. Justic. Rolls 1295–1303* 83 for admitted misuse of ecclesiastical justice in a case of lay debt to the dean of Slane.

[5] The bishop of Connor was impleaded for assault and wrongful imprisonment in 1297, *Cal. Justic. Rolls* 90. The upshot of the case is not known.

[6] Cf. *Cal. Justic. Rolls 1295–1303* 269–70.

worthwhile to undertake the labour and expense of such recourse to the king personally. The more usual route, however, would be to the justiciar and here the evidence suggests that effective redress was available to those clergy who had been misused by royal agents.

The point can be established from a number of cases of the one year 1295, the year nearest to the *gravamina* when evidence sufficient to put the matter to the test is available. All the cases concerned abuse of their jurisdiction by sheriffs. In 1295, the chancellor of Limerick successfully brought the sheriff of Limerick to court for unlawful arrest.[1] In the same year the justiciar was concerned with the misdeeds of the sheriff of Kerry. He had tried to force the bishop of Ardfert to make his brother precentor of the diocese. By false information laid by the escheator's agent in Kerry, the bishop's temporalities had been taken into the king's hand and the sheriff had made free of them.[2] Again in the same year, the dean of Limerick was complaining about the sheriff of that county in a matter concerning ecclesiastical taxation and tithe.[3] The abbot of Maigue was also complaining, successfully, against the same sheriff, for malicious retention of writs and unjust amercement.[4] Finally, still in 1295, the bishop of Kildare was able to prosecute a petition for unjust amercement in the courts.[5] It is quite clear that in some important respects ecclesiastics got more than fair words when they complained of being injured in their liberties.

There was another important way in which royal courts did service for ecclesiastics: they protected them from oppression by others of their own order, and this without trespass on the field proper to ecclesiastical jurisdiction. A case also selected from the year 1295 well illustrates this. Nicholas, bishop of Ardfert, was brought to court by his chancellor William Fynaly on a complaint that he had refused to honour an obligation to pay an annual pension of 2 marks which the Bishop was alleged to have made and also that he had ejected William from his vicarage. Nicholas pleaded that the election issue was of ecclesiastical jurisdiction and this was upheld. A jury called to hear the pension issue found that the Chancellor had in fact forged the instrument purporting to award him the annual sum. His punishment was imprisonment, redeemed by fine.[6] A case of more

---

[1] *Ibid.* 2.   [2] *Ibid.* 25.   [3] *Ibid.* 38.
[4] *Ibid.* 49.   [5] *Ibid.* 75.   [6] *Ibid.* 42.

far-reaching implications was brought in 1297 by the Dominicans of Ireland against William of Bermingham, archbishop of Tuam. The complaint was that this prelate through his archdeacon had issued instructions throughout his archdiocese that no one should supply the friars with food. The justiciar inflicted no penalty but got the parties to agree that the Archbishop and the vicar-general of the Dominicans should settle matters between them.[1] The same archdeacon was again brought to answer a charge that when the diocese of Annaghdown was vacant he had forcibly seized the mitre, crozier and other *pontificalia* of that see.[2] The record does not allow us to see the result of the case but since, in 1308, there was to be consecrated the first bishop of Annaghdown for over fifty years, it would seem that the justiciar had played some part in saving that diocese from extinction.[3]

These glimpses into the other side of the picture of how the clergy was affected by the common law suggest that it was as much supported as ill-used by it. Nevertheless there was some substance in the reiterated complaint of churchmen that what they had previously enjoyed as liberties of the Church were now taken from them. In the thirteenth century the boundary between the royal and ecclesiastical jurisdictions was being adjusted to the detriment of the latter. There were two particularly significant aspects of this.

The first was in the sphere of ecclesiastical property. Henry II had acknowledged in 1164 in the Constitutions of Clarendon that all disputes concerning land recognized as given to the Church in free alms were for the cognizance of the ecclesiastical courts. By a century later, however, this principle had been substantially modified. Frankalmoin was lay fee. The trend had been inexorably towards giving the royal courts exclusive jurisdiction over real property and ecclesiastical judges were forbidden to hear pleas concerning such, whether free alms or not.[4] Prelates in Ireland had a double basis for their protest against this development: it violated both what had been

---

[1] *Cal. Justic. Rolls 1295–1303* 108, 114–15.

[2] *Ibid.* 115, 144, 306–7.

[3] Because of the *temporalia*, the Crown had of course a vested interest in the continuance of the diocese.

[4] Maitland, *History of English Law* I. 240–51; G. B. Flahiff, 'The writ of prohibition' 274–5.

common law principle and what had been the practice (it was alleged) that prevailed in Ireland before the Invasion.

At the same time royal courts were increasingly suspicious of any ecclesiastical attempt to exercise a civil jurisdiction by way of jurisdiction *ratione peccati*. The common law was in process of making firm distinctions between the ecclesiastical and lay aspects involved when ecclesiastical judges punished sin in their courts. For example, in cases of defamation or breaking of pledge, canonists were wont to argue that the ecclesiastical courts had jurisdiction over the lay *accessoria* to the sin committed: civil proceedings for damages or civil remedy for breach of contract. It seems quite likely that ecclesiastical courts in Ireland had enjoyed quite considerable accessory jurisdiction of this sort; whether because of pre-Invasion custom or the particular circumstances of colonial settlement is difficult to say. By mid-thirteenth century, however, the ecclesiastical courts were being strictly confined to the sphere of penance only, even to the extent of being forbidden to inflict money fines instead of the traditional corporal or other penitential sanctions. As has been seen, however, in the case Fulk of Sandford fought against the city of Dublin in 1268 those found guilty of ecclesiastical crime were allowed to redeem corporal penances with money fines, even before *Circumspecte agatis* gave definitive permission.

Having reviewed both the operation of the common law where it touched ecclesiastical persons and causes and the protests made by the clergy against that operation, we are in a position to evaluate the *gravamina* submitted by the *ecclesia hibernicana* to the general council which met at Vienne in 1311–12. Such an evaluation will allow some final general observations to be made about the position of the clergy *vis-à-vis* the common law in our period.

On the agenda of the general council was the question of reform of the Church.[1] In this very general field the problem of upholding *libertas ecclesiae* was to receive specific attention. Submissions on this topic had been solicited from all the provinces of the Church and detailed complaints about violations of ecclesiastical liberty by secular rulers had fairly poured in from all quarters. A preparatory

---

[1] There are two excellent accounts of this council: E. Müller, *Das Konzil von Vienne 1311–1312: seine Quellen und seine Geschichte* (1934); J. Lecler, *Vienne* (*Hist. des conciles oecuméniques* 8: 1964).

commission of the council worked on this material to systematize it and condense it into a form suitable for the scrutiny of the council members. The *gravamina* of the Irish Church formed one small contribution among many to this great mass of ecclesiastical grievance. The working party had classified the articles of complaint under different headings. In the longer of the two forms in which the material has survived the actual content of the individual articles would not appear to have been substantially changed. It is possible that in the process of shaping a manageable format for the *gravamina* as a whole some articles were dropped. But when the thirteen articles of the *ecclesia hibernicana* are reassembled, it looks very much as if we are in possession of the whole submission in very much its original form. At any rate, there can be no doubt that with this reassembly there has been recovered a document recognizably in the tradition of earlier *gravamina*, with a marked family resemblance to the complaints of Lambeth MS 619 and the *Articuli Cleri* of 1291.

The prelates (there is no clue as to who they were) pulled no punches:

The Irish Church says that before the coming of the English to Ireland, it was free to the extent that it knew no superior in temporal affairs, possessing and exercising every kind of spiritual and temporal jurisdiction. Then however a certain king of England sought licence from the pope to enter this land and to subject it to himself, saving however the rights of the Roman and Irish churches. On pretext of this licence the king entered this land and conquered a part of it, and in the subject part he and his successors little by little unremittingly usurped, appropriated and occupied places, property, rights and jurisdictions of the church of that part, and he who is now king holds such a position at the present time that the ordinaries do not have free and full cognizance of any cause. What is worse, archbishops, bishops, abbots, priors and all other churchmen are forced to appear before secular judges in all cases; they are arrested, imprisoned, heavily fined and treated most harshly. Because of all this they have left their cities and sees and lead miserable lives hiding in caves.[1]

---

[1] Ed. Ehrle, 'Ein Bruchstück der Akten des Konzils von Vienne' 370. The *gravamina* of the various provinces had been classified by a preparatory commission of the council under different headings. This article, presumably the *proemium* of the submission of the *ecclesia hibernicana*, appeared under the rubric: 'Quidam compellunt etiam personas ecclesiasticas coram se super actionibus personalibus respondere'. That the claim to a *privilegium fori* was considered to apply as much to

Understatement was not the dominant characteristic of this protest. The obvious elements of exaggeration, particularly the last sentence, do not inspire confidence in the objectivity of the complainants. Nevertheless the general trend of the specific complaints is credible enough.

As do the other lists of *gravamina*, the particular articles fall generally into one or other of two main types: one where the principles themselves of the common law were complained of and the the other where the offending practices were quite clearly abuses of law, not its correct use.

To take the latter type first. Some of them refer to the illegal actions of barons and their officials rather than to royal officers. Thus there is complaint of being forced to raise hue and cry[1] and of being prevented from exercising their testamentary jurisdiction.[2] There is reference to war conditions when it is complained that benefices, temporarily vacated because of war or other valid reasons, were conferred by captains of armies as if they were permanently vacant or their fruits used as payment for service in war and if bishops protested they were treated as if they were traitors.[3] The prelates complained of royal officials that they arbitrarily prevented clergy from pleading their benefit.[4] They alleged that prelates were gaoled and fined for punishing such ecclesiastical crimes as sexual sin,[5] that they were prevented from exercising that jurisdiction over wills which was acknowledged to belong to the ecclesiastical courts,[6] that the approved custom whereby in lay presentations to churches candidates should be canonically examined by the bishop was not allowed.[7]

All of these complaints, which form eight articles in all, were about non-observance of the principles of the common law in matters where king and clergy were in agreement, It is likely that had they

personal actions as to criminal has not always been fully appreciated by historians of English law. See now, however, W. Ullmann, 'A decision of the Rota Romana on the benefit of clergy in England' *Studia Gratiana* 13 (1967) *Col. S. Kuttner* 3. 455–90.

[1] Ehrle, 'Ein Bruchstück der Akten des Konzils von Vienne' 380.
[2] *Ibid.* 382.
[3] *Ibid.* 383. For this entry the original allocation to *Ecclesia Ibernicana* has been altered to *Ecclesia Scoticensis*. However, the shorter version of the *gravamina* in Vatican Arch. Instr. Misc. 516 makes it clear that *Ibernicana* is the correct reading.
[4] *Ibid.* 377. [5] *Ibid.* 386.
[6] *Ibid.* 398–9. [7] *Ibid.* 399.

been put to the king answer would have been made along lines
similar to Edward I's in 1291: 'Let a case be shown; let the injured
party complain; let justice be done to him'.

Other complaints, however, raised issues of principles relative to
the respective functions of king and clergy. The prelates complained
that if royal officials could not distrain beneficed clerks on a lay fee
they would order the bishop to sequestrate their benefices in order
to compel them to attend court.[1] This was indeed the practice.[2] So
too was the procedure whereby an excommunicate could bring an
ecclesiastical judge to court to show cause of the excommunication.[3]
Finally there was reiterated a complaint first ventilated in 1255 that
bequests for pious causes, including bequests for the crusade, were
not permitted.[4] These were, no doubt, unpleasant practices for the
clergy and violations of the principle of the supremacy of the
spiritual power. They hardly seem to justify the full force of the
general denunciation contained in the proemium to these *gravamina*.

Documents of this sort of their very nature looked on the common
law critically and said nothing of the positive contribution which that
law could and did make towards clerical security and justice. That
gravamina continued to be compiled and presented testifies both to
the continued shortcomings of royal officials and to their energy in
seeking to bring practice in Ireland into line with that in England.
They are ample evidence that in Ireland, as in England at the same
time, 'a brisk border warfare simmered'[5] between the two sets of
courts. But they are also of their very nature evidence of the existence

---

[1] 'Ecclesia Ibernicana dicit, quod si ministri regii clericos beneficiatos, qui laycum
feudum, per quod distringi possint, non habent, ad suam presentiam evocent pro
causa quacunque; si non venerint, prelatis clericorum ipsorum districte precipiunt
et mandant, quod hos clericos ad respondendum coram ipsis per sequestrationem
beneficiorum suorum compellant; et si non fecerint, incarcerantur et pena pecuni-
aria puniuntur' *ibid.* 372–3. The *ecclesia anglicana* saw the matter differently. It was
prepared to accept sequestration of benefices. What it objected to was a bishop
being held responsible for the failure of the delinquent to appear after he had sequestrated the benefice.

[2] The *ecclesia anglicana* testified that sequestration was the custom, *ibid.* 372. There was
a case concerning Robert Walrand, bishop of Ferns, in 1306, *Cal. Justic. Rolls* 283,
302.

[3] The complaint was against the use of the writ *Quare excommunicavit.* Ehrle, 'Ein
Bruchstück der Akten des Konzils von Vienne' 391.

[4] *Ibid.* 398–9.

[5] Maitland, *History of English Law* 1. 479.

of process of law, that clergy did have access to authority for redress of grievance. The system might be imperfect but it was a system, a framework of reasoned order. Actual court records suggest that the royal courts showed a great deal more respect for the legal position of ecclesiastical persons and jurisdiction and had much more to offer for the security of individual clergy than *gravamina* would lead their reader to suspect.

The *ecclesia hibernicana* was not a single unified entity to speak with one voice as to its attitude to the common law. But some general attitudes may nevertheless be discerned. It is likely enough that Anglo-Irish and English prelates thought very much like their *confrères* in England. They grumbled, and not without reason, about certain principles and procedures of the common law and especially about the conduct of royal officials. *Libertas ecclesiae* was an important principle and the clergy was under obligation to fight to uphold it. Perhaps too there was an element of self-interest about its opposition to the royal courts of the sort which Maitland noted when he spoke of the comparable struggle in England, 'between professional classes each of which likes power and business and has no dislike for fees and perquisites'.[1]

On the Irish side no doubt similar considerations of principle and expediency had their part in shaping episcopal attitudes. But there was, too, for them a whole additional dimension. Irish prelates were confronted with a new and foreign order with which, some few remote areas apart, they had no option but to come to terms. There is no more difficult problem in medieval ecclesiastical history than to know the mind of an Irish bishop. Perhaps, though, the attitudes of two senior Irish prelates afford a good insight into the options open to Irish bishops.

Like some of the reformers of the twelfth century, Archbishop David MacCarwill of Cashel was apparently prepared to put his trust in English princes and therefore welcomed the common law as standing for 'peace and truth in the land' and so sought its extension to the native Irish. This enthusiasm did not, however, prevent his ignoring the law when it proved inconvenient nor protect him from incurring the deep suspicion of officialdom that he was actively anti-

[1] *Loc. cit.*

English. On the other hand Archbishop Nicholas Mac Maol Íosa, seeing the common law whittling away the traditional prerogatives of Armagh, sought to spur his episcopal colleagues to militant action in defence of ecclesiastical liberty against such inroads of the civil power. Yet his hostility to the encroaching sytem did not prevent his forming close alliances with English officials nor from being an indefatigable litigant in the royal courts in pursuit of his metropolitan and diocesan rights.[1]

[1] The attitudes of these two prelates are examined in more detail below, pp. 158–70.

Chapter 8

THE EPISCOPATE IN THE REIGN OF
EDWARD I

Just one hundred bishops held sees in Ireland in the thirty-five years
of the reign of Edward I. Fifty-one of these can be identified with
certainty, on the evidence of their names, as native Irish. Of forty-
eight foreigners, perhaps some thirty were of colonial or Anglo-Irish
stock, the other eighteen being born in England. The odd man out,
a papal appointment, was an Italian.[1]

The ratio of Irish to English varied considerably from province to
province. There was some change in the ratio over the reign as a
whole. In 1272, no native Irishman held a see in the Dublin province
nor had done so for nearly half a century nor was to do so in the
medieval period to come. By contrast, no Englishman held a see
in Tuam province. The other two provinces stood between these
extremes. In Armagh there were seven Irish and four foreign. In
Cashel, six Irish and five foreign. By 1307, however, three of the
Tuam dioceses, including the archbishopric, were held by Anglo-
Irishmen or Englishmen. Numerically the ratio remained the same
in Armagh as it had been in 1272. Qualitatively, however, it had
worsened in that the archbishopric was now held by an Englishman.
This was for the first time since Luke Netterville (1217–27). Armagh
was to have but one other Irish prelate in the remaining medieval
period. In Cashel province the ratio had changed quite markedly:
there were now seven foreign to four native Irish. The archbishopric
itself remained in Irish hands, though in 1317 it was to have its first
non-Irish archbishop. Thus in Edward I's reign, the anglicization of
dioceses was still proceeding. Expressed numerically the shift was
from seventeen native Irish to fifteen Anglo-Irish and English in 1272,
to fifteen and nineteen respectively, in 1307. Mere numbers conceal

---

[1] These, and the following calculations, are based on the Irish episcopal succession
lists as given in *Hbk Brit. Chron.*

the significance of the change in the two major sees of Armagh and Tuam.[1]

Were these bishops elected in freedom?

There were potentially three major threats to freedom of canonical election in Ireland: the hereditary monopoly of sees by strongly entrenched ecclesiastical families; the domination of Anglo-Irish sees by the Crown or by the Dublin administration or by local magnates; national discrimination against candidates by one or both peoples. The first of these situations had been prevalent enough before the twelfth century reform had attacked the abuse. There was, however, rarely any easy or quick solution of this problem and the effect of the Invasion and war conditions might well make a remote diocese even less open to external reforming influences. On the other hand, some of the earliest English bishops to occupy Irish sees had been put there by the Crown. Kings were never indifferent as to who became a bishop in Ireland. For a bishop was potentially useful politically, especially in a colony; a colonial bishopric might be used to give status and income to a royal official still on active service or as a reward to a retired one. Further, as has been seen, the regency government of Henry III had attempted a policy of national exclusivism. Influential voices were to be raised in Ireland urging Edward I to arrange the appointment of Englishmen to sees normally filled by Irishmen.[2] But there is more than a suggestion that discrimination might be advocated from the Irish side. In 1250, in response to a complaint of Henry III, Pope Innocent IV condemned the alleged attempt of Irish clergy to debar any Englishman from being admitted into a canonry in any of their cathedral churches.[3]

---

[1] Over the whole reign the ratios of Irish to Anglo-Irish and English in each province were: Armagh, 19 to 11; Cashel, 19 to 16; Dublin, 0 to 17; Tuam, 13 to 4. The Italian was Johannes de Alatre, bishop of Clonfert from 1266 to 1295 when he was translated to the see of Benevento.

[2] The recommendation was from the 1284 commission of enquiry into the conduct of the Irish administration of which details are given below. As far as can be made out from a much faded manuscript, the recommendation had specific reference to Armagh and implicit reference to other Irish dioceses: 'Et expediret Regi quod nunquam Hibernus esset archiepiscopus ... quia semper predicant contra Regem et provisiones faciunt in ecclesiis suis de Hibernis ... ita quod eleccio episcoporum possit fieri de Hibernis, ad sustinendam Linguam suam ...' PRO QR Irish Excheq. E.101/234/9 mem. no. 3.

[3] *Pont. hib.* 2. 325, 326. It has been suggested very plausibly that it was Bishop Geoffrey

Hereditary tenure of dioceses was no longer in the thirteenth century a leading characteristic of the Irish-speaking Church. But it had not disappeared completely, even by the second half of the century. The diocese of Derry was held by members of the O Cerbhallain family from 1185 down to the final breaking of its monopoly in 1293.[1] This example marks the extreme of how freedom might be restricted in a way typical of the traditional Irish pattern. On the other hand, Dublin, in the same period, provides an example of how it might be restricted in a way typical of the English compromise between the demand of royal and ecclesiastical service, where the latter came off second best. The chapter of St Patrick's cathedral Dublin was composed 'for the most part of king's clerks',[2] royal officials for whom a canonry was part of their emolument. Three archbishops of Dublin held the office of justiciar at one stage or another of their pontificates and most of the others were involved directly in royal service.[3]

These cases, however, were unique of their type. The majority of dioceses were in the pocket of neither family nor government. Nevertheless they represent what could have happened if certain permanent features of the Irish episcopal scene had gone to extremes.

Of course family influence was a factor in determining the composition of the episcopate and not merely in native Irish dioceses. There can be no question of tracing family connexions in any detail for the evidence does not exist. But there is a suggestive recurrence of certain names: of Irish families, O'Hogain in Killaloe, Mac-Carwill in Cashel; St Leger and Cusack of Anglo-Irish families; Sandford and Fulbourn, English born and in royal service. Perhaps the real point of significance here, however, is not that in these narrow, constricted ecclesiastical worlds there should have been such family influence, but that the influence was not very much stronger than appears to have been the case. Particularly when clerical marriage

of Tourville, the Irish treasurer who secured this papal condemnation, *Pont. hib.* 2. p. 155. The report cited in the previous note shows that English officialdom had not changed its reading of the situation some decades later.

[1] *Hbk Brit. Chron.* 314. Cf. A. Gwynn, 'Raphoe and Derry in the twelfth and thirteenth centuries' 84–100 for some light on an otherwise extremely dark sector of the Irish Church.

[2] *Rot. Parl.* I. 153.

[3] This involvement is examined in more detail below.

was by no means unknown in both Irish[1] and Anglo-Irish[2] dioceses.

There is no way of telling how far native Irish princes were involved in the making of the episcopate. The rôle of Edward I, however, is written quite clearly into the copious files of his government. He certainly did not seek to impose candidates on chapters. Only once, as far as can be seen, did he suggest a name to a chapter.[3] This was not to a native Irish see. There is no evidence that he pursued any policy of discrimination against the appointment of Irishmen, though as has been seen he was advised authoritatively at least once that he should try to arrange the appointment of Englishmen to sees normally filled by Irishmen. Edward I gave his assent to, and took fealty from, either personally or through his ministers, some twenty-nine native Irish bishops. There is no evidence that he ever refused assent to any bishop-elect, whatever his nationality.[4]

The conclusion is inescapable that, in this period, by far the greater part of the bishops appointed in Ireland were elected by their chapters, or their equivalents. With few exceptions, there is nothing to suggest that these were not, in the strict canonical sense, free elections. This is not to say that there were no local pressures at work to influence electors in their choice, though in the nature of things, evidence of this informal pressure does not exist. But intervention of a kind which would break the canon law was very uncommon. The papal curia stood open to all, hungry for business, and clergy from Ireland were never reluctant to use its facilities in disputed elections. We can be sure that any serious sustained attempt to ride roughshod over the rights of chapters or to frustrate the just expectations of candidates for ecclesiastical advancement would have left its mark on the records of papal and royal bureaucracies.

---

1 *Pont. hib.* 1. 53; *ALC* 1. 467.
2 Eustace bishop of Connor 1226–41 was described as 'filium sacerdotis et in sacerdotio genitum' *Pont. hib.* 2. 207. Cf. also Innocent IV to the bishop of Ossory, Geoffrey de Tourville in 1250: 'Ex parte tua fuit propositum coram nobis quod nimis per quosdam clericos tue diocesis et clericalis denigratur honestas et canonicis detrahitur honestatis dum quidam ipsorum uxores habentes ecclesiasticorum beneficiorum proventus percipere non verentur' *Pont. hib.* 2. 318.
3 That of Stephen of Fulbourn to Waterford in 1273, *Cal. Docs. Irel.* 1009, a suggestion for which the chapter professed itself grateful and accepted.
4 Though occasionally it was thought necessary to take security from the new bishop against possible future misbehaviour, as had been the practice in his father's reign, *Cal. Docs. Irel. 1172–1251* 2467, 2479; *idem 1301–07* 220, 232.

The episcopate in the reign of Edward I

The fact of canonical freedom of election, as it was recognized for the English context by the papacy, was not of course incompatible with an important measure of royal participation in the electoral proceedings. The king had his acknowledged rights.[1] No election could begin until the king had issued permission in the form of his *licencia eligendi*; every bishop-elect was subjected to examination before his suitability as far as concerned the king was recognized with the granting of assent; fealty was to be rendered before the episcopal temporalities, in royal control during vacancy, were restored to the new bishop. The Crown had fought consistently for the extension of the recognition in practice of these rights throughout Ireland and it had not been unsuccessful. Edward I, in this respect, took up where Henry III had left off.

Edward saw his rôle in the creation of the episcopate in exactly the same way as had his father in the later years of his reign. No attempt was made to intervene directly in appointments but a great deal of attention was given to ensuring that the proper electoral formalities were observed.[2] Edward I was not one whit less vigilant in maintaining the established procedure whereby custody of temporalities during vacancy, request for licence to elect, royal assent to the elect and performance of fealty before restitution of temporalities ensured that the king's right in the choice of a tenant-in-chief was maintained. There were fines for chapters that deviated from the proper forms and the courts ensured they were adhered to with exactitude.[3] Seizure of temporalities was unquestionably a cogent argument against disloyalty and misconduct. Though normally a latent threat it was used just often enough to persuade bishops that it was no empty one.[4]

---

[1] That the royal rights had full papal approval was always insisted on. Cf. e.g. Henry III in 1218, concerning an election performed without royal licence: 'Sed statim obiectum fuit eis a consilio nostro quod nulla fuit electio illa, nec rite celebrata, cum secundum dignitatem nostram multis diebus optentam et a domino papa confirmatam, debuit electionem suam petita et impetrata a nobis eligendi licencia prevenisse ...' *Cal. Docs. Irel.* 856; *Cal. Pat. Rolls* 183. In 1285: 'Quia indultum est Regibus Anglie per sedem apostolicam quod ecclesia hibernicana sit regulata et dignitati regis subjecta in premissis [i.e. custody of temporalities during vacancies and granting of licences to elect] ut est ecclesia anglicana' QR Irish Excheq. *ms. cit.*

[2] For the documentation of the formal stages of royal participation in the making of an Irish bishop, cf. my 'English law and the Irish Church' 163–7.

[3] *Ibid.* 144, n. 46. The case of 1306 there cited concerned Killala not Killaloe as was stated inadvertently.   [4] *Ibid.* 144, n. 47.

There can be little doubt that as the conquest of Ireland progressed and was consolidated by the establishment of routine administrative procedures, the Crown was increasingly in a position to exert pressure on bishops and chapters through threat of seizure of temporalities. Unfortunately, few pipe rolls have survived for the reign of Henry III and it is hardly possible to trace the gradual extension of the sway of the escheator. Escheatry accounts for the reign of Edward I are, however, adequate enough to provide a general account of which dioceses did actually have their temporalities taken into the king's hand during vacancy. Of the thirty-four dioceses, twenty-two figure in the accounts of escheators in this period. Not all of these temporalities were taken with the same comprehensiveness. It is clear that in a proportion of these twenty-two, the escheator accounted for only a part, sometimes a very small part, of the possessions of the diocese. He laid hold of what he could, and it might not amount to very much. Numerous entries on the rolls testify to the difficulties of the escheator's task in penetrating some areas. He was in the position of being totally excluded from some dioceses (in the north and west of the country, in Armagh and Tuam provinces), of taking only a fraction of the whole in other dioceses (notably in the outlying parts of Cashel province), and even in dioceses where normally his control was effective enough, there might be pockets of devastation and insuperable Irish hostility (as in Dublin and Meath dioceses).[1]

These twenty-two dioceses whose temporalities were in some degree subject to royal control normally conformed to the established electoral procedures, asking for licence to elect and for royal assent to the candidate. In addition, seven dioceses, of which no record has survived of any custody of temporalities, also often conformed to the procedures. All in all, looking at the position as it stood about the middle of the reign, only the five Armagh dioceses of Clogher, Kilmore, Dromore, Derry and Raphoe did not conform. The attempt to bring these into line will be examined in due course.

The papal curia functioned as a supplement when any defect in the ordinary machinery of capitular election made itself felt. Though it was not called on to any considerable extent in this period, it was invoked sufficiently often for there to be need of an examination of this aspect of Church–State relationship.

---

[1] *Ibid.* 141–2 where the surviving pipe roll evidence is analysed.

No Irish diocese conducted its elections so badly as Dublin.[1] This was, of course, because of the continuing wrangles of the two Dublin cathedral chapters who would not agree on how an election should be conducted. Dublin was vacant for nearly eight years at the beginning of the reign and for four at the end of it. Three of the four appointments made in this period were by papal provision after disputed elections. No other diocese had so high an incidence of papal provision and it is fitting, therefore, that an examination of the rôle of the papacy in the creation of the episcopate should begin with Dublin.

The three archbishops provided to Dublin were outstanding men of their type. John of Darlington O.P. (1279–84)[2] was a theology graduate of Paris, he had been a member of Henry III's council, his confessor and his intimate adviser in the troubled times of the Baronial Wars. He was important, too, to Edward I, acting as his agent in negotiations at the papal curia about taxation of the clergy. It was apparently because he continued to be of importance to Edward as a collector of taxes that, if indeed he ever set foot in Ireland at all, he was never resident for any sustained period. William of Hotham O.P. (1296–8)[3] was an Oxford doctor of theology, a Thomist of some note, a former Dominican prior provincial of England. He was among Edward I's most valued counsellors, accompanying him to Wales, Scotland, Gascony and Flanders, playing a significant mediatory rôle when relations between the King and Boniface VIII were strained. But he does not seem ever to have gone to Dublin. Richard de Ferings (1299–1306)[4] was an Oxford doctor of canon law and a former archdeacon of Canterbury, and had been busy about both the royal and papal courts. Clearly, as a lawyer and administrator and diplomat of quality and experience, he was a suitable choice. But he too spent little or no time in Ireland. Except for the period of John of Sandford's pontificate in the decade after 1284, Dublin was virtually without a ruling archbishop, through vacancy and absenteeism, from the death of

[1] Hand, 'Rivalry of the Cathedral Chapters in Medieval Dublin' tells the story authoritatively.
[2] Cf. T. F. Tout in *DNB* for an excellent sketch of his career.
[3] T. F. Tout in *DNB*; Emden, *Biographical Register, Oxford* 2. 970–1.
[4] T. F. Tout in *DNB*; Emden, *Biographical Register, Oxford* 2. 679.

Fulk of Sandford in 1271 to the appointment of John Lech in 1310.

The ill success of these provisions to Dublin prompts a closer look at the results of papal action in other dioceses. These archbishops were so closely connected with the Crown that it is difficult to resist the conclusion that it was the king of England who had put forward their names to the pope rather than the other way round. Three other appointments, where Englishmen were provided to sees hitherto held by native Irish, do nothing to weaken the conclusion that Edward I was able to influence the papacy in the making of bishops for Ireland. These were the appointment of William de Clifford, a former escheator in England to Emly in 1286, of Stephen of Fulbourn, justiciar of Ireland, to Tuam, also in 1286,[1] and of the English Dominican Walter Jorz to Armagh in 1307.[2] Each of these dioceses was to enter a period of English rule after these appointments. Another case is suggestive. Clonfert was very much a native Irish diocese and an Irishman would have been more appropriate than the Englishman Robert.[3] He was later to be treasurer of Ireland. The remaining provision made in the period, that of Nicholas Cusack to Kildare in 1279, seems unexceptionable. No native Irishman seems to have been provided in this reign, though the archbishops of Cashel were, in the normal way, confirmed by the pope.[4]

Consideration of the incidence of papal appointments to Irish bishoprics has raised the question of royal officials as bishops. It is a subject worthy of consideration in its own right. How significant an element in the Irish episcopate were officials of the Crown?

There can be no doubt that bishops played a significant rôle in the administration of the colony throughout the thirteenth century. Six

[1] Theiner, *Vet. mon.* 298, 303.
[2] *Ibid.* 381.
[3] *Ibid.* 346. He was a monk of Christ Church, Canterbury, and seems to have spent the major part of his pontificate as a Canterbury suffragan.
[4] *Hbk Brit. Chron.* is misleading about thirteenth century provisions to Cashel. It shows three archbishops as papally provided after capitular election. It did occasionally happen that a prelate about whose election there might be some query would resign his right to the pope who would then provide him *ex plenitudine potestatis*. But the Cashel cases are not of this sort; they are not provisions but ordinary canonical confirmations, cf. Theiner, *Vet. mon.* 166, 332, 375. A fourth archbishop shown as a provision, Marianus O Briain, is a translation from Cork after postulation by the Cashel chapter, *ibid.* 56.

bishops were justiciars or their deputies;[1] three were chancellors;[2] the office of treasurer was virtually an episcopal monopoly down to 1285;[3] other bishops were judges or held senior exchequer positions. Some of this type of bishop had a civil service career running *pari passu* with an ecclesiastical one. Geoffrey of Tourville, for example, achieved his first senior administrative post as chamberlain of the exchequer in 1226 and in the following year, his first major ecclesiastical office, the archdeaconry of Dublin. His ascent up both promotion ladders was steady if unspectacular: itinerant judge, 1230; deputy chancellor, 1232–4; treasurer, 1234–50; bishop of Ossory, 1244–50; deputy justiciar, 1245–6.[4] Other churchmen seem (absence of records may mislead us) to have been bishops before they achieved senior civil service positions. Hugh of Taghmon, Anglo-Irish and an Oxford M.A., held the see of Meath from 1250 to 1281. He became treasurer in 1260, an office he held for some fourteen years, and served too as a judge.[5] Stephen of Fulbourn was another of the same type: bishop of Waterford from 1273 to 1286, treasurer of Ireland 1274–85, justiciar 1281–8, archbishop of Tuam, 1286–8.[6] John of Sandford, archbishop of Dublin (1284–94) and justiciar (1288–90), with whom we will be concerned later, must also be mentioned in this context.

The significance of these men in the administrative structure of the colony should not, however, lead us to exaggerate their number. In the thirteenth century as a whole only fifteen bishops held senior appointments in the administration. In the reign of Edward I only eight of the forty-eight Anglo-Irish or English bishops held such posts. It is, therefore, not true that the typical colonial bishop was also a royal official.

Personal data about individual bishops are sparse enough in the

---

[1] They were: Henry of London (Dublin) 1213–15, 1221–4; Geoffrey of Tourville (Ossory) 1245–6 (deputy); Fulk of Sandford (Dublin) 1265; Hugh of Taghmon (Meath) 1265; Stephen of Fulbourn (Waterford and Tuam) 1280, 1281–8; John of Sandford (Dublin) 1288–90. These details and those following are from Richardson and Sayles, *Administration of Ireland* 76–82.
[2] Geoffrey of Tourville, 1232–4; Walter of Fulbourn (Waterford) 1283–6; John of Sandford, 1289–91.
[3] Richardson and Sayles, *Administration of Ireland* 98–9.
[4] *Ibid.* 2, 78, 92, 98, 118, 132.
[5] *Ibid.* 80, 98, 136; Emden, *Biographical Register, Oxford* 3. 2220.
[6] Richardson and Sayles, *Administration of Ireland* 81, 99.

colonial context. Data are even sparser in the native Irish context. It is typical of the materials from which the history of the Irish Church in the later thirteenth century has to be written, that we encounter bishops in the law courts rather than in churches or pulpits. We can know something of the religious activities and personalities of the great twelfth century bishops Malachy and Laurence because biographies of them are extant. No thirteenth century Irish bishop, so far as is known, achieved a biography. Nor do there exist any episcopal registers wherein might be traced something of the way they discharged their pastoral responsibilities. We must perforce be content to know bishops almost solely as officials and politicians, or in relationships with such, and especially as litigants. We can never see them as religious leaders.

Within this dimension of knowledge, there can be no doubt that the two most prominent Irish prelates of the period were David MacCarwill, archbishop of Cashel from 1253 to 1289 and Nicholas Mac Maol Íosa, archbishop of Armagh from 1272 to 1302. Through their public lives we can see some at least of the political and juridical problems and dilemmas with which the Irish clergy was confronted by the establishment of the English colony.

For long, Archbishop MacCarwill did not enjoy any high esteem among historians. James Ware thought many of his acts smacked of 'rashness and insolence',[1] while in the *Dictionary of National Biography* he was considered 'a quarrelsome prelate'.[2] More recently, however, a more sympathetic pen has assessed him as 'perhaps the ablest of the archbishops who ruled the see of Cashel in the medieval period . . . a man whose policies show strength of character and clearness of vision'.[3]

As for quarrelsomeness, it is certainly true that his long pontificate was punctuated by a wide variety of disputes.[4] Some of these were undoubtedly entered into in defence of the rights of his see or of his archiepiscopal borough of Cashel; some were caused by his failure to observe the principles of the common law about episcopal elections

[1] Ware, *Bishops* 474.
[2] C. L. Kingsford in *DNB s.n.* MᵃᶜCarwell, David.
[3] A. Gwynn 'Edward I and the proposed purchase of English law for the Irish c. 1279–80' *TRHS* 10 (1960) 111–27 at 112.
[4] There are adequate details and references in the works cited in the previous notes.

and the jurisdiction of the ecclesiastical court;[1] some show him capable of arbitrary action. As for the rashness, he does seem to have made enemies who could cause serious trouble for him in high places and he seems to have spent the best part of the years 1278 to 1283 in England seeking to clear his name at the royal court.

Yet there was evidently quite another side to this disputatious prelate. Cashel had a traditional connexion with the Cistercians. Between 1185 and 1237 four successive archbishops had been of that order. In 1269 Archbishop MacCarwill himself became a Cistercian.[2] The renewed interest, in the early 1270s, of the Cistercian general chapter in the well-being of houses in or near the Cashel province may fairly be attributed to his reforming endeavour. In 1272 he established a Cistercian monastery in Cashel itself. In 1274, those decrees the general chapter associated particularly with the visitation of Stephen of Lexington whereby monasteries had been reallocated to different mothers, were repealed and the former visitation system restored. It seems reasonable to assume that this intense personal interest in the Cistercian order[3] represents a conscious attempt to foster the traditional Irish monastic spirituality. It aroused the deep suspicions of colonial officialdom which saw in all this a deliberate anti-English conspiracy.[4]

[1] He claimed that in confirming elections in his province he had not known that such elections should first be presented to the king before he confirmed and that he should not confirm when an election has been held without licence to elect having been sought. *Cal. Pat. Rolls 1266–72* 270.

[2] 'David archiepiscopus Cassellensis indutus est habitu monachali' state the Annals of Multyfarnham *s.a.* 1269, ed. A. Smith, *Tracts relating to Ireland* 2 (Irish Archaeol. Soc. 1843) 15. That the habit was the Cistercian must be deduced from his strong personal connexion with that order.

[3] Canivez, *Statuta* 3 (1262–1400) 101, 128, 133, 137, 179.

[4] '... the archbishop of Cashel has put all the monasteries of the order of Citeaux in subjection to Mellifont where all are Irish, and there are five houses and this he has obtained from the chapter of Citeaux and he has deprived other houses which are in his province of a great part of their property and appropriated it to Irish houses ...' Mem. to Edward I, ed. Otway-Ruthven, 'Request of the Irish for English law' 267, 269. Fr Gwynn has drawn attention to the comment of another hostile English witness about the same change: 'On his way back from the council [of Lyons in 1274] the archbishop of Cashel went to the chapter at Citeaux and at his request the paternity of the Irish abbeys was restored to its former state; and so they went back to the bad old ways (*in antiquam silvam*)' Continuator of William of Newburgh, *Chron. reigns Stephen, Henry II and Richard* (ed. R. Howlett) RS 2. 567; 'Edward I and the proposed purchase of English law' 120–1.

Yet if Archbishop MacCarwill was hostile, as was claimed by English officials, to the Anglo-Irish part of the Cistercian order and acted in other ways, 'to humiliate the English',[1] how are we to reconcile this with his championship of the extension of English law to the Irish? Whatever may be thought about the wisdom of the request for English law or the possibility of its being granted and being successfully implemented in practice, there seems no reason to doubt the Archbishop's good faith when he spoke of his and his colleagues' intentions in approaching Edward I. They professed themselves concerned 'without dissimulation of heart or mind' to forward 'peace and truth' and to promote the 'honour of God and the salvation of souls'. They protested their loyalty to the king equally strongly.

We just do not know enough about David MacCarwill to come to any very firm conclusions about either his character or his policies. But the conflicting evidence about both is itself an expression of the conflict facing every Irish prelate who ministered in the *terre Engleis*: between the pull of natural, instinctive sympathy towards the 'community of the Irish tongue' and its ecclesiastical traditions and the need to establish some viable relationship with the Crown.

The same tension can be seen in a different way in Armagh in the career of Archbishop Nicholas Mac Maol Íosa, a prelate we have already encountered in connexion with episcopal *gravamina* and with the attempt in 1291, at the Trim council, to establish some sort of constitutional unity in the *ecclesia hibernicana*.

Nicholas was perhaps the outstanding prelate of thirteenth century Ireland, whose career, almost coterminous with the reign of Edward I, touched nearly every point of Irish public life. Without doubt he was the most energetic of thirteenth century primates in seeking to preserve native Irish traditions throughout the provinces of Armagh,[2]

---

1 'It is to be remembered that he has made an Irish boy of 22 years bishop of Cork to shame the English' *Mem. cit.* ed. Otway-Ruthven, 'Request of the Irish for English law' 267, 269. Fr Gwynn has pointed out that, boy or not, Robert Mac-Donnchada O.Cist. appointed to Cork in 1277 was given royal assent, performed fealty and secured restoration of temporalities, 'Edward I and the proposed purchase of English law' 122.

2 Fr Gwynn has presented a skilful portrait of him as 'the last representative of old Irish traditions (in Armagh)', 'Nicholas Mac Maol Íosa, archbishop of Armagh (1272–1303)' *Féilsgríbhínn Mhic Néill* (1940) 394–405.

in upholding *libertas ecclesiae,* in striving to remedy the financial debility of his see. Nicholas himself claimed that Armagh, once 'the most abundantly endowed of Irish churches' was in his time extremely poor, 'through the oppression of evil men and the lack of skill of certain of his predecessors'.[1] The claim has much to support it. Of all dioceses, Armagh had suffered most since the Invasion. Its primacy had been severely restricted[2] and its finances gravely weakened; its archbishop could not show his primatial cross in the provinces of Dublin and Cashel without incurring opposition and the evidence of ecclesiastical valuations[3] shows Armagh's poverty relatively to the other three metropolitans. It had suffered more than any other diocese through disputed succession; in the period 1201–60, in six vacancies, there were three occasions when vacancy lasted three years or more. Nor were the other three appointments accomplished without difficulty. These disputes reflect the intensity of the struggle in this area between the two nations.

Six years after his elevation, Nicholas sought to improve that part of his financial distress which was remediable by royal action. Six of the seven points of his petition to Edward I had reference to royal rights which the Archbishop considered might be amended or waived in his favour. One of them was concerned with the custody of the temporalities of Armagh suffragan sees during vacancies. Nicholas claimed that both before and after the coming of the English into Ireland, the church of Armagh was accustomed to have custody of the temporalities of all the dioceses of the province during vacancy. Through the negligence of some of his predecessors this right had been lost *de facto,* though in some dioceses the primate still enjoyed his right. Nicholas asked the king if he might retain the right in these dioceses and to consider restoring it to him in its integrity and to forbid royal officials to seize temporalities in the Armagh province.[4]

There was little in the known attitude of Edward to this question, or indeed to any right of the Crown, to suggest he would hear this

---

[1] Gwynn, 'Armagh docs.' 2 (1278)   [2] See ch. 5 above.
[3] The major evidence comes from the fourteenth century and is calendared, *Cal. Docs. Irel. 1302–07* 202–323 (with corrigenda, ix–xxi). It must be read with G. J. Hand, 'The dating of the early fourteenth-century ecclesiastical valuations of Ireland' *Irish Theol. Quart.* 24 (1957) 271–4.
[4] Gwynn, 'Armagh docs.' 2. p. 10.

request sympathetically. But he proceeded in a painstakingly formal way. The matter was referred *ad generale parliamentum* whilst the justiciar, Robert of Ufford, was ordered to make discreet investigation as to the facts and legality of the archbishop's claim. His report was that the *de iure* position of Armagh in respect of vacant sees was exactly the same as any other archbishop in Ireland but that *de facto* an illegality was practised because of the inability of English officials to penetrate 'into Irish forest land'. The Archbishop had himself taken over the temporalities at vacancies and usurpation had been transformed 'into a counterfeit right'.[1] The Archbishop was answered at a parliament when the King claimed to have recovered by judgment custody of these sees, on the principle that vacant dioceses in Ireland stood in the same relationship to the Crown as dioceses in England.[2]

In the meantime, Archbishop Nicholas had become deeply involved in the politics of the Anglo-Irish colony through an episcopal vacancy in the diocese of Meath. Though legally a diocese of the Armagh province, Meath was very much within the area of strongest English influence and its bishops had been English or Anglo-Irish from 1194. Already before the accession of Nicholas, there was some history of tension between Meath and Armagh. Between 1252 and 1254 there were two claimants to the see;[3] one who had been elected and was consecrated after receiving royal assent and a second who had been provided by the metropolitan and consecrated without royal assent having been asked. The matter was settled by the pope in favour of the former, Hugh of Taghmon. Whether or not the dispute was due to sheer misunderstanding, as the arch-

---

[1] 'Quare excellentie vestre significo per presentes quod non plus iuris habet dictus archiepiscopus Ardmacanus in episcopatibus sui archiepiscopi vacacionis tempore quam alii archiepiscopi per Hyberniam constituti habent in episcopatibus sibi subditis seu subiectis: set quia quidam episcopatuum dicto archiepiscopo subiectorum situantur in terra Hybernica et silvestri, ubi Anglici vacacionis tempore secure accedere non valebant, archiepiscopus predictus temporalia episcopatuum predictorum vacacionis tempore usurpavit, et ita illa usurpacio per huiusmodi abusum in ius quodammodo transiit simulatum. Nec alio iure nisi tali subreptitio dictus fulcitur archiepiscopus in premissis.' For the chronology of the investigation, Watt, 'English law and the Irish Church' 148. 59.

[2] Gwynn, 'Armagh docs.' 6. p. 15; Watt, 'English law and the Irish Church' 148 n. 59.

[3] The course of the disputed election has been accurately traced by M. Sheehy, *Pont. hib.* 2. 218–19.

bishop claimed,[1] it was the prelude to a serious conflict between the new bishop and his metropolitan. Bishop Hugh made a determined effort to escape from any subjection to Armagh. His specific aim was exemption from archiepiscopal visitation of Meath and he pursued it vigorously though unsuccessfully at the papal curia.[2] How far Meath's acceptance of the *status quo* and its formal promulgation in provincial council put an end to controversy cannot be decided. But the appearance previously of such aspirations to autonomy in Meath suggests that on the death of Hugh of Taghmon, the Archbishop would be more than usually interested in his successor and in the election of someone more sympathetic to the rights of Armagh than the deceased bishop.

Be that as it may, Archbishop Nicholas made his bid for control of the appointment. But his choice of candidate had much wider implications than merely the question of Meath independence. Walter of Fulbourn was the brother of the justiciar and treasurer, Stephen of Fulbourn, and nephew of the chancellor Adam of Fulbourn.[3] For Nicholas to advance him to Meath was to strike an accord with the most powerful group of royal administrators in Ireland. He refused to confirm the elected candidate, claimed that the Meath appointment had lapsed to him as metropolitan through neglect of the electors, and duly nominated Walter to the see.[4] He had cause to hope that the Dublin administration would take no steps to implement the judgment concerning custody of temporalities of vacant Armagh sees. As long as he maintained his understanding with the Fulbourns he was free of the threat of *quo warranto*.[5]

---

[1] According to canon law, if those who had the right to elect to a vacant see had not done so within three months, the right of election devolved on the immediate superior, *Decretales* 1. 6. 41. Archbishop Reginald, then at the curia, had understood that the Meath clergy had failed to proceed to an election within the specified canonical period and had therefore assumed that their right had devolved on him as metropolitan.

[2] Cf. p. 114 above.

[3] Walter acted as deputy treasurer while his brother though justiciar continued to act as treasurer, Richardson and Sayles, *Administration of Ireland* 54. Adam apparently continued to act as chancellor for a period when Walter was drawing the salary for that office (*ibid.* 93). Little wonder that it was complained of them 'they are everything and without them there is nothing' *Cal. Docs. Irel. 1285–92* 2. p. 2.

[4] Theiner, *Vet. mon.* 301 tells part of the story. The rest is in the next note.

[5] The nature of the bargain appears clearly from the findings of the royal commission of enquiry into the conduct of Stephen of Fulbourn's administration: 'The justiciar

The days of the Fulbourn ascendancy were, however, numbered. Complaints of extortion, oppression, fraudulent conversion and many another crime from the stock catalogue of charges against unpopular medieval officialdom had led Edward I to set up a commission of enquiry into the conduct of the Irish administration. Throughout the summer months of 1284, the commission was at work auditing, examining records and witnesses, compiling charges.[1] To the commission of enquiry, it appeared that the Justiciar and the Primate had conspired together against the Crown. Their causes were intimately linked; the issue of the exercise of rights of the Crown by the Archbishop, including the matter of the custody of temporalities, was about to be reopened.

The commission compiled a formidable array of charges of misgovernment and corruption against the Fulbourns. The final charges against Nicholas were less than originally investigated[2] and amounted in effect to two: one concerned with the custody of vacant sees, the other with the provision of Walter of Fulbourn to Meath. It was alleged that the Archbishop appropriated for himself temporalities during vacancies in his province as well as requests for licences to elect, and appointed bishops, all *contra regiam dignitatem*.[3] When

caused the archbishop of Armagh to be summoned before him at Drogheda and accused him of usurping vacancies of cathedral churches and abbeys to the king's disherison, of appropriating to himself the custodies of the temporalities thereof and of instituting prelates in the same without obtaining the king's licence as in the churches of Kilmore [the editor's "Kildare" is incorrect] and Raphoe and others which the escheator can name; and of holding pleas belonging to the Crown to the king's disherison. The justiciar left these excesses unpunished and uncorrected out of favour to the archbishop who by simoniacal irregularity had unjustly provided the brother of the justiciar to the see of Meath' *Cal. Docs. Irel. 1252–84* 2332.

[1] Composition and terms of reference, *ibid.* 2153, 2337; aspects of the investigation, 2274, 2332–40; draft of the final report (?), *Cal. Docs. Irel. 1285–92* 2. For comment, Richardson and Sayles, *Administration of Ireland* 54–6.
[2] Archbishop Nicholas was investigated on five counts: generally, custody of temporalities during vacancy of dioceses and abbeys in his province and confirming and consecrating bishops where licence to elect had not been granted nor fealty sworn; specifically, having done this in respect of Meath; holding pleas of the Crown; harbouring his relatives who were the king's enemies (for the hostility of his family to the English in Ardagh, Gwynn, 'Nicholas Mac Maol Íosa' 395); the coining of money without licence. *Cal. Docs. Irel. 1252–84* 2274.
[3] 'et ad magnum dampnum Regis et contra libertates Regis' QR Irish Excheq. E/101/234/9 mem. 3; Watt, 'English law and the Irish Church' 150 at n. 71; *Cal. Docs. Irel. 1285–92* 2.

writs had been issued lately against the Archbishop on this charge it was said he had replied with a repetition of his earlier claim of privilege on this matter and had threatened to interdict the province if it were violated.[1] More specifically, issue was made of the alleged course of recent events in the diocese of Dromore. There, it was claimed, the escheator had been expelled by the Archbishop and a bishop installed without reference to the King.[2] For this offence Nicholas was in fact fined and bound in a large sum as to his future conduct.[3] As a general deduction from the behaviour of Nicholas, it was recommended that no Irishman should ever be archbishop or bishop because of their disloyalty and their care to provide to canonries only those of their own race so that only Irishmen should be elected bishops.[4]

In the Trinity term of 1285, Stephen of Fulbourn was cited to appear before the barons of the Exchequer in England who had found his account too insufficient to be admitted.[5] It is clear that there was more to the investigation into his conduct than the personal jealousies and rivalries of officials in Dublin. But in August, the King pardoned him all offences on account of his past great services to the Crown.[6] Nicholas shared in this act of clemency to the extent of having his fine for the Dromore irregularity halved, and his security remitted.[7] The rescue of the Fulbourns was completed in 1286 when Pope Honorius IV solved the Meath dispute. Both Walter of Fulbourn and Thomas St Leger had resigned their claims for settlement *ex plenitudine potestatis*, and Honorius found a neat solution. Through a disputed election, there were currently two candidates to the vacant see of Tuam and the case had gone to Rome. There were clear irregularities involving each of the candidates. The Pope

[1] 'De nouo sunt breuia leuata super Ardmachanum super premissos et expediret quod alia privilegia si que essent visa, quia Ardmachanus minatur interdicere (?) terram ...' QR Irish Excheq. *ms. cit.*
[2] 'Item est in Ultonia unus episcopatus qui uocatur Drumorensis, et subest predicto Ardmachano de ... Rex habuit custodiam per mortem unius episcopi illius loci, per magistrum Johannem de Saunford exchaetorem suum ut patet per inquisicionem inde factam uideatur de qua quidem custodia expulsus fuit dominus Rex ... et ille Ardmachanus sine Rege contulit temporalia Thiermath modo episcopo Drumorense. De isto episcopatu ... leuatum est breue super Ardmachanum' *ms. cit.*
[3] *Cal. Docs. Irel. 1285-92* 150, 151.
[4] See p. 150 above.
[5] *Cal. Docs. Irel. 1285-92* 59.
[6] *Ibid.* 121.
[7] *Ibid.* 150, 151.

therefore disqualified them both, translated Stephen of Fulbourn from Waterford to Tuam, provided Walter to Waterford (of which he was dean), and allowed St Leger to hold Meath; solutions which gained royal assent.[1]

For Nicholas, there was no such providential way out of his troubles. The new treasurer, Nicholas de Clare, who had been one of the commissioners of inquiry, resumed the struggle to bring the whole of the Armagh province into line with the English law view of the Crown's rôle in the making of bishops. The justices of the common pleas of Dublin held a *quo warranto* inquisition into the alleged privilege by which Nicholas held custody of temporalities in Armagh vacancies, and it was adjudged yet again that he had no right to them. Nicholas seems to have been willing to defy all such judgments. But after being heavily fined for contempt of the king, he petitioned Edward for a reversal of the judgment or at least that he should have compensation in lands or rents for the rights he had lost.[2] There is reason for thinking that the Armagh chapter thought that Edward had left Nicholas in hope of some such recompense. The King did not admit this and the formal records offer no support for any such contention,[3] desirable as it might seem, as a gesture of real support to a poverty-stricken diocese to help to draw closer the links between the Crown and this important diocese only on the very fringe of the *terre Engleis*.

Some documentary evidence survives from this period to remind us that most Irish bishops, outside the Dublin province at least, fought the battle for *libertas ecclesie* on two fronts. For the Crown

---

1 Theiner, *Vet. mon.* 298, 301, 302; *Cal. Docs. Irel. 1285–92* 258.

2 '... responsum fuit eidem in parliamento Westm' quod Rex recuperavit per iudicium custodiam episcopatuum vacancium in Hibernia tenendam sicut episcopatuum in Anglia' Gwynn, 'Armagh docs.' 6; *Cal. Docs. Irel. 1285–92* 558.

3 After Nicholas's death, the dean and chapter petitioned the King: '... quod concedat Archiepiscopo suo futuro aliqua tenementa in recompensationem exituum de vacationibus quinque Episcopatuum scilicet de Rathoth, Chogian, Drummoth, Dere et Tirconil unde dominus Rex posuit Nicholaum quondam Archiepiscopum ejusdem loci in spem gratiae suae etc. Dictum est eis quod expectent creationem futuri Episcopi ad quem pertinet hujus petitionis prosecutio etc.' *Memoranda de Parliamento* (ed. F. W. Maitland) *RS* 239–40. There is some confusion about the place names as given in the text which gives Raphoe, Clogher, Dromore, Derry and Tyrconnell (Raphoe). For the first Raphoe should presumably be substituted Kilmore.

was not the only lay power with which they were compelled to achieve a legal and political relationship. In many parts of the country, especially in Armagh and Tuam, native Irish kings remained a force to be reckoned with. Indeed, in these provinces they counted far more, in most of the ordinary routine business of administering a diocese, than the distant, less menacing English authorities. Unfortunately there is not much to be learned of the relationships of bishops and Irish kings, but a fragment from a now lost register of the Clogher diocese allows us to glimpse Archbishop Nicholas pressing leading Irish rulers within his province to acceptance of general and particular principles of ecclesiastical liberty.

It is safe to say that Pope Boniface VIII did not have in mind the kings of Tir Eoghain and Oriel in northern Ireland when, in February 1296, he promulgated *Clericis laicos* in an attempt to preserve ecclesiastical property from exactions arbitrarily imposed by secular rulers. But the bull, though obviously aimed at the kings of France and England, was couched in general terms and Archbishop Nicholas, quite legitimately and astutely, took advantage of its appearance to extract promises of respect for ecclesiastical liberty from the rulers of his province. The Archbishop read and explained the bull, along with certain other constitutions touching the liberty of the Church, to Domnall O'Neill, king of Tir Eoghain and his sub-kings and made them solemnly promise to maintain its principles.[1] That Nicholas was not content with mere generalities is made clear from the record of the repetition of the process in neighbouring Oriel where Brian MacMahon was king. Affirmation was sworn to a detailed series of specific points.

There were eight main articles, some of which were subdivided. They were described as constituting the *gravamina* afflicting the Church in these parts and are of a type comparable to those which the *ecclesia hibernicana*, as has been seen, was wont to present to the king of England. But there is a very significant difference in tone and emphasis. To Henry III and Edward I, articles of complaint were submitted as petitions and the king conducted himself as master of the situation. To O'Neill and MacMahon, and to Maguire of Fermanagh who was also brought into line, the articles were laid

[1] H. J. Lawlor, 'Fragments of a lost register of the diocese of Clogher' *Louth Archaeological Journal* 4 (1916–20) 226–57 at 249.

down as a matter of ecclesiastical right to which they, of their regal
duty, were required to give unquestioning religious assent.

What the Archbishop wanted from these rulers had both negative
and positive aspects. The articles were very detailed about what the
lay power might not do. It was required to guarantee the immunity
of the clergy, clerical property, ecclesiastical tenants and artisans who
worked ecclesiastically, from all manner of lay imposition: fiscal,
alimentary, violence to persons, quartering of soldiers, feeding of
animals, even, in the case of the artisans, from agricultural labour
services. They were to refrain from penalizing those who helped to
protect ecclesiastical persons and property from felons. They were to
respect jurisdictional boundaries. Delicts, pleas of debt and contract
touching ecclesiastics or ecclesiastical tenants were to be heard *coram
episcopo*. So also were certain aspects of jurisdiction concerning
miserabiles personae.[1] Finally, the testamentary jurisdiction of Church
courts was to be respected in full.[2]

On the positive side, secular rulers were expected to perform
certain police duties. They must help to enforce a penal code against
those who violated the immunities.[3] This code combined canon,
common law and native Irish law principles. Rulers committed
themselves to cooperate in the caption of excommunicates on something very like the common law model and in the levying of a scale
of fines, assessed not in money but in cows,[4] payable to the bishops

1 *Ibid.* 250–2.   2 *Ibid.* 253.   3 *Ibid.* 250–1.
4 We are here in contact with customs of a very different society. The full estimation
of this passage demands knowledge in depth of medieval Irish legal principles and
procedures: '... concedentes, et tenore praesentium nos obligantes, quod si alicui
ecclesiae vel ecclesiasticae personae in terra alicuius nostrum existenti per quos-
cunque homines nostros factum fiat aut rapina aut aliquod genus exactionum
praedictarum per nos vel nostros, eisdem vel alicui earundem imponatur, nos pro
quolibet furto aut rapina vel incendio, dummodo sex vacarum numerum vel earum
estimationem non excedat, et etiam pro qualibet exactione supradicta, quoties
furtum rapina incendium vel exactio fiat qualiscumque, viginti quatuor vacas a
delinquente seu delinquentibus, cum rei prosecutione, leuabimus nomine poenae;
de quibus duodecim vaccas praedicto Domino Matheo nostro episcopo [Matthew
MacCathasaigh, bishop of Clogher 1287–c. 1316] liberabimus, aliis duodecim vacis
reservatis illi nostrum qui pro furto, rapina aut pro qualibet alia consimili trans-
gressione, temporibus retroactis emendam recipere consueuit, nisi ipse in exigendo
illam poenam negligens fuerit vel remissus, quo casu poena ipsa inter Regem et
Dominum episcopum supradictum equaliter dividebatur; sed si furtum rapina
incendium vel preda numerum sex vacarum vel earum estimationem excedat, tunc

by those who offended. Thus was the canonical principle of the *brachium seculare* given its specifically Irish interpretation. Clearly the Archbishop expected more in the way of ecclesiastical liberty from Irish rulers than he got from the king of England. Whether or not it was conceded in practice as well as by verbal assurance is a question that lies beyond solution in any extant documentation. Nor is there any comparable evidence from elsewhere in Ireland for this or any other period. It is not therefore possible to generalize about the relationships of Church and State in Irish Ireland.

It is possible, however, to generalize about the attitudes of bishops to the Crown. Possible, but not easy, because the *ecclesia hibernicana* could not speak with a single undivided voice. *Tot episcopi, quot sententiae:* there was every shade of opinion between two poles—one of total opposition to the intrusion of any foreigner, seeking to ignore the Crown completely, the other of total identification, seeking to unite the purposes of Church and State more than a bishop should. Perhaps a cross-section of the episcopate will reveal in microcosm the abiding types of episcopal attitude to the Crown and perhaps the four metropolitans in office in 1290 afford such a cross-section. They each represent a type: they were of very different national backgrounds, ruling dioceses where anglicization had penetrated to very different extents, their policies were very different.

John of Sandford was *par excellence* the civil servant bishop—a competent and industrious administrator, zealous in the royal service. The second illegitimate member of the Basset family of Wycombe to become archbishop of Dublin, he achieved this office by way of the treasurership of Ferns (*c.* 1269) and the deanship of St Patrick's, Dublin (1275). His ascent up the ranks of the civil hierarchy was equally steady: escheator (1271–85), justice in eyre (1275) and justiciar (1288–1290).[1] His promptitude in meeting the

quadraginta vacas a delinquente sive delinquentibus cum rei prosecutione, similiter levabimus nomine poenae, et earum dimedietatem eidem Domino episcopo dabimus, salva tumelialie [sic] medietate illi nostrum qui hactenus emendam habere consuevit, ut superius est expressum' *ibid.* 250–1 (I have made some minor changes to Lawlor's text).

[1] He was also Keeper of the Seal (chancellor), 1289–91. See Richardson and Sayles, *Administration of Ireland* 82, 93, 126, 140 for the correct dating of his various posts. T. F. Tout has supplied a good summary of his career in *DNB*, and there is another in Emden, *Biographical Register, Oxford* 3. 2213–14.

king's requests for money attracted the attention of contemporary observers in England;[1] in his justiciarship he was very active on campaign, in parliament and in general eyre. His days were ended in royal diplomatic service on the Continent.

Closely associated with John as 'clerk and companion' was a native Irishman, Stephen O'Brogan, an Ulsterman and archdeacon of Glendalough, the pre-eminently native Irish part of the Dublin diocese. He was also a canon of Cashel and in 1289 was elected its archbishop. Whether the influence of the justiciar–archbishop had a place in this election cannot be determined, but John of Sandford hastened to assure the chancellor in England that his *protégé* was a man of quality. Stephen rewarded this confidence by his support of Thomas Quantok in 1291.[2] There seems no reason to suppose that this harmony was interrupted when Quantok became Irish chancellor.[3] He was what a later age would call a king's man.

The attempt of another northern-born prelate, Nicholas Mac Maol Íosa, to achieve an understanding with the administration took a different course. John of Sandford and Thomas Quantok were an altogether different proposition from the Fulbourns, whose corruption and arrogance brought about their own downfall. With their fall there ended apparently any close working agreement between the Primate and the administration. Thereafter Nicholas was pursued as a usurper of Crown rights whilst he fought to retain what he held to be his primatial and feudal rights. He despised no legal means of upholding the position of Armagh as diocese, province, primacy and fief, whether it was petitioning the king in England, suing in his courts in Ireland, allying with the Dublin administration, attempting to rally the whole Irish clergy to resist lay oppression or imposing a strict observance of *Clericis laicos* on the Irish princes of

1 *Ann. Dunstable*: 'Iste [the dean of St Paul's who is not here relevant to Irish history] multum favebat regi, quando rex auxilium petiit a clero. Item Joannes de Saunford archiepiscopus de Develyn, qui similiter in omnibus regi favebat ...' *Annales monastici* (ed. Luard) RS 3. 39.
2 Quantok told Robert Burnell, chancellor of England: 'Set, ultra omnes quos in Hibernia sum expertus, archiepiscopus Cassellensis, ex immensis fidelitate et affeccione quas gerit erga dominum nostrum regem, est merito commendandus'. Richardson and Sayles, *Parliaments and Councils* 199.
3 An office he held 1291–1308. Though he never became justiciar he acted as chief governor on some occasions when there was no justiciar in office, Richardson and Sayles, *Administration of Ireland* 83, 93, He was bishop of Emly 1306–09.

his province. In the last analysis, however, he had less need than
Cashel for the close support of the administration, for the bulk of
his province lay outside its effective control. He was never a king's
man.

Even more than the archbishop of Armagh could the archbishop
of Tuam evade the mandates of the administration and the decision
of its courts. William de Bermingham, son of the second lord of
Athenry, was the first Anglo-Irishman appointed to this see. That he
was elected testified to the growing influence of his family in the
west. That the family was not native Irish did not make Archbishop
William an ally of the Crown. When he figures in the records of the
Dublin administration, it is because other clergy are having recourse
to the royal courts for protection against him—the Connacht
Dominicans and the clergy of Annaghdown, as has been seen, and
the abbess of Casta Silva (Kilcreevanty, co. Galway).[1] The evidence
is not conclusive but it suggests that the position of archbishop was
being exploited to further local and dynastic interests. At any rate,
Archbishop William pursued his own interests in ways which brought
him into opposition with the Crown and, despite his fair words to
the king in 1291, he had no intention of giving financial help to
him.[2] The administration was not able to mount pressure on Tuam
as it could on south Armagh, and, on the whole, the archbishop had
matters his own way.

The attitude of these four prelates—two Irish, one half-Gaelicized
Anglo-Irish, one English—reflect accurately enough, though in
general terms, how the political attitudes of bishops in Ireland could
vary according to the geographical limitations of the common law

---

[1] *Cal. Justic. Rolls. 1308–14* 31–2, 113–14.
[2] His letter has been printed by Richardson and Sayles, *Parliaments and Councils* 197–8.
He pleaded, not implausibly, that the poverty of a war-torn region made it impossible to raise money for his province, much though he would have liked to
oblige the king. But he took a firm line about liberty of the Church, telling the
king that such a grant could not be made *inconsulto Romano pontifice*. His account of
how he encouraged his clergy to pay up is not without subtlety: '... intimantes
(nostro clero) ac nostris suffraganeis eorumque clero quod, licet per concessionem
huiusmodi modice crederent pregravari, per eam tamen possent vestram et vestrorum beneuolenciam ministrorum et vberiorem graciam indubitanter captare, ac vos
ipsi per hoc induci ad grauamina hibernicane ecclesie et personis ecclesiasticis
ibidem illata hactenus reuocanda et fortassis ad eandem ecclesiam restituendam in
solidum pristine libertati' *ibid.* 197.

area. The bishoprics of the Dublin province were sometimes held by the civil-servant class. They were invariably held by men loyal to the Crown. Part of the Cashel province, including the Cashel diocese itself, lay so well within the area that an attitude of cooperation with the Crown was essential, though native Irish influence was strong enough to ensure that only Irish-born prelates were elected to Cashel throughout the thirteenth century. But such men might well be loyalists. Armagh also was compelled, for defensive purposes, to seek a *modus vivendi* because of the increasing pressure of royal officials upholding the principles of English law which conflicted with traditional Armagh rights. Tuam, whether ruled by native Irish or Anglo-Irish, was relatively immune from similar pressure and might, with few limitations, follow its own path. In sum, the political attitudes of bishops in Ireland was decided not so much by the national origins of the individual bishop as by his proximity, geographical or functional, to the civil administration.

Chapter 9

FOURTEENTH CENTURY DEVELOPMENTS

ACCEPTIO PERSONARUM

Surveying the history of Ireland throughout the thirteenth century it is possible to extract two different, even contradictory, lines of interpretation of the main trends of development. On the one hand, there is the trend towards the consolidation of the control of the Crown whose authority became progressively more effective and extensive as the century wore on and was still expanding even after the death of Edward I. With this royal progress, it might be argued, came a certain lessening of the hostility of the peoples, even movement towards integration, shown in a certain disposition, on the one side, to admit Irishmen to parity of status at common law and, on the other, to acknowledge the desirability of achieving such status. On the other hand, however, the history of the thirteenth century may be read as the progressive revelation of the impossibility of such integration, of the unbridgeable nature of the cleavage between the nations, demonstrated, on the one side, by the absence of any disposition to statesmanship in the form of generosity or magnanimity towards the conquered, and, on the other, by obstinate refusal to submit to *force majeure.*

Whether or not these two antithetic lines of interpretation form a valid approach to the general history of Ireland in the thirteenth century, they can certainly be seen in the history of the Irish Church. Both trends can there be seen in operation. The adoption in Ireland of the practices of the Church in England gave a framework within which it was not impossible for churchmen of both peoples to work together. In their different chequered ways, the careers of Archbishops David MacCarwill, Nicholas Mac Maol Íosa and Stephen O'Brogan show this. So too does the progress of the native Irishman John MacCarwill from the see of Cork (1302–21) to that most

173

English of sees, Meath (1321–7) and thence to Cashel (1327–9). The presence of native Irish bishops at parliaments, either in person or by proxy,[1] is perhaps the clearest proof that a real degree of integration, if not already attained, was certainly attainable. All this, however, was especially in the context of the episcopate and diocesan church, where the pressures towards reaching an accommodation with the Crown were strongest. When attention is directed to the regular church, however, a contrasting picture emerges. The history of the religious orders tends to exemplify the other, divisive trends in Irish history. For among religious, racial trouble tended to increase rather than to disappear. The trend is the more deplorable in that the hostility was manifested not merely in the older orders of monks and canons but also in the orders of friars whose introduction and spread constituted the most impressive sign of religious vitality in thirteenth century Ireland.

There is no documentation comparable with Stephen of Lexington's Register to provide evidence concerning hostility between monks and canons of both nations and discriminations against each other in the later thirteenth century. But what has survived is suggestive enough. In 1274, as has been seen, the Cistercian general chapter had been persuaded by Archbishop David MacCarwill to abolish Stephen of Lexington's changes in the subjection of houses and to restore the *status quo*. The general chapter asserted the principle that all postulants should be admitted to any house irrespective of nationality, especially if they were native inhabitants, since their claims were the greater.[2] English officialdom, however, was not prepared to credit the Archbishop with any intention of promoting the interests of religion through the abolition of *acceptio personarum*. It was deeply suspicious of his motives and in 1277 warned Edward I that 'the archbishop of Cashel has made all the monasteries of the

---

1 Cf. Richardson and Sayles, *Irish Parliament* 120–7 for an examination of the parliamentary position of the clergy of both nations: 'A line was not easily drawn, perhaps no line was desired to be drawn, between English and Irish bishops' *op. cit.* 121.

2 'Item, cum quidam abusus inoleverit in Ordine, ut dicitur, quod quidam abbates nullos recipiant nisi de gente et natione sua, omnibus abbatibus praecipitur auctoritate Capituli generalis, ut omnes, dummodo boni sint, pro indifferenti recipiant, et maxime indigenos, cum ad illos maxime teneantur, cum non sit apud Deum aliqua personarum acceptio ...' Canivez, *Statuta* 3. 13 (1275).

English tongue of the order of Citeaux subject to Mellifont where all are Irish and there are five such houses and this he has obtained from the chapter of Citeaux and he has deprived other houses in his province of a great part of their tenements and has appropriated them to Irish houses'.[1]

Edward I received a more general warning about Irish religious when Nicholas Cusack, Franciscan bishop of Kildare, reported that he had learnt that the peace was frequently disturbed by parleys between 'certain arrogant Irish speaking religious' and Irish rulers whom they made to revolt, assuring them that such action against the English was justified by divine and human law.[2] The Bishop's letter is probably to be dated about the time (1284–5) of the commission of enquiry into the conduct of the Fulbourns and Archbishop Nicholas Mac Maol Íosa, which warned Edward against the dangers of Irishmen being appointed to bishoprics because they discriminated in favour of men of their own nation, as did the Dominican and Franciscan friars.[3]

In 1297, the bishop of Down, who was Anglo-Irish, was accused in the justiciar's court of promulgating decrees forbidding the reception of those of English origin into the religious houses of his diocese.[4] The accusation seems to have had specific reference to the canons of Saul. The bishop was made to disavow any such legislation and to promise to revoke it, if such existed. It rather seems that the justiciar was holding him accountable for the existence of such discrimination in his diocese, whether or not he himself had initiated it (which seems unlikely). Archbishop Nicholas Mac Maol Íosa stood accused of the same charge, but what happened in his case does not appear.

Stephen of Lexington's changes in the Cistercian visitation system

---

[1] Otway-Ruthven, 'Request of the Irish for English law' 267–9.

[2] E. B. Fitzmaurice and A. G. Little, *Materials for the history of the Franciscan province of Ireland 1230–1450* (1920) 52–3.

[3] See pp. 150 and 165 above.

[4] 'The bishop of Down (being present was demanded wherefore he, together with the archbishop of Armagh, made ordinances in their dioceses, in which is contained that clerks of English origin be not received in monasteries in those dioceses, in prejudice of the Crown) comes and disavows such constitutions, and allows that the abbot of Saul and other abbots, priors and convents of his diocese may receive clerks of English origin when they may wish, at their own risk, saving to him due visitation; and he undertakes that the said constitutions, if there be any such, and orders under them, he will completely revoke' *Cal. Justic. Rolls 1295–1303* 102–3.

do not appear to have been conspicuously successful in eliminating national strife within the order. The restoration of the *status quo* does not seem to have been conspicuously more successful. Further to the evidence of 1277 cited above, there is a little more, from 1307, when the affairs of Mellifont and Maigue were brought to the notice of the justiciar.

Mellifont, as reported, was in a state of chaos, torn by contention for the abbacy of such violence that the various contenders were employing private armies to back their claims. The strife involved other Cistercian houses for the rivals conspired with other abbots. It was reported that because of this: 'many abbots of other houses are deposed by the Cistercian chapter'.[1] The record does not state specifically that the ambitious monks were of the different nations, though this of course would be likely enough. The report went on to speak of the situation at Maigue. There, it was said, its abbot continually alienated the tenements and goods of the monastery and, 'in hatred of the English tongue, maintains that no monks of England may dwell there, as was accustomed'.[2]

The coming of the friars to Ireland forms a major chapter in the history of medieval Irish Christianity. But like many another promising development in the medieval Irish Church it was to be seriously damaged by national hatreds.

First of the four major orders of friars into Ireland were the Dominicans.[3] Established in Dublin and Drogheda in 1224, there were twelve foundations in the first quarter century and a further twelve in the next half century. These twenty four friaries were all save five of Anglo-Irish foundation, and were administered by a vicar-provincial appointed by and subject to the English provincial. In 1314, a general chapter of the English province decided that the Dominicans of Ireland could submit three names to the English provincial from which the Irish vicar-provincial would be chosen. The Franciscans arrived in 1231 or 1232. Their history will be considered in more detail later.

---

[1] *Cal. Justic. Rolls 1305–07* 350–1.

[2] *Ibid.* In both the Mellifont and Maigue cases the royal administration virtually took over the abbeys pending further action, which we do not know about. The Cistercian *Statuta* are silent on these matters.

[3] The facts used here are from Gwynn and Hadcock, *Medieval Religious Houses, Ireland*.

The Carmelites and Augustinians established themselves in the second half of the thirteenth century. The former seem to have had at least nine houses by 1300 and at first formed a part of the English province. A separate Irish province was established, however, at some date between 1303 and 1307. The Augustinians may have been established in Dublin *c.* 1259 but their other foundations were later: six in Edward I's period and a further six in Edward II's. They too were subject to the English provincial, though they were to receive a modicum of self-government in the late fourteenth century.

The introduction and spread of the friars was then predominantly an Anglo-Irish phenomenon. But it was by no means exclusively so. All four orders were patronized by native Irish rulers and though houses of friars were for the most part situated in the towns of the colony, each had a significant native Irish element both in the form of houses established in predominantly Irish areas and at least sometimes, in the form of Irishmen in houses in the predominantly English areas. It was to be in the biggest and most mixed of the orders that the potential danger of this situation was realized. There seems no evidence of trouble among the Augustinians and Carmelites and not much in the Dominican order. But the story was different with the Franciscans.

There was no Thomas of Eccleston to write a first chapter of Irish Franciscan history, *de adventu fratrum minorum in Hiberniam*.[1] But it is Brother Thomas himself who has supplied the first hard fact about the establishment of the Franciscans in Ireland when he recorded the appointment by the minister-general of a minister-provincial for Ireland. This was Richard of Ingworth, 'the first minorite to preach to the people north of the Alps' (in Eccleston's words) and a prominent and senior member of the first mission to England.[2] His arrival in Ireland must be dated either 1231 or 1232. There is no medieval evidence that the Franciscans came to Ireland from Spain and in the

---

[1] The difficult subject of Irish Fransciscan origins has been well discussed by A. G. Little, Fitzmaurice and Little, *Franciscan materials* xi–xv; 1–2.

[2] 'Ricardus de Ingewurde, natione Anglicus, sacerdos et praedicator et aetate provectior, qui primus extitit qui citra montes populo praedicavit in ordine; et processu temporis, sub bonae memoriae fratre Johanne Parent, missus est minister provincialis in Hiberniam' *Fratris Thomae vulgo dicti de Eccleston Tractatus de adventu fratrum minorum in Angliam* (ed. A. G. Little, 1951) 4.

lifetime of St Francis. This pious tradition must yield before Brother Thomas's clear testimony that the Irish province was of English provenance. To make the point clearer still he recorded the appointment of another Englishman, John of Ketton, who succeeded Richard of Ingworth as provincial in 1239 and was to rule until 1254.[1]

By the 1230s English settlement in Ireland was widespread and well established. The Franciscans spread rapidly throughout the colony. Beginning with the foundations of Youghal and Cork in the south east—almost certainly the region of Richard of Ingworth's arrival—by c.1239, houses were in existence at the two principal Leinster towns of Kilkenny and Dublin, in the principal towns of the Ulster earldom, Carrickfergus and Downpatrick and on the western, Shannon, frontier at Athlone. Under the steady patronage of the great but especially of townspeople, some sixteen houses were in being by the end of John of Ketton's period as provincial,[2] and by c. 1280 the number had risen to twenty-seven.[3] They were situated in all the English towns in Ireland of any significance though three of them (Ennis, Armagh and Buttevant) were of native Irish foundation. In the second-half century of the province's history some five houses were added, three under native Irish auspices (Killeigh, Timoleague and Cavan).[4] In 1331 these thirty-two houses were divided into five custodies.[5] (Map 5).

Springing immediately from England, spreading predominantly within the confines of the English colony in Ireland and preserving links with England, through visitation in particular, the Franciscans in Ireland were not constitutionally a part of the English province. Unlike the Dominicans whose progress in Ireland ran *pari passu* with that of the Franciscans, who were subject to the English provincial, the Franciscans were autonomous, with, however, one qualification. Their provincial was not apparently elected in provincial chapter as was customary, but as was the case with the provinces of the Holy

---

[1] *Ibid.* 42.

[2] In approximate order of foundation: Youghal, Cork, Dublin, Carrickfergus, Athlone, Ennis, Kilkenny, Downpatrick, Drogheda, Waterford, Dundalk, Castledermot, Claregalway, Nenagh, Ardfert, New Ross.

[3] The additional eleven were: Kildare, Clane, Armagh, Cashel, Limerick, Wexford, Wicklow, Multyfarnham, Clonmel, Buttevant, Trim.

[4] The remaining two were Galway and Monasteroris.

[5] Fitzmaurice and Little, *Franciscan materials* 133–4.

Map 5. The five custodies of the Franciscan province in Ireland.

Land and Romania, was appointed by the minister-general.[1] The succession list of provincials is not without gaps and confusions but it is clear that some Anglo-Irishmen, as well as Englishmen, were nominated. No native Irish name appears in this period.[2] There is singularly little information available as to the place and proportion of native Irish friars in the province. The argument *ex silentio* suggests that there was no deliberate policy either in theory or practice of excluding them from any houses of the order, in the first half-century. That a friar of the name O'Quinn was *custos* of the very English Drogheda custody in 1252 suggests very strongly, with other evidence, that *acceptio personarum* has as yet at any rate little or no place in Irish Franciscan life.[3]

As mentioned already, there is no chronicler in whose light we may see, in Professor David Knowles's words, 'the leaven of Francis at work in a distant country'.[4] Nor is there for Franciscan Ireland any Grosseteste to give convincing testimony of the pastoral success of the first Minorite generation. Ireland had no university and therefore no intellectual world to sustain, and be sustained by, the friars as in other countries and though there is no reason to suppose that theological studies did not flourish to some degree in individual houses, nothing of this remains for the historian's scrutiny. It is perhaps surprising that there is virtually no trace of any regularity of attendance at Oxford of friars from Ireland, though there is such a trace for attendance at Paris at least from the end of the century. All due allowance for the limitation of source material made, however, it does not seem unreasonable to see the first half-century of the Franciscan province in Ireland as a period of creditable development. Comparing comparable things, its rate of growth measured in numbers of houses stood well by comparison with the Dominicans in Ireland who had reached twenty-one houses in their first fifty years and with the Franciscans in Scotland and in Wales, who had achieved three and four, possibly five, respectively, in a similar period. The province was established throughout the length and breadth of the country, the friars were obviously popular with all classes of society and with

---

[1] *Bullarium Franciscanum* (ed. Sbaralea) 5. 85; Fitzmaurice and Little, *Franciscan materials* 93–4.
[2] *Ibid.* 209.
[3] *Ibid.* 18.
[4] M. D. Knowles, *The Religious Orders in England* (1948) 139.

both the Anglo-Irish and Irish peoples. There was a certain demand for friars as bishops, particularly in Irish dioceses where capitular organization was less strong than in Anglo-Irish dioceses.[1] If no outstanding personality emerged from their ranks, two Irishmen, one from each nation, were known beyond the bounds of their own island. A John of Ireland was one of the principals who collaborated in the drawing up of Nicholas III's famous decretal *Exiit qui seminat* (1279),[2] whilst Malachy of Limerick accomplished a near best-seller with his treatise on the seven deadly sins, the so-called *Venenum Malachiae*.[3] What is striking about this first period of growth, this first half-century, is the absence of that strife, both within and without, which was endemic in other parts of the Church in Ireland in this period. The Franciscans succeeded (it seems) in remaining uninvolved in the never-ceasing struggle between the two peoples, and this was no mean achievement.

It was not, however, destined to be a permanent one. The history of the province in the second half-century has to be written in almost exclusively political terms. This was a time when not merely did individual Franciscans, in some numbers, become deeply involved in the strife between colonists and native Irish which was the dominating theme of life in thirteenth century Ireland, but the order came to reflect within itself the strife of the country as a whole, as it moved inexorably to the separation of an Irish from an Anglo-Irish part of the province.

It was in the 1280s that the English government received its first warning that some of the Franciscans were a political risk. As has been seen, the commission of enquiry sent from England in 1284 to investigate complaints about the alleged maladministration of the justiciar, Stephen of Fulbourn, drew Edward I's attention to the nationalist sentiments of native Irish friars and recommended that steps should be taken to check it. What these precise steps were is not known, because of the defects in the manuscript of the commission's report. But it was likely enough that it was along lines already recommended for Cistercian houses earlier in the century and currently being urged on Edward I for adoption in the religious orders gener-

---

[1] They are conveniently listed in Fitzmaurice and Little, *Franciscan materials* 211 but the entries should be controlled by *Hbk Brit. Chron.*
[2] Fitzmaurice and Little, *Franciscan materials* 56–8.   [3] *Ibid.* 46.

ally by the Anglo-Irish Franciscan bishop of Kildare, Nicholas Cusack. This was the policy of removing the security risks from houses which were predominantly native Irish, especially from houses in march districts, filling the vacancies thus caused with sound, handpicked English religious, who would be in charge of the house.

Variations of this theme recur frequently in the various schemes for reforming the state of Ireland with which official circles fairly bristled in the later thirteenth century and well on into the fourteenth. The problem of arresting the treasonable activities of Irish monks and friars was not the most important one which the Dublin administration faced, but it was thought to be an important one and a good deal of effort by different authorities went into trying to find a solution. There were no doubt really two distinct problems: one a purely political one of how to keep Irish religious loyal to the Crown and a second, an ecclesiastical one, of how to maintain the unity of religious orders split along national lines into two hostile factions. In no other religious order was this double problem felt more acutely than in the Franciscan, and in no other order was a more determined attempt made by the various governments involved (royal, papal, Franciscan) to solve it. The story of the various governmental interventions in Irish Franciscan affairs with the object of reducing the tension between the two nations forms the main theme of the second half-century of Irish Franciscan history.

Of the seriousness of the crisis there can be little doubt. In 1291 when the provincial chapter met in June at Cork, tension between the two peoples exploded into violence. Of this incident the Worcester annalist, the best source, narrates baldly that the Irish friars came armed with a papal bull (unspecified and not traced); 'a dispute having arisen concerning this, they fought against the English friars; and after many had been killed and wounded, the English at length gained the victory by the help of the city, and with scandal to the order'.[1] The scandal brought Raymond Gaufredi, the minister-general, himself to Ireland and Edward I placed the full strength of the secular arm at his disposal. Whatever resulted from this visitation, and no information has survived, it was no final solu-

[1] The evidence has been assembled in *ibid.* 63–4.

tion. Conflict was to break out again in particularly virulent form during the invasion of Ireland by Edward Bruce and in the aftermath of that very considerable disaster.

Suspicion of Irish religious by the colonial authorities reached its climax in 1310. A statute was promulgated by a parliament held at Kilkenny forbidding the profession or reception of any native Irish religious, monk, canon or friar, among the colonists.[1] The prohibition was underwritten by several bishops.[2] The decree was, however, speedily revoked.[3] But, repealed or not, legislation of this type reveals how far the two nations forming the Irish Church were from integration. Nothing was to happen in the fourteenth century to draw them closer together.

REMONSTRANCE AND COUNTER-REMONSTRANCE

The main thrust of development in the fourteenth century, in the Franciscan order, in the friars and other religious orders, in the Irish Church, in Ireland generally was towards further disunity. First of the many events that either caused or revealed the gulf between the nations was the Bruce invasion: 'the most decisive three years in Irish history since Strongbow arrived', because it ushered in the age of the decline of the colony.[4]

Edward Bruce landed in Ireland in May 1315, was crowned king of Ireland a year later and continued to ravage the country savagely

---

[1] 'It is also agreed that it be forbidden to all the religious who dwell in a territory at peace or in English land (*terre Engleis*), to receive, into their order or into their profession any save those who are of the English nation, and if they do otherwise, the King shall act towards them as in the case of those who are despisers of his command; and their patrons shall demean themselves towards them as in the case of those who are disobedient and opposed to this ordinance, made by the common consent of the land' *Stat. Irel. John-Henry V* 270–7 at 272–3.

[2] They were: Maurice MacCarwill (Cashel), William FitzJohn (Ossory), William Roughhead (Emly), Maurice de Blancheville (Leighlin). One, listed as R. of Lismore, is probably a mistake for Robert Walrand (Ferns). The prelates threatened to 'excommunicate, anathematize, condemn and from the threshold of holy mother Church' to exclude any who disobeyed these ordinances, *ibid.* 274–5.

[3] By the justiciar, John Wogan (who had been present at the Kilkenny parliament), apparently on the advice of Walter Jorz, archbishop of Armagh (22 May 1310). Cf. J. F. Ferguson, 'The "mere English" and "mere Irish" ' *Trans. Kilkenny Archaeol. Soc. (RSAIJn.)* 1. (1850–1) 508–12. The letter of annulment is now apparently lost.

[4] Curtis, *Medieval Ireland* 197. 'it will continue to hold its place as a great dividing line in our history' J. F. Lydon, 'The Bruce Invasion of Ireland' *Hist. Studies* 4 (ed. G. A. Hayes-McCoy, 1963) 111–25 at 112.

until he was killed in October 1318.[1] John Clyn, the Kilkenny Franciscan whose chronicle is a major source for this period stated that almost all the native Irish threw off their faith and loyalty to the Crown and supported the Scots.[2] It has been suggested that this is an exaggerated statement of the degree of support Bruce could command. But certainly he drew considerable support from the native Irish, at least for a time. And more. He drew support also from the Anglo-Irish. Some of these associated themselves with the Invasion for much the same reasons as did the native Irish, as an opportunity to work off old scores and to claim by force what in the way of rights they felt they had been denied.[3]

Silent leges inter arma. It might be thought that amid the destruction, the only interest for the historian examining the relations between prelates and royalty would be in the compilation of an inventory of destroyed churches and a list of rebel churchmen. But there is one facet of the situation which merits attention. The papacy found itself brought prominently into the picture. Pope John XXII has a unique place in Irish medieval history: no pope before or after him in the medieval period, was quite so sought after by the different interests which were clashing in Ireland.

Clement V had died in April 1314 and it was August 1316 before the College of Cardinals could decide on a replacement. Edward Bruce was thus already proclaimed king of Ireland before John XXII became pope. Edward II was first with his bid for papal support. Inevitably so, since the English government maintained a permanent diplomatic presence at the papal curia and in any case, at this time, was already deeply involved with negotiations about the Scots. Even before news of the election had reached him, Edward II had been complaining to the cardinals about the 'fierce and ignorant' Irish. Specifically, he was seeking the promotion to the archdiocese of Cashel where there had been a divided election of the English Franciscan Geoffrey of Aylsham. Edward urged that in the present rebellions among the Irish induced by the Scottish Invasion, it would

---

[1] Narrative account and analysis of its aftermath in Otway-Ruthven, *Medieval Ireland* 224–51.

[2] John Clyn, *Annales Hibernie* in *Annals of Ireland* ed. R. Butler (Ir. Archaeol. Soc. 1849) 12.

[3] See the pertinent comment of Lydon, 'The Bruce Invasion of Ireland', 115–16.

be very dangerous to have an Irishman promoted to a see *inter anglicos*.[1] The King had other plans too for Geoffrey of Aylsham. He was cast for a rôle in curbing the seditious activities of some Franciscans. Already shortly after the landing of Edward Bruce in Ireland, the government had become uneasy about the activities of Irish friars and other clergy who were living among the English.[2] Now, in August 1316, Geoffrey of Aylsham was sent, along with the minister of the Irish Franciscan province, Thomas Godman, to the order's minister-general, Michael of Cesena, with the complaint that Irish Franciscans were working up support for Edward Bruce in Ireland.[3] In March, Edward again pressed hard for a decision about Cashel, urging the need for politically reliable bishops at a time when some Irish bishops were inciting the populace to rebellion, supporting the Scots and trying to destroy the royal power in Ireland. He asked especially that no native Irishman should be promoted archbishop or bishop during the present trouble except with royal assent previously obtained.[4]

There is no question as to where the papal sympathies lay. Through the spring of 1317, John XXII issued a series of instructions offering practical support for Edward II: permission for the King to retain the crusading tax ordered by the general council of Vienne;[5]

[1] '... considerantes ... quod, si quisquam Hibernicus preficiatur in archiepiscopum ecclesie supradicte, que inter puros Hibernicos, homines siquidem bestiales et indoctos, situatur, maiora pericula nobis et fidelibus nostris in dicta terra poterun de facili evenire; presertim cum iam quamplures ex illis, relicta ligiantia sua, Scotis, inimicis nostris, nuper quasdam partes in dicta terra hostiliter ingressis, et varia ibidem committendo flagitia, proditionaliter adheserunt, et nobis, una cum ipsis, inimice palam effecti sunt et rebelles ...' Rymer, *Foedera* 3. 567 (20 August 1316).
[2] *Cal. Cl. Rolls 1313–18* 307–8.
[3] Rymer, *Foedera* 3. 568.
[4] 'Per machinationes fraudulentas, malitiosamque collusionem atque falsam quorumdam prelatorum Hibernicorum, de terra nostra Hibernie, nos de terra illa exheredare malitiose nitentium pro viribus et fraudare, inimici nostri Scotie in eadem terra nostra receptantur, et de ipsorum prelatorum assensu, dampna quamplurima contra nos et fideles nostros dictarum partium perpetrarunt et adhuc perpetrare non desinunt, quodque prelati Hibernici natione publicis predicationibus, contra ipsorum fidelitatem et iuramenta non cessant contra nos populum dictarum partium provocare ... non permittendo si placet quod aliquis Hibernicus natione in terra nostra predicta, saltim durante turbatione iam ibidem existente, ad dignitatem archiepiscopalem seu episcopalem, nisi prius noster assensus regius adhibitus fuerit, sicut decet, quomodolibet assumatur' Rymer, *Foedera* 3. 616–17.
[5] *Jean XXII. Lettres communes* (ed. G. Mollat) 1 (1904) 3393.

the appointment of the chancellor of Ireland, William FitzJohn, to Cashel;[1] appointment of judges-delegate to restrain the clergy from preaching rebellion;[2] general condemnation of all supporters of the Bruces;[3] specific condemnation of disloyal Mendicants.[4]

Somewhat belatedly, the native Irish put their case to the Pope early in 1318 when through the cardinal-legates who had gone to England to mediate between Edward II and Robert Bruce, they sent him a 'remonstrance',[5] essentially an apologia for their rejection of English lordship of Ireland. This document has a strong claim to be regarded as chronologically the first major formulation of Irish nationalism.

It was addressed to the Pope by that same Domnall O'Neill, king of Tir Eoghain whom we have already encountered in connexion with Archbishop Nicholas of Armagh's implementation of *Clericis laicos*. Describing himself, pretentiously, as king of Ulster and heir to the high kingship of Ireland and submitting his letter, optimistically, in the name of all the Irish people, Domnall's specific purpose was to justify the recognition of Edward Bruce as king and to ask the Pope to acknowledge him as such, 'or at least be pleased to render us . . . our due complement of justice'.

The Remonstrance began with a brief history of sovereignty in Ireland, to establish that Ireland was validly independent of foreign rule before and after it became Christian and that its kings had always maintained 'their birthright of freedom unimpaired'. In 1170, however, the Irish had been made over into slavery, when Henry II, slayer of Thomas Becket, falsely and wickedly persuaded his fellow

---

1 Rymer, *Foedera* 3. 622–3. FitzJohn had been bishop of Ossory since 1302 and as such had lent the weight of his authority to the ban on the reception of Irish religious into English religious houses promulgated by the Kilkenny parliament of 1310. He had had a short spell as chancellor in 1314 and served again as such 1316–22, acting as keeper (chief governor) for some months in 1318, Richardson and Sayles, *Administration of Ireland* 84, 95.

2 Rymer, *Foedera* 3. 630–1.

3 Rymer, *Foedera* 3. 620–2.

4 *Ibid.* 630–1; Theiner, *Vet. mon.* 411.

5 Its text survives in the continuation of Fordun's *Scotichronicon* ed. T. Hearne 3. (1722) 908–26 and ed. W. Goodall 2 (1759) 259–67. I cite here from the translation of C. McNeill printed in E. Curtis and R. B. McDowell, *Irish historical documents 1172–1922* 38–46. For general discussions, Curtis, *Medieval Ireland* 191–3; Otway-Ruthven, *Medieval Ireland* 235–6 and for the light it throws on the legal status of the Irish at common law, Hand, *English law in Ireland* 201–6.

countryman Adrian IV, blinded by his English prejudice,[1] to grant
him lordship of Ireland. From the time of their entry into Ireland
under the cloak of religion, the English had striven with all their
might to wipe out the Irish nation. Further, Adrian's grant (a copy
of which accompanied the Remonstrance) was a contract. The kings
of England were given the lordship on condition that they extended
the bounds of the Church, preserved its rights intact, improved the
morals of the people. They had done none of these things. Every
liberty of the Church had been violated, ecclesiastical property
seized and clergy imprisoned, the Irish people corrupted. From such
generalities, the writer proceeded to particular and accurate articles
of complaint of the legal incapacity of the Irish in civil pleas and
their unequal status in criminal law. Further, there was especial
complaint about the 'English inhabiting our land, who call themselves of the middle nation' men of the utmost perfidy whose rule is
quite intolerable and for whom the Irish feel insuperable aversion:

For such is their arrogance and excessive lust to lord it over us and so
great is our due and natural desire to throw off the unbearable yoke of
slavery under them and to recover the inheritance so wickedly seized by
them that as there has not been in the past, there cannot be in the present
or in the future, any sincere goodwill between them and us.

So much for thoughts and hopes of integration.

For the ecclesiastical historian, the Remonstrance has a number of
points of interest. It furnishes an important example of how Adrian
IV's *Laudabiliter* was accepted as an authentic document by the Irish
though the legal validity of its grant of lordship was called into
question, and how it continued to influence the way men thought
politically.[2] It provides evidence that the suspicions of English
officials about discrimination by Irish against English religious was
fully reciprocated. Recalling the statute passed at the Kilkenny
parliament of 1310 against the reception of Irish religious among the
English, it asserted:

[1] In a letter soliciting support for another Irish prince and not meant for papal eyes,
Domnall allowed himself to be even more frank about Adrian IV: 'qui dici meruit
potius antichristus quam iustus pontifex' cf. H. Wood, 'Letter from Domnall
O'Neill to Fineen MacCarthy, 1317' *PRIA* 27 sect. C (1926) 141–8.
[2] See further, my '*Laudabiliter* in medieval diplomacy and propaganda' *IER* 87
(1957) 420–32.

Even before this statute was made, and afterwards, the friars, both preachers and minors, monks, canons and other English religious have been observing it strictly enough, being in the highest degree respecters of persons; yet the monasteries of monks and canons where at the present day the Irish are refused were, generally speaking, founded by them.

Further, the Remonstrance testified that English clergy nurtured most unchristian sentiments towards the native Irish:

For not only their laymen and secular clergy but also some of their regular clergy dogmatically assert the heresy that it is no more a sin to kill an Irishman than a dog or any other animal. And in maintaining this heresy some of their monks assert boldly that when, as often happens, they kill an Irishman, they do not on that account refrain from saying mass, even for a day. It is indisputable that Cistercian monks of Granard in the Ardagh diocese and of Inch in the Down diocese shamelessly fulfil in act what they profess verbally. Bearing arms without concealment, they attack and kill Irishmen and yet celebrate mass.

Finally, there was the response of the Pope to this burning appeal. It was of course scarcely to be expected that John XXII would recognize Edward Bruce as lawful king of Ireland. The papacy had condemned the Bruces and there were too many reasons of immediate practical policy why John should not suddenly abandon the traditional papal support of English lordship of Ireland.[1] He wrote to Edward II in tones of paternal admonition advising him, 'You should scrupulously refrain from all such courses as may justly provoke against you the wrath of God, the Lord to whom all vengeance belongs, who never disregards the groaning of those who are unjustly afflicted and who is described as having rejected his own chosen people and transferred their kingdom to others because of the acts of unrighteousness which they had committed.'[2] It does not seem likely that John himself contemplated any parallel transfer, whatever the supplications of the Irish. Instead the Pope offered counsel, shrewd enough in itself, that it was precisely in its beginnings that unrest should be dealt with before it was too late. The medicine for the early stages of the illness was justice. The papal legates in

[1] Cf. Watt, 'Negotiations between Edward II and John XXII concerning Ireland' *IHS* 10 (1956) 1–20 at 3–4.
[2] Theiner, *Vet. mon.* 422, 423 (30 May 1318).

England were charged with keeping the Irish case before the King's attention. The cardinals did this. Edward II, the more anxious for papal goodwill the more Robert Bruce prospered, replied respectfully and tactfully, disclaimed knowledge of any misconduct towards the Irish by his ministers, promised investigation and justice for the Irish 'all the more willingly because urged thereto by your salutary admonitions'.[1] Such polite exchanges made no balm for the running sore of race hatred in Ireland.

They did nothing, for example, to make peace between the contending nations within the Cistercian order. In 1321, Edward II complained to the general chapter about Irish discrimination against English Cistercians. His case comes to us more fully in an instruction he issued to his justiciar:

Recently it came to the King's attention in full parliament that in the Cistercian abbey of Mellifont and in other houses of that order in Ireland it has become the practice that no one is admitted to the religious habit unless an oath is taken, or it be known on other evidence or common knowledge, that he is not of the English nation or related to the English. The King therefore wrote to the abbot of Citeaux asking for the abolition of this partiality [*acceptacio*], since it appears to be designed not only for the dissolution of charity but in contempt of the king, in opprobrium of all his nation [*lingua*] and in subversion of his lordship. The abbot has written to the king in reply that the king's letters were discussed in the next chapter-general and the abbots of Dore and Margam were commissioned and enjoined by authority of the chapter to go in person to Ireland and to dispose and ordain concerning the houses of the order, and to compel the abbots of these houses to receive without distinction any who wish to enter the religious life in that order without any partiality, so long as they are able and suitable. The King now instructs the Justiciar to encourage these abbots when they arrive in Ireland, to fulfil diligently the mandate given to them and to compel the other abbots of that order in those parts to obey them and the instructions they have been given. The Justiciar is commanded to carry out this work and to coerce rebels and conspirators when necessary, so far as justice demands.[2]

---

[1] Rymer, *Foedera* 3. 727–8 (25 August 1318).

[2] *Cal. Cl. Rolls 1318–23* 404. I have here corrected the editor's misreading of the passage concerning *acceptacio personarum*. The Cistercian *Statuta s.a.* 1321 must obviously be understood in the context of this royal complaint and instruction: 'Item, damnabiles divisionis parietes suasu capitalis humani generis adversarii

National partialities likewise continued to dog the fortunes of the Franciscans. On 7 April 1324 the provincial chapter met in Dublin. Its main business was the promulgation of a mandate concerning the hostility between Irish and English Franciscans by judges-delegate appointed by the Pope, chief of whom was the dean of St Patrick's, Dublin, William of Rudyard.[1] Present at the chapter were Durandus and Romanus whom the minister-general had sent to Ireland as Visitors.[2]

William of Rudyard first defined the problem with which he was concerned. Sworn investigations which had been made of Franciscans, other religious, diocesan clergy and lay magnates in various parts of Ireland had found, he said, that in the communities of Irish Franciscans in Cork, Limerick, Buttevant, Ardfert, Nenagh, Claregalway, Galway and Athlone the conduct of the friars was deeply suspect. They revealed that the dwelling of these men in these places constituted a serious danger to the king's peace and to the common welfare of society (*status reipublice*) unless English and Irish friars lived together.

For the greater security of the peace, therefore, the Dean thought it necessary to issue a series of commands in the name of the Apostolic See, binding under penalty of *ipso facto* major excommunication for any violation and hindrance, and recourse to the secular arm against rebels where necessary. Irish friars living in these places were to be allocated to other houses in Ireland except for three or at the most, four of the less suspect who might remain to ensure that there was cohabitation of friars of both nations in a fashion appropriate to the circumstances of these places. Further, it was forbidden for any

introductos detestans Capitulum generale praecipit patribus abbatibus Ordinis universi et specialiter illis de Hibernia, pro quibus gravis quaerimonia delata nuper extitit ad Capitulum generale, quod tales ibi reperti facientes partes coniungere studeant in concordia et unitate, et indifferenter de omni natione ad regularem habitum, dum tamen reperiuntur idonei, admitti facient et procurent; alioquin patres abbates, vel alii quicumque, si super hoc culpabiles fuerint reperti, gravissime se noverint per Capitulum generale puniendos' Canivez, 3. 353. It is not possible to follow the story further. There is no Irish entry in the *Statuta* after this until 1352.

1 It is not surprising to find him in royal service, deputy treasurer of Ireland 1331, justice of the common bench 1327–9, 1331–2, Richardson and Sayles, *Administration of Ireland* 101, 156, 158.

2 Texts in full in *Calendar of Ormond Deeds 1172–1350* ed. E. Curtis (Ir. MSS Comm. 1932) 575. 237–42. The translation there offered must be treated with caution.

Irishman to be guardian of any of these eight houses. Each *lector* of Irish nationality must be transferred to a house among the English. Finally, all members of the order must make solemn oath to the minister-provincial and Visitors, or to one of them, that in the future they would not say or do anything to disturb the peace. The minister-provincial and Visitors were to certify to the Dean within one month how his mandate, 'or more truly the apostolic mandate' had been carried out, under pain of excommunication.

On 21 May, when parliament was meeting in Dublin, the Dean issued a clarificatory instruction. He had been led to understand, he said, that his original mandate had been badly understood and interpreted against his intention. The vacancies caused by the transference of Irish friars were to be filled by English friars, allocated at the discretion of the minister-provincial. He modified his original veto on the presence of Irish *lectores* in the eight named houses, permitting Claregalway and Galway of special grace to retain them. The same two houses were also to be allowed to have guardians of Irish nationality along with four others (not named) which had been founded among the Irish. These six houses should form a single Irish custody. No friar of Irish nationality should have any general administrative post either as bishop or as vicar-provincial.[1] Finally, it was ordered that some English friars should be in each 'pure Irish' house, just as there should be some Irish friars in English houses. Three bishops, Ossory, Waterford and Connor, presumably in Dublin for the parliament,[2] added their confirmatory approval of these instructions.

A brief record of a decision made at the next general chapter of the Franciscans, held at Lyons in 1325, gives some additional details about the reorganization of the custodies of the province along national lines. It confirmed the establishment of a fifth custody, that of Cork, formed by removing Cork, Buttevant, Limerick and Ardfert from the Irish.[3] It thus seems clear that the policy of William

[1] 'Nolumus eciam immo simpliciter prohibemus ne aliquis frater Hibernice nacionis regimen habeat generale in tota Hibernia nec ut prelatus nec ut vicarius eiusdem propter causas in prioribus annotatas' *Cal. Orm. Deeds* 241.
[2] Richard Ledred of Ossory was certainly at the parliament which was the occasion of his famous quarrel with Arnold le Poer, Richardson and Sayles, *Medieval Irish Parliament* 72–3. The bishop of Connor was an Irishman, James O'Kearney.
[3] Friar John Clyn: '(1324) Fuit discordia ut communiter inter religiosos pauperes

of Rudyard was ratified, at least in general terms, by the supreme authority of the order. Presumably the two Visitors played an intermediary rôle. There was to be a further consideration of houses and custodies at the Perpignan general chapter of 1331. The establishment of a single Irish custody was confirmed, somewhat larger than that established by William of Rudyard. This was the custody of Nenagh, with Athlone, Ennis, Claregalway, Galway, Armagh, Cavan and Killeigh.[1] The other four custodies were predominantly English or at least intended to be. But there was no finality to be found. In 1345 the custodies were again reduced to four, a change necessitated by the changing balance between the two nations.[2]

This increasing disorder in Ireland and the worsening of relations between the Irish and English peoples set English official opinion moving towards other organizational expedients in the Irish Church. These too were to involve the papacy. In 1324 Philip of Slane O.P., a member of the Irish council and bishop of Cork (1321-7)[3] undertook two journeys to Avignon to promote a scheme for the *reformatio* of the Irish Church. The first, exploratory in nature, was received sympathetically by John XXII but he expressed the wish for further discussion and clarification of the reform proposals.[4] Philip returned home to fulfil this request, leaving with the Pope a *Libellus de descriptione Hibernie*, his abbreviation of the *Topographia Hibernie* of Giraldus Cambrensis.[5] Edward II was to tell the Pope in a letter announcing Philip of Slane's return to Avignon that the reform plan for the curbing of the 'obstinate malice' of the Irish which the Bishop

---

Hybernie quasi omnes, quidam eorum nacionis sue et sanguinis et lingue partem tenentes et foventes ac promoventes ... 1325 in Pentecoste capitulum generale celebratum Lugduni: ubi loca de ˙Cork, Boton (Buttevant), Lymyric et Tartdart (Ardfert) auferuntur ab Hybernicis fratribus et Anglicis et quinta custodia assignatur, cum ante tantum fuissent quatuor custodie ...' *Ann. hib.* 17; Fitzmaurice and Little, *Franciscan materials* 120.

[1] *Ibid.* 133-4.
[2] Clyn, *Ann. hib.* 31. Cf. Fitzmaurice and Little, *Franciscan materials* 139 for pertinent comment.
[3] Cf. *DNB* (C. L. Kingsford) for a summary of his career. For his membership of the Irish council, Richardson and Sayles, *Medieval Irish Parliament* 30-1.
   Rymer, *Foedera* 4. 53-4, 54-5.
[5] Cf. R. Flower, 'Manuscripts of Irish interest in the British Museum' *Anal. hib.* 2 (1931) 317.

brought with him was the fruit of very thorough investigation and discussion by the archbishops of Dublin and Cashel with Philip of Slane, the Irish council and magnates in Ireland and the King's council in England.[1] Three specific proposals were laid before the Pope.[2] There is a very familiar ring about the first:

Discord is fomented and wars promoted in that monks in some areas and regular canons having extensive possessions among the English and other religious in the mendicant orders in various places wish only to allow pure Irishmen to make profession in their houses, though in English religious houses Irishmen are received without discrimination. For this it would seem sufficient remedy if Englishmen were to be received into Irish houses just as Irishmen are received into English houses, and especially so in houses among the English and they should be kept in order by the archbishops, as would seem expedient for the peace and concord of the nations. And native Irish friars should act impartially and not continue to do as some have done recently, namely, buy certain places for friars of their own nation, but should live communally and mixed throughout all the houses of their order in Ireland.

The Pope had already gone some way towards implementing the second proposal at the time of the Bruce invasion. It was complained now of 'the peoples of the Irish nation' that they considered the king of England no true lord of Ireland but a usurper. The Pope was urged to write to all prelates and religious ordering them to use the pulpit and confessional to instruct the Irish in their political duty and to promulgate sentences of major excommunication on those who rejected English lordship.

If, given the nature of Edward's Irish problem and the amount of cogitation which allegedly had gone into their formulation, these seem relatively unoriginal solutions, the third proposal was more novel and radical. The King asked that the poorer dioceses of Ireland which were ruled by bishops of Irish nationality who, he claimed, were responsible for sowing dissension either personally or through their relatives, should be united to other dioceses. The scheme was to approximately halve the number of dioceses, siting

---

[1] Rymer, *Foedera* 4. 54–5.
[2] The translations following are from Vat. Library Barberini Latini MSS no. 2126 fo. 120r–121r, edited as Document A in Watt, 'Negotiations between Edward II and John XXII concerning Ireland' 16–18.

each wherever possible in an English stronghold. The plan was put to John XXII in this form:

The peace and concord of Ireland are disturbed because Irish prelates hold sees adjacent to the English and sometimes among the English. These prelates and their clergy help their own nation by promoting and encouraging wars against our lord king of England and his subjects. Since the bishoprics of Ireland are very poor and number thirty-four, a remedy would seem to be to make unions of some of them and especially that additional bishoprics be annexed to royal towns in which there are episcopal seats, to the great security of peace and the king's estate. It should be done as follows:

[ARMAGH]

To the archiepiscopal see of Armagh should be united Clogher which borders on it.

To Down should be united neighbouring Dromore.

To Connor should be joined neighbouring Derry and Raphoe.

To Meath which is in the province of Armagh should be joined the three adjoining dioceses of Kilmore, Ardagh and Clonmacnois of which the total revenue is scarcely more than one hundred marks.

[CASHEL]

To the archiepiscopal see of Cashel should be united neighbouring Killaloe.

To Limerick, a royal city, should be joined neighbouring Kilfenora.

To Waterford, a royal city, and whose revenue is scarcely more than fifty marks, should be united neighbouring Lismore, as was the case in former days.

To Cork, a royal city, and whose revenue is scarcely more than sixty marks, should be joined neighbouring Cloyne.

[TUAM]

To the archiepiscopal see of Tuam should be united neighbouring Annaghdown as was the case formerly, and Achonry and Kilmacduagh.

To Elphin should be united neighbouring Killala and the seat transferred to Roscommon where there is a noble royal castle and thus it should become a city.

It was obviously considered that the organization of the Dublin province with its five dioceses was satisfactory. Armagh was to be reduced from eleven to four dioceses. Three dioceses of Cashel province were not mentioned: Ardfert, Emly and Ross. It seems likely that the omission of the small Irish diocese of Ross was accidental. Its union with Cork would be in accordance with the logic of the scheme, as would the union of Emly to Cashel, leaving Ardfert intact. Thus the province of Cashel would be reduced from eleven to five dioceses. Clonfert of the Tuam province was not mentioned and it is likely that it was envisaged as remaining as it was. Thus Tuam was to be reduced from six to three dioceses.

There was a good case for reorganization of the diocesan structure. Medieval Ireland had too many dioceses, and unions of dioceses in modern times by both the Catholic and Church of Ireland hierarchies are testimony of this. From Edward II's point of view, which was primarily political, it was a scheme with much to commend it and could well have served its purpose—if it could have been brought about. But it was quite impracticable. John XXII was not hostile to the plan. But he made it subject to a condition which was certain to kill it: 'Let what is asked be done if the bishops who have charge of the dioceses to be united give their assent.'

Yet the Pope did not completely shelve the matter. John was apparently sufficiently impressed by the need of some diocesan changes to issue instructions in July 1327 for three unions of dioceses.[1] With the archbishopric of Tuam were to be amalagamated Achonry, Kilmacduagh and Annaghdown. Lismore and Waterford were to be joined, as were Cork and Cloyne. The first two of these unions already had a history of attempted amalgamation, and Edward claimed that his plan was a return to an earlier state of affairs. The third concerned the diocese whose bishop, Philip of Slane, John had had ample opportunity of consulting personally. It is impossible to say whether this was the limit to which John was prepared to go in acceptance of the plan, or whether it was the first step, along the safest lines open to him, to a wider measure of reform.

The difficulties encountered by even this limited measure of change indicate how unrealistic, in the last analysis, Edward's plan really was. Of the three unions ordered by John XXII not one was

[1] Details in *art. cit.* 11–12. Cf. further *Hbk Brit. Chron.* 304–5, 325–6, 332, 334–5, 344–5, 350.

effected according to the instructions issued. It is certainly true that one union was thereby achieved—that of Annaghdown to Tuam. For Malachy, archbishop of Tuam, was able to assimilate the diocese and claim papal authorization for his act. This result is a stroke of real irony—for Malachy had been trying for many years to get control of Annaghdown and had encountered lively opposition from both Edward II and John XXII. And it was Edward III, in protest against this development, who pointed out to John that this union meant that a diocese of 'mere Anglici' was being absorbed 'inter mere Hibernicos' and the rule of an Irish bishop being substituted for that of an English one.[1] This was hardly a step towards the realization of Edward II's plans.

The Achonry union seems to have remained effective until *c.* 1348, when a bull of Clement VI mentions the recent 'dissolution of the union with Tuam'. Kilmacduagh remained unaffected by John's instruction for amalgamation with Tuam. For Cork and Cloyne, John seems to have changed his mind early, for in 1330 he was taking steps for a new appointment to Cork alone. It was to be left to Martin V in 1421 to complete the work begun by Edward II and John XXII for this union. In the final accomplishment of the union of Waterford and Lismore the influence of John was more direct. In 1355 Innocent VI, at the instance of Edward III, confirmed the letter of union granted by John. But the process was not finally completed until in 1363, Lismore being vacant, Roger Cradock of Waterford was translated to Llandaff in Wales, and Urban V united the dioceses in a union that was to endure.

There is one last appeal from Ireland to John XXII to be noticed, that despatched by the justiciar and Irish council *c.*1331.[2] No document conveys more strongly the strength of Irish opinion, or some sections of it, about the Crown and the colony than the Remonstrance presented by Domnall O'Neill. The parallel remonstrance of *c.*1331 from the English side conveys equally strongly how the sentiments were reciprocated. This document has so many general features similar to that of the O'Neill document, that it is difficult to resist the conclusion that it was consciously intended as a counter-

[1] Rymer, *Foedera* 4. 418–19 (11 February 1330).
[2] Text as Document B, 'Negotiations between Edward II and John XXII concerning Ireland' 18–20 (see ref. in p. 193 n. 2 above).

blast to it. It too made its appeal to *Laudabiliter*, invoking it as the basis on which rested a special longstanding relationship between Ireland and the papacy and claiming, against the Irish Remonstrance, that the English kings had fulfilled those stipulations which Adrian IV had laid down. As the Irish had presented the English as heretics, as despoilers of the Church, oppressors of the clergy, as wanton slayers of Christians, so here the counter-charges. As the colonists stood accused of vices peculiar to their own nation, so the Irish were accused of vices special to them; namely, the practice of incest and adultery, justified by recourse to the custom of the country. As the Irish had accused the English of claiming that it was no sin to kill an Irishman, so here the argument *e converso*. The English document was not, however, so concerned with specific cases, though it did mention the case of Adam Duff O'Toole who had been burnt in Dublin for heresy in 1327.[1] The purpose of the appeal was to present to the Pope the desperate plight of the Irish Church where ordinary methods of government had broken down, with bishops too terrified to act through fear of death and the king's courts powerless. What was wanted, it was urged, was authority to wage a crusade on these Irish (and their Anglo-Irish supporters), a holy war against the Church's and the Pope's enemies. It was not a very intelligent suggestion.

There are perhaps two conclusions that stand out. One is particular. Since the Pope's response to O'Neill did nothing to change the situation and there is no record of any response to the justiciar and his council, there is here demonstration of the essential inability of the papacy, whatever its will, to ameliorate the situation, however hard each side might solicit its support. The other is general: Remonstrance and Counter-Remonstrance constitute a striking revelation in literary form of the failure to integrate the two nations.

[1] 'Per decretum ecclesie', *Chart. St. Mary's Dublin* 2. 366.

Chapter 10

THE STATUTE OF KILKENNY

In the time of King Edward the Third the impediments of the conquest of Ireland are so notorious as I shall not need to express them; to wit, the wars which the King had with the realms of Scotland and France, but especially the wars of France, which were almost continual for the space of forty years. And, indeed, France was a fairer mark to shoot at than Ireland, and could better reward the conqueror.[1]

That Sir John Davies was unquestionably right in emphasizing the part played by distractions elsewhere in the decline of the colony is vividly illustrated by Edward III's frank admission in 1359. As he departed for France, he conceded that he left England so 'empty of armed power and destitute of lords, whereby there is no room to send men or money to Ireland at present, although it is said they are needed there'.[2] The Dublin administration certainly believed men and money were essential and pressed urgently for the despatch of a military commander *estofféz et efforcéz de gentz et tresore.*[3] By 1361 it had persuaded the King that Ireland was now 'subjected to such devastation and destruction that unless God avert and succour the same it will be plunged into total ruin'.[4] The situation was not perhaps as bad as that nor was the colony plunging to catastrophe with the celerity that some historians have suggested. Nevertheless there was a crisis situation and an extraordinary effort of defence and reform was needed from England. In 1361, in the period of truce with France following the Treaty of Brétigny, Edward III sent his third son, Lionel, duke of Clarence, to Ireland to redeem the situation.

1 Sir John Davies, 'A discovery of the true causes why Ireland was never entirely subdued ...' in *Ireland under Elizabeth and James I* ed. H. Morley (1890) 254.
2 *Cal. Cl. Rolls 1354–60* 595–6; Otway-Ruthven, *Medieval Ireland* 284–5.
3 H. G. Richardson and G. O. Sayles, *Parliaments and Councils of Medieval Ireland* i (1947) 21.
4 *Cal. Cl. Rolls 1360–64* 253–4 (15 March 1361).

The legislation whose title stands at the head of this chapter was part of his contribution to the redemption attempt.

Particular historical documents may symbolize periods of history. If there is a sense in which the period of Edward II and Edward Bruce in Irish history may be aptly termed the age of Remonstrance and Counter-Remonstrance, the period of Edward III is the age of the Statute of Kilkenny. This is not, as is often asserted, because the document marks any turning point or watershed or 'Great Divide'[1] in Irish medieval history. For the Statute in general marked no major new departure, no radical change of policy. Rather does its significance rest, in many respects, in its very absence of novelty. It was essentially a codification of earlier legislation, the origins of some of which at least go back to the earliest extant statutes of an Irish parliament and all of it bearing the mark, directly or indirectly, of the numerous ordinances and mandates formulated by the king and council in England, themselves usually as a response to recommendations and representations from the Irish council or the petitions of the 'liege commons' of Ireland. It presents the historian with a most significant part of the contemporary diagnosis of what ailed the colony in the half century following the Bruce invasion and with the governmental response to that diagnosis. That the Statute was to be repeatedly repromulgated down to the end of the middle ages shows that medieval policy makers came to accept it as the right diagnosis and, could it only be properly applied, the correct remedy for arresting the decline of English power in Ireland, in so far as it was remediable by legislation.

A short analysis of the Statute is a necessary preliminary to consideration of its considerable ecclesiastical significance. There were thirty-six clauses, of heterogeneous nature, not arranged in any systematic order. No doubt there are different ways of classifying them. Five main divisions are suggested here.

Firstly, there were twenty-four clauses, forming the bulk of the measure, which related to the preservation of public order and the reform of the administration. Very little of this had any originality. Many of the clauses, particularly those relating to defence, were the

---

[1] Curtis, *Medieval Ireland* 234. The most recent analyses of the Statute are G. J. Hand, 'The forgotten Statutes of Kilkenny: a brief survey' *Irish Jurist* 1 (1966) 299–312 and Otway-Ruthven, *Medieval Ireland* 291–4.

platitudes of half a century of legislation on the topic. There was
one major direct source: an ordinance issued by a great council held
by Sir Thomas de Rokeby in Kilkenny in 1351.[1] Ten of the clauses in
this category relate directly to the making of war and peace and six
of these had been adopted from the 1351 ordinance.[2] The remaining
fourteen clauses in this category covered a miscellany of topics
relating to public order, concerning particularly criminal law and its
administration and the conduct and remuneration of royal officials.
Ten of these had been taken from the 1351 ordinance.[3] One of the
fourteen clauses (c. 7) concerns the Church.

Secondly, five clauses which have given the Statute its especial
niche of notoriety in Irish history.[4] These were concerned with what
a Tudor lawyer was to call succinctly 'the extincting of amyties
betweene the Englishrie and the Irishrie and thencrease and con-
tynuance of Englishe maner and habite'.[5] The propensity of English
settlers to forsake their own culture and, as the Statute itself said in
its proemium, 'live and govern themselves according to the manners,
fashion and language of the Irish enemies' had appeared even in the
days of the colony's strength.[6] It had increased as the tide of English
power began to ebb. The phenomenon was looked on by officialdom as a major cause of the falling away of English authority and
these clauses of the Statute were designed to preserve intact the
'Englishness' of the colonists and hence their loyalty to the Crown.

[1] *Stat. Irel. John–Henry V* 374–96. For the detail of the connexion *ibid.* 374. The text
and translation of the Statute is *ibid.* 430–68.

[2] They were cc. 6, 10, 12, 15, 17, 19, 21, 24, 27, 28. The last six mentioned are from
the 1351 ordinance.

[3] They were cc. 18, 20, 22, 23, 25, 29, 30, 31, 32, 33. The other four were cc. 7, 11, 16, 26.

[4] See the most recent judgments, putting a long historiographical tradition in
modern garb: '[The Statute is] chiefly remembered for the policy of racial exclusive-
ness—one is tempted to say *apartheid* . . .' Hand, 'The forgotten Statutes of Kilkenny'
299; '[The Statute] bore a striking resemblance to the modern *apartheid* law of
South Africa'. T de Vere White, *Ireland (New Nations and Peoples Library* 1968) 27.
Such comparisons seem to me to confuse the purposes of each of the laws in
question and fail to take account of the fact that there was a procedure in being before
and after the Statute, frequently used, by which Irishmen could be granted exactly
the same legal status as any Englishman.

[5] Robert Cowley, later Master of the Rolls in Ireland, writing to Thomas Cromwell
in 1537, cf. J. Hardiman, *A statute of the fortieth year of King Edward III . . . Ir.
Archaeol. Soc.* 2 (1843) 6.

[6] There was legislation in an Irish parliament of 1297 against those 'Englishmen who
have become degenerate in recent times' *Stat. Irel. John–Henry V* 194–213.

This was certainly not the first legislation on this subject but it was the most comprehensive. The colonists were forbidden to use the Irish language, law, dress, manner of naming, way of riding a horse. They were forbidden too to intermarry, have their children fostered by Irish people or enter into any other sort of familial or sexual relationship with the Irish. The separateness of the English nation was to be enforced under severe penalties. There was an ecclesiastical dimension to this separateness and clauses 13 and 14 treated of the position of Irish clergy, secular and regular, living and exercising their ministry among the English.

Thirdly, there were three clauses (cc. 1, 8, 9) which dealt with the relations of the civil and ecclesiastical jurisdictions. Two clauses (cc. 5, 34) relating to economic matters, the control of merchandise and manpower, constitute our fourth category. Finally come two clauses (cc. 35, 36) which were an attempt to put teeth into the Statute. Its penultimate clause established two commissioners for each county to make inquisition twice yearly as to its observance. The last clause made the Statute binding on pain of excommunication by the authority of three archbishops and five bishops.

Eight clauses of the Statute, then, have ecclesiastical relevance: liberty of the Church was the concern of cc. 1, 8, 9; c. 7 was about using the clergy as a quasi-police instrument to maintain public order; the position of Irish clergy among the English was the subject of cc. 3, 13, 14; c. 36 raises the question of the political attitudes of the eight prelates, three of whom were native Irish, who lent their spiritual authority to the enforcement of the Statute.

Actions by the civil authority could still in the first half of the fourteenth century provoke prelates into angry retaliation against royal officials. And despite so long a period of interaction between the two jurisdictions when mutual adjustments of the respective positions had extended to the minutiae of the relationship, new and important issues of principle could arise.

A case in point was the dispute in 1346 between Ralph O'Kelly O. Carm., archbishop of Cashel and three of his suffragans: Limerick (Maurice Rochfort), Emly (Richard le Walleys) and Lismore (John Leynagh) with the Dublin administration.[1] The justiciar, Walter de

---

[1] The original source for the case, an Irish Plea Roll of 21 Edward III, is now lost but a transcript survives in the Harris *Collectanea, Anal. hib.* 6 (1934) 348–9.

Bermingham, had held a council at Kilkenny at which some magnates and communities had granted a subsidy to be spent on defence against the Irish. It is not clear whether or not the bishops were present, but they did not assent to any subsidy. Nevertheless, the king's collectors for Munster sought to levy it on ecclesiastical properties. The four prelates, meeting at Tipperary, decreed strong measures. All beneficed clergy who contributed would be *ipso facto* deprived of their benefices and rendered incapable of holding one within the province. Lay tenants who contributed would be *ipso facto* excommunicated and their children, to the third generation, be deemed incapable of holding benefices. Later, the bishops, in public and solemn ceremony at Clonmel pronounced excommunication on all who broke the king's peace, violated the liberties of holy Church or levied any subsidy on ecclesiastical property without episcopal consent. In particular, William of Epworth, archdeacon of Cork, the king's chief collector in Munster, found himself excommunicated for defying his metropolitan. The excommunication of a royal official brought the bishops into the king's court. Absence of records prevents us from seeing the outcome of the case. There can be no doubt, however, of the importance of the principle at stake, apparently here professed explicitly and defended vigorously for the first time in Ireland, namely no taxation without consent, nor of the interest of a clear example of how the mutual interest of churchmen in opposing the operations of the civil power easily transcended differences of nationality.

The Statute of Kilkenny had nothing to say about the principle of episcopal consent to taxation. Its approach to the question of ecclesiastical liberty was generally formal and conservative though there were some points of originality. Its first clause was an affirmation that holy Church should be free and enjoy without injury all the liberties recognized in England and Ireland by the king and his forbears. If this was a conventional enough form of opening a statute, it should not be immediately concluded that it was an empty one. The first clause of *Magna Carta* was meaningful to churchmen in Ireland in this period, Irish as well as English. Archbishop Ralph O'Kelly had defended himself with the claim that by *Magna Carta* the Church was guaranteed all its liberties unharmed. It had decreed the *ipso facto* excommunication of those who violated these liberties, he claimed, and this was his authority for the steps he had taken.[1] ArchbishopThomas Minot of Dublin, one of the eight prelates who underwrote the Statute, also took *Magna Carta* seriously. He held a provincial council in Kilkenny at a date approximate to that of the parliament which promulgated the Statute.[2] The first constitution promulgated included a history of *Magna Carta* as a guarantee of ecclesiastical liberty from its reissue by Henry III to its confirmation by Edward I and reaffirmation by Edward III in the English parliament of April–May 1341.[3]

The Statute sought to strengthen the enforcement of respect for ecclesiastical liberty. Clause 1 continued with a provision that anyone who was excommunicated for violation of any of the liberties of the Church and did not make satisfaction should, after the requisite certification procedure had been used, be taken into custody by the secular power. Caption of excommunicates was of course a familiar enough procedure. What is new here, however, is the alteration of the period within which the delinquent must make satisfaction. Forty days was the usual period, established by custom of very long standing.[4] The Statute shortened it to a month.[5]

It is appropriate to notice at this point c. 9 of the Statute, which also was concerned with excommunication. It was there provided that those who had been excommunicated should not, on the points for which they had been excommunicated, be received into the favour of the king nor into *communion ou d'alliaunce* by the king's ministers. Nor should they be supported by any of the king's lieges, under pain of fine and imprisonment. It is clear that the prelates had influenced the Statute in the direction of strengthening the effectiveness of the Church's own weapon of defence of its liberties.

---

[1] *Loc. cit.* 349.

[2] The constitutions of this council were published by A. Gwynn, 'Provincial and diocesan decrees of the diocese of Dublin during the Anglo-Norman period' *Arch. hib.* 11 (1944) 90–117. Dr Hand has traced the provenance of some of them to Archbishop Stratford's London council of 1342 (Wilkins, *Concilia* 2. 702–9), 'The forgotten Statutes of Kilkenny' 305.

[3] Gwynn, 'Provincial and diocesan decrees of the diocese of Dublin' 92–3 with reference to 14 Edw. III St. 1 and 4.

[4] Cf. F. D. Logan, *Excommunication and the secular arm in medieval England* (1968) 72–3. The English custom of caption of excommunicates was specifically decreed for Ireland in 1227, *Cal. Docs. Irel. 1171–1251* 1481.

[5] The period apparently recognized also by c. 1 of Minot's constitutions, Gwynn, 'Provincial and diocesan decrees of the diocese of Dublin' 94.

Clause 1 had a third point to make about the liberty of the Church. It included a general affirmation that writs of prohibition would not be issued in cases where it was established that the ecclesiastical courts had jurisdiction and an assurance that in cases where prohibition was disputed, there should be no delay in allowing a bishop to make his case against it in the 'consultation' procedure. Recent legislation in England had contained comparable affirmations.

In c. 8 the Statute contained another general affirmation concerning respect for a major aspect of ecclesiastical liberty and laid down appropriate penalties of fine and restitution for its violation. No layman whatsoever was to take arbitrary action against tithes or any other type of spiritual property. Perhaps the Cashel controversy of 1346 was among the incidents which formed the background to this clause. But in a war-torn land, which was also a supply base for wars elsewhere, arbitrary seizure and extortion were obviously perennial threats to clerical incomes.

Clause 7 was classified above among those which looked to the preservation of public order. It is concerned with measures to suppress conspiracy, champerty, maintenance and the like. The Statute applied to Ireland those provisions concerning enquiry into these crimes by royal judges which had been decreed in the English statute 4 Edw. III c. 11. A clue to the immediate origin of the clause lies perhaps in Archbishop Minot's apparent reference to the same statute in c. 2 of his constitutions, where he laid penalties of *ipso facto* excommunication on all those guilty of these crimes. The Statute, however, went on to demand much more cooperation from prelates than that:

The archbishops and bishops of Ireland, each within his diocese, shall have letters patent of the king from his chancery of Ireland to enquire into the aforesaid articles at their discretion and thereupon to proceed against them by the appropriate penalties of the law of the Church and to certify into the chancery the names of those they have found guilty of those crimes so that the king may inflict due punishment on them, for the honour of God and holy Church, the rule of his laws and the preservation of his people.

It is appropriate at this point to notice another contemporary practical expedient for harnessing clerical support in the maintenance of public order. The Statute's c. 7 had been concerned with the co-operation of the clergy *inter Anglicos*. Archbishop Minot's provincial council promulgated legislation on the same topic, but this time concerning the clergy *inter Hibernicos*. Though the province of Dublin contained some of the most anglicized parts of the Irish Church, there still remained considerable numbers of native Irish interspersed among the settlers, still preserving the basic structure of their own society and culture. Naturally these 'nations of the Irish' under their own *capitanei*, had their own Irish clergy. But it was a clergy which generally speaking would be ordained by Anglo-Irish or English bishops and was jurisdictionally subject to them. The Dublin provincial council of 1366 attempted to make this clergy an instrument of peace:

Because priests and other clergy serving churches and chapels among the Irish contribute greatly to the lawlessness and crime of the Irish, sometimes by expressly giving evil advice, commonly by tacit consent, approval and tolerance, we decree and command by authority of this council, the following. If rulers of the Irish, parishioners of these clergy, rise in war against the Church and the peace of the king and his faithful people, in violation of their oaths about keeping the peace and against the admonitions of ecclesiastical law issued to them by their prelates that they must desist and abstain from war, should they refuse so to refrain or stop, then their rectors, vicars, parish priests and other clergy who minister among them shall denounce this refusal to their prelates and on the command of their prelates, shall publicly excommunicate them, suspend them and forbid them entry into church. They shall add further weight to these ecclesiastical censures by forbidding intercourse with them and make them heavier still by leaving their society, so that mass shall not be celebrated for them nor any sacrament of the Church be ministered to them, other than the sacraments of penance and baptism of infants until through the command and decree of the Church they shall be led to return to the unity of peace. Rectors, vicars, parish priests and other clergy living among the Irish who act against these instructions and encourage malefactors in their evil ways or assist them, shall on the judgment of their local ordinaries be suspended from office and the fruits of their benefices sequestrated and put to pious uses, as he or whoever acts in his place shall judge best.

The council sought also to ensure that the Irishmen who were ordained were politically reliable. It required them to take an oath not to support rebellion against the Crown. The constitution already cited continued:

Further, by authority of the present council, we command and decree that for the future, ordinands of pure Irish nationality of our diocese and province shall be presumed to have lived continuously among evil people and to come from an evil background until witnesses or letters are brought to prove the contrary and that they are of moral and honourable family. They shall be required to take an oath in the presence of whoever ordains them that for the future they will not go treacherously to war against the peace of the Irish Church, the king and his faithful people nor give advice or help or encouragement to those who do go to war. Should they do so, they will incur *ipso facto* sentence of major excommunication with absolution reserved to the diocesan bishop or whoever acts for him.[1]

This legislation draws attention to the real nature of the problem about Irish clergy, as English officialdom saw it. There were two distinct aspects of it. There was, firstly, the question of the loyalty of those priests whose pastoral care lay among the native Irish, and it was with these that Archbishop Minot and his colleagues were concerned. There was, secondly, the question of the conduct of Irish clergy whose ministry lay among the English. It was with these that the Statute was concerned. Clause 3 makes it clear that there were Irish clergy working among the English. It commanded:

Those holding benefices of holy Church among the English shall use the English language and if they do not do so, their ordinaries shall have the issues of their benefices until they do use the English language in the manner aforesaid. They shall have respite in order to learn the English language, and to equip themselves with saddles, between now and the next feast of St. Michael.

This ordinance is to be read as a more explicit formulation of an existing policy. This had been defined in 1360 when Edward III had ruled that while it was forbidden for anyone of native Irish birth to hold an official position in any town, borough or castle or the like, Irish clergy of proved loyalty were not to be excluded from any ecclesiastical office or benefice.[2]

---

[1] *Loc. cit.* 100–1.

[2] *Stat. Irel. John–Henry V* 420–1. This was a withdrawal from a royal instruction of 20 July 1359 which had forbidden the appointment of Irishmen to canonries, prebends and benefices among the English, *Cal. Cl. Rolls 1354–60* 575–6.

Clause 3, however, was far from saying the Statute's last word on the place of the Irish clergy among the English. That clause was concerned with the position already in being, with those who already held benefices. The Statute apparently looked further ahead to a position where no Irishman should hold a benefice at all. Clause 13 laid down the principle:

Further, it is ordained that no Irishman of the nations of the Irish shall be admitted into any cathedral or collegiate church by provision, collation or presentation of anyone, nor to any benefice of holy Church amongst the English of that land; and that if any be admitted, instituted or inducted into such a benefice, it shall be deemed to be void and the king shall have the presentation to the benefice in that vacancy, no matter to whom the advowson of the benefice may belong, saving their right to present or make collation in future vacancies.

Here undoubtedly is a change of policy. It was a change, probably, that brought policy closer to what had long been the practice of many Anglo-Irish ecclesiastical bodies, which had, for example, ensured that the cathedral chapters of the province of Dublin were strictly Anglo-Irish preserves. Nevertheless it is permissible to doubt that it was enforced simply as a flat prohibition. It seems much more likely that while the veto would in some circumstances be rigorously enforced, in others it might be dispensed from by virtue of that discretionary power over the enforcement of laws of this type which the king or his representative might exercise. There is later statutory evidence that licences for Irishmen to hold benefices among the English were in fact granted by the king's lieutenant.[1] It is very likely that the practice was known before the earliest date (1416) of this evidence, as it was certainly known, witness the evidence of the 1360 ordinance, before the Statute.[2]

Clause 14 presents an exactly analogous problem of interpreting the degree of concordance between statutory theory and actual practice. It was concerned with a very familiar problem:

Further, it is ordained and established that no religious house, exempt or not, situate among the English, shall for the future receive any Irishmen

---

[1] Cf. the examples collected by Hardiman, *A statute of the fortieth year of King Edward III* 46–8.

[2] The Act of 1416 re-enacted the position of c. 13 without, however, succeeding in stopping its circumvention either by the issue of letters of licence or probably more usually, by grant of English legal status.

as professed religious but may receive Englishmen without any consideration of whether they were born in England or in Ireland under pain of seizure of temporalities.

Here again, this has every appearance of being a new policy. It has already been seen that English official policy had supported the principle of mixed nationality houses and the one official express departure from it, in 1310, by Anglo-Irish authority, had been quickly countermanded from England. Further, there had been a very explicit reiteration of the same principle by Edward III when he cancelled an attempt to restate the 1310 exclusion principle and allowed those native Irish who were faithful subjects to be admitted into religious houses among the English.[1] In this context too, however, there is later evidence to suggest that the flat prohibition of the Statute did not make any very considerable change from the position before it. There is evidence that procedure for licensing the presence of native Irishmen in houses considered to be English remained in being after the Statute, and even after its reissue in 1380.[2] The same evidence establishes what could readily be believed *a priori*, that both the statutory prohibition and the dispensatory licence were often ignored.

It remains to consider the ecclesiastical personalities connected with the promulgation of the Statute.

Three metropolitans were present at Kilkenny. The absence of the archbishop of Armagh was no accident. As long as the primates were not allowed to have their primatial crosses borne before them in the province of Dublin they would not set foot in it and the Crown continued to give them permission to absent themselves from parliaments held in that province. Far from dying down after Armagh ceased to have native Irish archbishops, the primatial controversy had flared afresh in the fourteenth century. It had been reopened when Roland Jorz of Armagh (1311–22) had tried to have his cross carried in Dublin and had been abruptly evicted from the province by Archbishop John Lech (1311–13).[3] Alexander Bicknor (1317–

---

[1] *Stat. Irel. John–Henry V* 420–1.
[2] Cf. the examples given by Hardiman, *A statute of the fortieth year of King Edward III* 49 from 1385. The topic needs further investigation.
[3] *Ann. St. Mary's Dublin* 1313: 'Frater Rolandus Joce, Primas Ardmachanus, applicuit in insula de Houth, in crastino Annunciationis Beate Marie, de nocte surgens furtive

45) was apparently the first archbishop of Dublin since Henry of London to style himself *primas Hiberniae*,[1] and though Armagh fought back vigorously in the person of the formidable Richard FitzRalph (1346–60),[2] the archbishops of Dublin conceded not an inch. Papal and royal attempts to resolve this damaging conflict were unsuccessful, though both had already arrived at the formula which was finally to be accepted: Armagh to be *primas totius Hiberniae* and Dublin, *primas Hiberniae*, a solution already adopted in the analogous Canterbury–York dispute.[3] Meanwhile, however, Milo Sweetman (1361–80) and Thomas Minot (1361–75) continued the controversy.[4]

levando crucem suam, illam portavit usque Prioratum de Gratia Dei. Cui occurrebant quidam de familiaribus Archiepiscopi Dublin illam crucem deponendo, et ipsum Ardmachanum tanquam confusum a Lagenia effugarunt' *Chart. St. Mary's, Dublin RS.* 2. 342.

[1] Cf. the proemium to his provincial constitutions of *c.* 1320, A. Gwynn, 'Provincial and diocesan decrees of the diocese of Dublin' *Arch. hib.* 11 (1944) 71. If his were the definitive adoption of the title, this would perhaps explain the otherwise rather odd remark made by Archbishop John Alen in 1529 about the history of the controversy about the primacy, that 'it was brought to an end in the time of Archbishop Alexander'. Presumably he meant that it ended any doubts there might be in Dublin about Dublin's status, *Cal. Abp Alen's Reg.* 217. But it must be observed that neither of Archbishop Alexander de Bicknor's two successors used the title when promulgating their provincial constitutions, Gwynn, *art. cit.* 84, 91.

[2] FitzRalph got Edward III to recognize his right to have his cross borne before him in Dublin, a recognition which led to considerable unrest there and its eventual retraction, *Cal. Abp Alen's Reg.* 207–8.

[3] Archbishop Alen reported: 'While I was at Rome eleven years as proctor of the most reverend lord William, archbishop of Canterbury, primate of all England, as I was reading in Innocent VI's Register in the pope's private library the suits and other controversies there pending, I discovered entirely by chance that the beforementioned suit had been settled by the pope's authority and with the approval of the college of cardinals in the following form, namely that each should be primate but for distinction in writing the archbishop of Armagh should entitle himself primate of all Ireland, and the Metropolitan of Dublin should style himself primate of Ireland after the manner (says the sovereign pontiff) of the archbishops of Canterbury and York in England, the first of whom writes himself primate of all England, and the other writes primate of England' *Cal. Abp Alen's Reg.* 217. The original of this alleged papal decision (there seems no reason to doubt Alen's good faith) has not so far come to light. For Edward III's recommendations about the adoption of the Canterbury–York solution, cf. H. J. Lawlor, 'A calendar of the register of Archbishop Sweteman' *PRIA* 29 (1911) 213–310 nos. 16, 17; *Cal. Abp Alen's Reg.* 216.

[4] *Cal. Abp Sweteman's Reg.* 20 (22 October 1363). Among the other pacificatory functions the King had assigned to the duke of Clarence was that of acting as mediator between the two archbishops.

The absence of any suffragan bishop for the province of Tuam, now for the most part beyond the reach of the common law, was to be expected. The presence of only one from the province of Dublin was much less predictable. Killaloe, Cloyne, Waterford and Lismore gave Cashel the largest representation.

The official element was prominent. Minot himself, an Englishman and an Oxford graduate, was a senior Irish Exchequer official for at least six years before his appointment to the see of Dublin.[1] Thomas Reeve, Anglo-Irish, canon of Lismore, was to become Irish chancellor in 1367.[2] John Young, also Anglo-Irish, treasurer of Leighlin chapter, was to serve for two short spells during his long pontificate as Irish deputy treasurer.[3] These are very typical members of the Anglo-Irish episcopate. The bishop of Cloyne, John de Swaffham, was a more rare type. An English Carmelite and a Cambridge doctor of theology, later as bishop of Bangor (1367–98), he was to make his mark as a forceful opponent of the opinions of John Wyclif.[4]

Little though we know of these Anglo-Irish and English bishops, there is even less to be known about the three Irishmen whose support for the policy of national discrimination in the Statute is not the least intriguing feature of the history of episcopal attitudes to politics in medieval Ireland. What is known suggests that they are, in an Irish way, as typical as the bishop–officials are in an English way. Thomas MacCarwill was the fourth member of his family to be archbishop of Cashel in a period rather longer than a century. Thomas O'Cormacain was the third of his family to be appointed bishop of Killaloe in very much the same period.[5] There was a close link between Cashel and Tuam which at least in part drew its strength from family associations. Thomas MacCarwill, archdeacon of Cashel, had been elected to Tuam in 1349 and held that see until his translation to Cashel in 1365. He was succeeded at Tuam by

1 Emden, *Biographical Register, Oxford* 3. 2199; Richardson and Sayles, *Administration of Ireland* 103, 113, 128.
2 Ware, *Works* 554; Richardson and Sayles, *Administration of Ireland* 97. It was during his pontificate that Lismore and Waterford were finally united.
3 Ware, *Works* 458.
4 Ibid. 577; Emden, *Biographical Register, Cambridge* 569.
5 For his *curriculum vitae*, Gleeson in Gleeson and Gwynn, *Diocese of Killaloe* 367–71.

another archdeacon of Cashel, John O'Grady.[1] There is very suggestive evidence of a strong bond of union between these three Munster ecclesiastical families.[2] More unexpectedly, it appears very likely that some of the members of these families also had in common a training at the university of Oxford.[3] All in all, considering these links, we are perhaps entitled to conclude that the appearance of these bishops at the Kilkenny parliament and their support of the Statute was a considered joint policy, not a merely fortuitous association of three individuals. It represented an attitude to the Crown consistent with attitudes commonly adopted by archbishops of Cashel and bishops of Killaloe in the past. Whatever steps towards total separation of native Irish from Anglo-Irish clergy were being taken in the fourteenth century, no iron curtain had come to divide the episcopate into two irreconcilable parts. But the trend towards that position had grown very pronounced.

Judged overall from the ecclesiastical standpoint, the Statute of Kilkenny with its related legislation, lay and ecclesiastical, may be seen as being but the latest instalment of various processes whose history goes back to the earliest days of the colony.

There is to be seen, still operative, that continuous process whereby the common law understanding of the relationship of the Church and civil power was adapted, modified and adjusted to changing circumstances. The experience in colonial Ireland of this process for

---

[1] Ware, *Works* and *Hbk Brit. Chron.* supply the appropriate information.

[2] Gleeson, in Gleeson and Gwynn, *Diocese of Killaloe* 369.

[3] A Nicholas O'Grady of the Killaloe diocese, a canonist, was certainly at Oxford, on the evidence of a papal dispensation, *Cal. Pap. Pet.* I. 19, Emden, *Biographical Register, Oxford* 2. 1393. John O'Grady, the archbishop of Tuam, was a bachelor of canon law, but his university is uncertain. Emden has claimed him for Oxford, *op. cit.* 3 (Appendix) 2203 as 'one of [those] whom it is fair to assume ... pursued at least part of their academical studies at Oxford'; a plausible conjecture in this case, since he was clearly a near relation of Nicholas and because there was an established link between the Killaloe clergy and the university of Oxford. The bishop of Killaloe, Thomas O'Cormacain who with Nicholas O'Grady was a protégé of Archbishop MacCarwill, was also a canon law graduate of an unknown university, which Gleeson, *Diocese of Killaloe* 369, has very reasonably presumed to be Oxford. Emden has overlooked this bishop. There was nothing new about a connexion between the diocese of Killaloe and the university of Oxford. At least two of its bishops, Matthew O Hogain (1268–84) and Maurice O Hogain (1282–98) had apparently studied here (Emden *op. cit.* 3. 2204). There is no record of Archbishop Thomas MacCarwill's being at Oxford though there was a connexion between his family and the university, Emden *op. cit.* 2. 1199–2000; 3. 2193.

the most part mirrored developments in England. *In singulis obser-vatio similis regnum colligaret utrumque* was no less the guiding principle in the reign of Edward III than it had been in the reign of Henry II. But the days when the episcopate sought to achieve significant change in principle and practice were over. Rumbles of episcopal discontent there were from time to time, particularly when royal taxation was in the offing. Nevertheless, in the fourteenth century, each power seemed reasonably satisfied with the mutual accommodation of respective interests which the common law had come to enshrine.

If the volume of clerical protest against violation of the liberty of the Church had died down in the fourteenth century, the Crown, for its part, showed a heightened awareness of the Church's potential as a political instrument. It was, of course, one of the great truisms of medieval political thinking that it was God's will that the powers should cooperate. The common law had its own procedures by means of which this principle could be implemented in practice, some of which it shared with the rest of Christendom and some of which it had devised for itself. One important aspect of this cooperation had preservation of the peace as its purpose. There was always a spiritual arm to royal authority. In Ireland, particular attention was given to making the Church useful in deterring rebellion and promoting loyalty to the Crown. The pope, the hierarchy, the diocesan clergy, Anglo-Irish and Irish, the religious orders were all in different ways called upon to play their part in this process. Excommunication should fall on the king's enemies and his laws were to carry spiritual as well as temporal sanctions. The national composition of the episcopate, of the priesthood, of cathedral chapters, of religious orders was to be regulated, as never before, to preserve English power. The very diocesan structure was to be remodelled for the same purpose. Ecclesiastical court, pulpit, confessional were all to be put to the service of the royal cause. However, in mid-fourteenth century, these expedients were the symptoms of governmental weakness. The spiritual arm might be an effective adjunct to the efficient police measures of the civil power. It most certainly could not be a substitute for them.

The rôle of the papacy in Anglo-Irish relations calls for more specific consideration. It had countenanced the Anglo-French

Invasion of Ireland and continued to support the *dominium* of the king of England. This had certain practical consequences. It meant that the introduction into Ireland of the common law system with all its implications for the relations of the two jurisdictions had papal approval, tacit or explicit, at least in its main lines. The papacy continued to act in accordance with this first approval. But it did not play a major rôle as an adjunct of English power. The Crown was likely to find that any voice it might raise at the papal curia about particular cases, episcopal appointments for example, was heeded. It could count, too, on general political support, for what that was worth. Popes were ready enough to instruct the Irish about their political duty and threaten those who refused to take any notice with sentences of excommunication. On the other hand, popes did not countenance *acceptio personarum*, they protested against infringements of *libertas ecclesie* and occasionally condemned other English malpractices. It was open to any Irish prelate or prince to lay his grievances before the universal ordinary and many did so. English kings were thus from time to time rebuked for what they had done or failed to do in Ireland. But the effectiveness of such papal action depended entirely on the conscience of him who received the admonition. Nothing occurred which brought seriously into question the *de jure* principle of papal support for English lordship. Nothing that the papacy did, or could do, halted the *de facto* decline of that lordship.

That attempts to use the Church as a buttress of royal power had the support of the English and Anglo-Irish section of the episcopate will not cause surprise. That such attempts were often conceived and always promoted by the clergy of the colony may be readily believed, especially when the Dublin administration contained such a significant clerical element. The more interesting phenomenon is that such expedients commanded a not insignificant degree of support from the native clergy. The Statute of Kilkenny presents us with the spectacle, by no means unique, of Irish bishops underwriting with their spiritual sanctions the legislation of the colonial administration. This time, Irish bishops, including the two senior of them, were giving their support to a policy (laid down in c. 13) by which their fellow-countrymen were excluded from monasteries, benefices and offices. Herewith the Statute of Kilkenny highlighted that most fundamental problem of all: the relationship between the colonists and the native Irish clergy.

By the period of the Statute of Kilkenny, it was manifest that the sort of integration of the peoples that had been brought about in England through comprehensive conquest had not been paralleled in Ireland. Part only of Ireland had been colonized and political instability was endemic in this *terre Engleis*. It followed from the incompleteness of conquest and the unevenness of the English hold within the allegedly conquered areas, that Irish clergy did not adopt any uniform attitude towards the English authorities. Neat classifications are rarely in order amid the turbulence of the medieval Irish scene. The positions adopted by Irish churchmen towards the Crown went the whole gamut from complete independence to full cooperation. In general terms, however, it is true that so far as the colonists were concerned, there were three main categories of Irish clergy.

There were those, firstly, outside the confines of the colony, who went their own ways virtually unaffected by the English who had no access to these regions. Even in the days of the colony's health, anglicization had touched these parts scarcely at all. Abbot Stephen of Lexington, for example, had recognized that he had no choice but to leave certain of the Cistercian houses of Connacht and Ulster with their own Irish superiors, at a time when other Irish houses were being given foreign abbots. When the colony was at its apogee, Edward I's attempts to assert his rights in five dioceses of the Armagh province met with minimal success. Any reduction of the independence of this category of Irish clergy grew increasingly less likely as the fourteenth century wore on.

The second category was composed of all those Irish clergy who lived within the colonized area or had contact with them: their different degrees of independence were treated with a proportionate amount of suspicion by the English authorities. Most distrusted of these were the regular clergy who sought to exclude all save Irishmen from their monasteries and friaries. Such discrimination was read automatically as the overt symptom of disloyalty to the Crown. Hardly less suspect were those who ministered to the Irish in the marches or in the Irish enclaves *inter Anglicos*. They were suspect as spies or fomenters of rebellion or harbourers of rebels and felons. The English civil and ecclesiastical authorities did their best to control dissident and potentially dissident elements. Obviously control did not become any easier when the colony continued to decline.

In the third category ranked those Irish clergy who conformed to certain conditions in order to live and work *inter Anglicos*. What the English authorities wanted to operate was a system of licensing or controlled entry analogous to that which obtained for Irishmen *inter Anglicos* in the civil capacity. An Irishman could be accorded reception to English law—in effect, granted English citizenship. He would undertake to keep the peace, be loyal to the king of England, learn to speak English, follow English customs. A priest would be allowed to remain *inter Anglicos* if he complied with such conditions, otherwise he was excluded from benefice or office. Though there were Irish bishops still prepared to promote this policy, it is not to be expected that the numbers of Irish clergy in this category should have been on the increase in the second half of the fourteenth century.

This study began at a point in time when a note of optimism was sounding strongly throughout the ecclesiastical life of Ireland. A reform movement, revolutionary in some at least of its spiritual, disciplinary and organizational facets, was revitalizing the Church, making progress despite formidable difficulties. It ends in a period when that note had long since faded and bleak pessimism had become the prevailing mood. The lamentable condition of the Irish Church by the fourteenth century stands typified in the state of three of its major sections: diocesan clergy, monks and friars. The enfeeblement of Armagh, the frequent estrangements of the metropolitans, divisions in the episcopate generally, meant that the *ecclesia hibernicana* had neither constitutional nor any other sort of unity. The Cistercian order, one of the most promising developments of the twelfth century reform, was racked with conflict between the nations. The Franciscans, whose outstanding progress in the first part of the thirteenth century testifies to the continuance of reform even after the Invasion, were in their turn victims of the same canker. It would be wrong to suggest that all the strife which was tearing at the heart of the Irish Church had as its primary cause conflict between the two nations. Grounds of dispute abounded: in Ireland no less than in other countries, rivalries of ecclesiastical jurisdictions, both in relation to each other and in relation to civil jurisdictions, were a fertile seed-bed of sharp, often bitter, even violent controversy. But in Ireland where the natural antagonisms of invaded and invader were never assuaged, this endemic conflict, even when not itself the direct cause of dispute, was always a poison to fester the sores of other frictions.

Appendix 1

CANTERBURY'S CLAIM TO PRIMACY OVER IRELAND

From 1074 until its promotion to the status of an archbishopric in 1152, Dublin acknowledged its subjection to Canterbury. Each of the five bishops whose pontificates cover this period was consecrated by the archbishop of Canterbury after first rendering a profession of faith and an oath of obedience. The precise form of this oath evolved somewhat. The first of the series, that of Bishop Patrick to Lanfranc in 1074, ran as follows:

Whoever rules over others must not think it beneath him if he himself is sub-ordinate to others; but rather let him humbly show to those who are appointed over him, in all things and for the love of God, that obedience which he wishes to receive from his own subjects. Wherefore I, Patrick, who have been chosen to rule Dublin, the capital city of Ireland, do hand to thee, my reverend father Lanfranc, primate of Britain [*Britanniarum primas*] and archbishop of the holy church of Canterbury, this charter of my profession; and I promise that I shall obey thee and thy successors in all things which pertain to the Christian religion.[1]

This version was severely pruned when Lanfranc consecrated Donngus in 1085. The title *Britanniarum primas* was dropped.[2]

The oath was standardized by Anselm in 1096 at the consecration of Samuel, the form being retained at the other Irish episcopal consecrations at which he officiated, as well as for Bishop Gregory consecrated by Ralph d'Escures in 1121:

[1] The text, edited by Ussher, *Sylloge* 564 is: 'Quisquis aliis subjaceat, dedignari non debet: sed potius obedientiam quam a subjectis suis desiderat habere, propter Deum studeat praelatis sibi per omnia humiliter exhibere. Propterea ego Patricius, ad regendam Dublinam metropolem Hiberniae electus antistes, tibi, reverende pater Lanfrance, Britanniarum primas et sanctae Dorobernensis ecclesiae archiepis-cope, professionis meae chartam porrigo: meque tibi tuisque successoribus in omnibus, quae ad Christianam religionem pertinent, obtemperaturum esse pro-mitto.' The translation is that of A. Gwynn, 'Lanfranc and the Irish Church' *IER* 57 (1941) 498.

[2] 'Ego Donatus, Dublinensis Ecclesiae antistes, quae in Hibernia sita est; canonicam obedientiam tibi promitto et successoribus tuis, o Lanfrance, sanctae Dorobernensis ecclesiae archiepiscope' Ussher, *Sylloge* 564.

Appendix 1

I, Samuel, having been chosen for the rule of the Church of Dublin, which is situated in Ireland, and being about to be consecrated by thee, reverend father Anselm, archbishop of the holy church of Canterbury and primate of all Britain [*totius Britanniae primas*], do promise that I shall keep canonical obedience in all things to thee and all thy successors.[1]

Obedience to Canterbury was professed also by Malchus, first bishop of Waterford to Anselm in 1097, though no other bishop of this see seems to have followed his example.[2] Another Norse–Irish bishopric was established about this time, Limerick, but its bishop, Gilbert, was not consecrated by Anselm.[3] A later bishop of Limerick, Patrick, was consecrated at Canterbury, though it seems likely that he did not secure possession of his see.[4] Both Malchus and Patrick professed canonical submission to the *totius Britanniae primas*, in the formula devised by Anselm.[5]

These oaths promise full obedience and it is obedience to the see of Canterbury, not to the persons of Lanfranc or Anselm. Both these archbishops saw their relationship to Irish bishops in the same way; if the form of oath adopted by Anselm is just possibly a shade less emphatic than that used by Lanfranc in 1074, there is no real difference of substance. *Britanniae* and *tota Britannia* are equivalent terms and significance should not be read into the adoption of the one rather than the other.

The oath stands as the one tangible manifestation of the primatial authority, for other marks of dependence—attendance at provincial councils, exercise of appellate jurisdiction, for example—are totally lacking. That Irish dioceses, particularly Dublin, received help from the archbishops of Canterbury in the form of consecrations, advice and instruction, gifts of books and church ornaments, the despatching of

1 'Ego Samuel, ad regimen ecclesiae Dublinensis quae sita est in Hibernia electus, et a te, reverende pater Anselme, sanctae Cantuariensis ecclesiae archiepiscope, et totius Britanniae primas, antistes consecrandus; tibi et omnibus successoribus tuis canonicam obedientiam me per omnia servaturum promitto' Ussher, *Sylloge* 565.

2 Ussher, *Sylloge* 565. Cf. also Eadmer, *Hist. nov.* 76–7 where it is made clear that canonical examination of the elect took place: 'Electum ergo pontificem diligenter in iis quae sacra iubet auctoritas examinatum . . .' Eadmer also makes clear that he read the request for Malchus's consecration from Murtagh O'Brien and four Irish bishops as a recognition of Canterbury's primacy: '. . . petentes quatinus ipse [Anselm], primatus quem super eos gerebat potestate et qua fungebatur vicis apostolicae fretus auctoritate . . .'

3 Gilbert had written to Anselm to tell him that he was bishop of Limerick as Anselm's acknowledgment of this information makes clear, *PL* 159 Ep. 143. 174–5.

4 Cf. A. Gwynn, 'The diocese of Limerick in the Twelfth Century' *North Munster Antiquarian Journal* 5 (1946–7) 35–48 at 40.

5 Ussher, *Sylloge* 565–6.

monks,[1] is not in itself evidence of a claim to primatial authority. The services of the archbishops of Canterbury had been used in this way at an earlier period by the bishops of Scandinavia without their thereby incurring canonical subjection.[2] As four of the six bishops of Irish dioceses who were consecrated by the archbishops of Canterbury were formerly monks in the Canterbury province it is not surprising that with difficult circumstances in Ireland, they should have recourse to Canterbury. That there should be intercourse between Canterbury and Dublin need occasion no surprise. What, however, stands in need of explanation is why Canterbury could claim a primacy and exact an oath of obedience in return for services rendered.

On what grounds did the archbishops of Canterbury lay claim to primatial authority over Ireland?

The texts of the oaths of submission offer no evidence on this score. Neither do the letters sent by Lanfranc and Anselm to different people in Ireland; there is not a mention of a primacy in them, not even in the title each archbishop used of himself. No circumstances arose in which an archbishop of Canterbury found it necessary to justify his primacy in response to any Irish challenge. There is no source which bears directly on the subject. But Ireland is mentioned very occasionally as an incidental detail in the dossier of the great controversy between Canterbury and York about the primacy of Britain. It is among the material relating to that struggle that we must look for the answer to our question.

Lanfranc began the fight to assert the supremacy of Canterbury in 1070 when he demanded of the archbishop-elect of York, Thomas of Bayeux, an oath of obedience to Canterbury as a condition of his consecration. It was thought in York that in addition to gratification of personal ambition,[3] his main object was a political one. He saw the ecclesiastical unification of Britain as an essential precondition of the due subjugation of the 'fickle and treacherous Yorkshiremen'.[4] Modern

1 Nothing is known in detail about these gifts nor of the sending of monks. That they were sent by Lanfranc to Bishop Donatus is known only because Anselm had occasion to reprove Donatus' successor, Samuel, for disposing of books, vestments and other church ornaments as if they were his own property, and for expelling monks from his church at Dublin. *PL* 159 Ep. 72. 109–10.

2 Cf. F. Barlow, *The English Church 1000–1066. A constitutional history* (1963) 233.

3 Hugh the Chantor, *The History of the Church of York:* 'Audistis immanem et superbam prelacionis et elacionis ambicionem' ed. with transl. C. Johnson (1961) 4.

4 Hugh the Chantor: 'porro utile esse ad regni utilitatem et firmitatem conservandam ut Britannia tota uni quasi primati subderetur; alioquin contingere posse, vel suo vel successorum suorum tempore, ut de Dacis, seu Norensibus, sive Scotis, qui Eboracam navigio venientes regnum infestare solebant, unus ab Eboracensi archi-

Appendix 1

judgments of Lanfranc's motives have mitigated the severity of this inevitably subjective view in pointing out that there were undoubted advantages for reform progress in this projected ecclesiastical centralization[1] and that the strengthening of primatial sees for this purpose was at this very period a fairly universal phenomenon.[2]

Lanfranc alleged that the swearing of such an oath as he was demanding from Thomas was an established custom. Thomas denied this.[3] He allowed himself to be persuaded—'misled by bad advice and terrified by threats', said Hugh the Chantor[4] —to agree to swear obedience to Lanfranc, whilst reserving his position and that of his successors towards the see of Canterbury. Inevitably the matter was taken to Rome, where Alexander II in effect evaded the issue with all its difficult political by-products, by referring the dispute back to England. The matter, it was ruled, was one of history. Decision could only follow the discovery of the ancient traditions of the Church, a task entrusted to the churchmen of the kingdom aided by a papal legate.[5] This ruling of the Pope began a large-scale research operation into the history of the origins of the sees of Canterbury and York and their relations which continued for half a century. Many sources were pressed into service, some legitimately so, but others, as the heat was turned on, not so legitimately. It is as well to say at this point that forged

episcopo et a provincie illius indigenis mobilibus et perfidis rex crearetur, et sic regnum turbatum scinderetur' *ibid.* 3.

[1] Z. N. Brooke, *The English Church and the Papacy* (1931) 119–20.

[2] R. W. Southern: 'It was just at this time that primatial claims similar to those of Lanfranc were being asserted by the archbishops of Rheims, Lyons, Mainz and Hamburg; and it must have seemed to many that the future ordering of church discipline lay in the hands of metropolitan overlords of this type.' 'The Canterbury Forgeries.' *EHR* 73 (1958) 193–226 at 206.

[3] Hugh the Chantor, *The History of the Church of York* 2–4; *Chron. pont. eccl. Ebor.*, *Historians of the Church of York* ed. J. Raine *RS* (1886) 2. 357–8.

[4] *Ibid.* 4.

[5] The sources for Alexander II's instructions and their fulfilment are: (1) Lanfranc's own account given in a letter to the pope, J. A. Giles ed., *Beati Lanfranci Opera* (1844) 1. 23–7 and in a rather shortened form, William of Malmesbury, *Gesta pontificum Anglorum RS* 44–6. (2) The form of composition drawn up between Lanfranc and Thomas of York and signed by William I, his queen, the papal legate, the two archbishops and four bishops, ed. J. B. Sheppard, *Literae Cantuarienses RS* 3. 351–2. (3) Another text of this composition, with an additional sentence in the text and a much longer list of witnesses, Eadmer, *Hist. nov.* 252–4. The difference between these two versions of the composition began the investigation of H. Boehmer which led him to the conclusion that Lanfranc had been guilty of the forgery of documents to prove his case, *Die Fälschungen Erzbischof Lanfranks von Canterbury* (Leipzig 1902). For an authoritative review of the whole question, including the complete exoneration of Lanfranc, cf. R. W. Southern, 'The Canterbury Forgeries'.

papal privileges which came to be adduced in Canterbury's favour are not relevant to the Irish issue.

The first part of the great historical debate came to an end in 1072, when, before York had marshalled her forces, Lanfranc had demonstrated to the satisfaction of both king and pope that his case for the all-Britain primacy of Canterbury was historically well-founded. For the nature of his arguments we must rely on the summary account he presented by letter to Alexander II. Primary among them was Bede's *Ecclesiastical History* which told of the mission of Augustine to England, of Pope Gregory I's instructions concerning the diocesan structure to be established there and concerning Augustine's jurisdiction, of the early history of the see of Canterbury. It was this source only which yielded anything material to Canterbury–Irish relations. Ireland entered the story as a detail not without significance but nevertheless very incidentally to the main issue. That it was mentioned at all was not because Lanfranc thought it of any urgency to vindicate claims over Ireland which in any case had not yet in 1072 been asserted in practice, but because it helped to buttress his argument against York. The more geographically extensive his primacy, the more impressive its solidity.

As this Bede reference is the only one in the whole primacy debate which affords any clue to the grounds on which the primacy over Ireland was based, it must be stated in full:

In the council which you [Alexander II] had ordered to be held in England where the complaints of Archbishop Thomas were presented and discussed, there was cited the Ecclesiastical History of the English People written by the doctor of the English, Bede, who was a priest of the church of York: different extracts were read and in general agreement [*pace omnium*] it was shown that from the time of the blessed Augustine, first archbishop of Canterbury down to the time of Bede himself, that is to say, about 140 years, my predecessors have exercised primacy over the church of York, over the whole of the island called Britain, as well as over Ireland and pastoral care over all . . .[1]

Lanfranc did not specify which passages from Bede he had in mind, and at

---

[1] 'In concilio quod Angliae per vestram auctoritatem coactum est ubi querelae Thomae archiepiscopi prolatae et ventilatae sunt allata est ecclesiastica gentis Anglorum historia, quam Eboracensis ecclesiae presbyter, et Anglorum doctor, Beda composuit; lectae sententiae, quibus pace omnium demonstratum est a tempore beati Augustini, primi Doroberensis archiepiscopi, usque ad ipsius Bedae ultimam aetatem, quod fere centum et xltᵃ annorum spatio terminatur, antecessores meos super Eboracensem ecclesiam, totamque insulam quam Britanniam vocant, necnon et Hiberniam, primatum gessisse, curam pastoralem omnibus impendisse . . .' William of Malmesbury, *Gesta pont.* 44.

least one investigator has denied that there was any passage which would bear the construction placed upon it by him.[1]

There is, however, one source which helps to reveal how Lanfranc could read a case for Canterbury's authority in Ireland and indeed helps to clarify Lanfranc's reading of Bede about the primacy generally. In 1119 in circumstances that are not relevant to the present examination, Archbishop Ralph d'Escures went over the ground again, in a letter to Calixtus II, rehearsing all the arguments for Canterbury's claim.[2] His presentation of the case is very similar to Lanfranc's but it was presented in much more detailed form. Where Lanfranc was content to summarize Bede, Ralph quoted chapter and verse *in extenso*. It is unlikely that his selection of texts and their interpretation would differ very substantially from Lanfranc's. But there is no need to try to put Ralph's words on to Lanfranc's pen. It is sufficient to use them as a general guide to the elucidation of Lanfranc's thinking on the Irish primacy question. When they have all been scrutinized for their significance from this point of view, two in particular call for examination.

The first was the reply of Gregory I to a query put to him by Augustine: 'How ought we to act towards the bishops of the provinces of Gaul (*Galliarum*) and Britain (*Britanniarum*)?' The Pope replied that he should have no authority in Gaul, 'But as for all the bishops of Britain [*Britanniarum vero omnes episcopos*], we commit them to your care, that the unlearned may be taught, the weak strengthened by persuasion, and the perverse corrected by authority'.[3] Here surely is the origin of Lanfranc's title *Britanniarum primas* used in the submissions of Thomas of Bayeux and Bishop Patrick of Dublin. Ralph d'Escures explained the use of the plural form *Britanniarum* as denoting the various provinces and linguistic divisions of the island (in the singular) of Britain.[4] We may note that there is thus an implicit claim to the authorization of Pope Gregory for this primacy. But was Lanfranc also claiming papal authority for a primacy over Ireland by including it among the *Britanniae*? The evidence is inconclusive. Ralph d'Escures clearly did not include Ireland in the plural form. On the other hand, Lanfranc's use of it in Bishop Patrick's oath of submission might

1 'No single text in Bede, it need hardly be said, can be quoted as historical justification for this claim', A. Gwynn, 'Lanfranc and the Irish Church' *IER* 57 (1941) 481–500 at 491.
2 Printed by J. Raine, *Historians of the Church of York RS* 2. 228–51.
3 'Britanniarum vero omnes episcopos tuae fraternati committimus, ut indocti doceantur, infirmi persuasione roborentur, perversi auctoritate corrigantur' *Historia ecclesiastica* (hereafter *HE*) 1. 27 (ed. Loeb) 130.
4 Ralph was explaining *HE* 1. 27: 'Britannias siquidem pluraliter appellat propter diversas eiusdem *insulae* provincias et linguarum divisiones' *Ep. cit.* 235.

suggest that he did include it. But there is no confirmation of this from another source.

A second passage, however, reveals that there was a more definite position in relation to Ireland to be won from Bede. It was not, however, concerned with any papal instruction. It concerned the alleged practice of a primacy over Ireland initiated by Augustine's successor, Laurence. Bede related how Laurence built up the British mission on the foundations already 'so nobly laid'. He thus summarized his labours: 'In short, he not only took care of the new church formed among the English, but endeavoured also to employ his pastoral solicitude among the ancient inhabitants of Britain, as also the Scots, who inhabit the island of Ireland, which is next to Britain.'[1] Bede then went on to tell of how Laurence wrote to the Irish bishops and abbots 'an exhortatory epistle, entreating and conjuring them to observe unity of peace',[2] part of which he cited.

This is, of course, a far cry from the language of precise legal definition of the *maioritas* of Canterbury. It is the sum total of what Bede had to say about Canterbury's relations with Ireland. Nevertheless it was a key passage for Lanfranc and his successors as the following textual comparison shows:

BEDE	LANFRANC	RALPH
Denique non solum novae quae de Anglis erat collecta, ecclesiae curam gerebat, sed et veterum Britanniae incolarum, necnon et Scotorum qui Hiberniam insulam Britanniae proximam incolunt, populis *pastoralem impendere sollicitudinem curabat*[3]	...antecessores meos super Eboracensem ecclesiam, totamque insulam quam Britanniam vocant, necnon et Hiberniam, primatum gessisse, *curam pastoralem omnibus impendisse*[4]	[After quoting the Bede text] Quam videlicet *pastoralis curae sollicitudinem* nunquam postea Cantuariensis ecclesia, tam universae Britanniae quam Hiberniae beneficio simul et primatu, *impendere* cessavit[5]

1 *HE* 2. 4; actual words cited in the textual comparison above.
2 '... scripsit cum coepiscopis suis exhortatoriam ad eos epistolam: obsecrans eos et contestans ...' *HE* 2. 4 *ed. cit.* 220.
3 *HE* 2. 4 *ed. cit.* 218.
4 *Ep. cit.* William of Malmesbury, *Gesta pont.* 44.
5 *Ep. cit.* 236. The use of the word 'beneficium' is interesting. F. Barlow has stressed the feudal element in Lanfranc's view of the hierarchy: 'What however had been a loose confederacy of bishoprics was reorganized on a strictly hierarchical principle and it must be recognized that feudal ideas quite as much as ecclesiastical discipline contributed to the result. The southern bishops were firmly subordinated to their Canterbury metropolitan, and oaths of canonical obedience were required which resembled the fealty of a vassal' *The Feudal Kingdom of England* (1955) 123. R. Foreville: 'Il est frappant d'ailleurs de constater, pour une fois qu'elle nous est décrite, l'analogie de la profession canonique d'obédience avec l'hommage féodal

Appendix 1

Bede, *Ecclesiastical History* 2.4 was the best they could do in supplying an authentic basis for claiming primacy over the Irish Church.

The continuity of doctrine from Lanfranc to Ralph d'Escures is plain to see. There is, however, no evidence in Ansel㎡'s writings that he subscribed to this reading of Bede, nor indeed is there any other argument to be found there relevant to the question at issue. As has been seen, he used the term *totius Britanniae primas* in the forms of submission required from Irish bishops. As with Lanfranc's *Britanniarum primas*, there is some ambiguity as to whether it was intended to include Ireland. It will be noted that in the passage of Ralph d'Escures just cited, *universa Britannia* did not include Ireland. A search for a use of the Anselmian or similar forms which unquestionably included Ireland has been unsuccessful. The trend of the evidence suggests that while it is beyond doubt that the archbishops of Canterbury considered they had primatial right over Ireland, the titles they used to describe themselves as primates of Britain, whether in the submissions of Irish bishops or elsewhere, were not in fact the result of any considered attempt to include that right expressed in precise language.

If there is nothing to be learned of Anselm's position from his own pen there is something to be noted of the view he came to represent in Canterbury propaganda. Anselm's intimate and biographer is not perhaps the most reliable of witnesses for his attitude to the primacy. For even though now cleared of the charge of being the Canterbury forger, he has not been freed of suspicion of duplicity in that connexion.[1] But if Hugh the Chantor can be heard on Lanfranc, Eadmer can claim a hearing on Anselm. The relevant passages can be quickly presented:

[Eadmer's own description of the church of Canterbury]
ipsam totius Angliae, Scottiae et Hiberniae, necne adjacentium insularum matrem.[2]
[The bishops of the Canterbury province are said to have told the king of Anselm]
Primas est non modo istius regni, sed et Scottiae et Hiberniae necne adjacentium insularum.[3]
[Anselm is alleged to have described himself]
primas totius Angliae, Scottiae, Hiberniae et adjacentium insularum.[4]

quant à la forme extérieure qu'elle revêt'. *L'Eglise et la royauté en Angleterre sous Henri II Plantagenet* (1942). The reference is to Anselm's reception of the profession of Gerard of York in 1107, 'Annuit Gerardus, et, sua manu imposita manui Anselmi, interposita fide sua pollicitus est . . . ', Eadmer, *Hist. nov.* 187.

[1] Cf. Southern, 'The Canterbury Forgeries' 225–6. For Eadmer as forger, A. J. MacDonald, 'Eadmer and the Canterbury Privileges' *Journal of Theological Studies* 32 (1931) 39–55.

[2] Eadmer, *Hist. nov.* 26.

[3] *Ibid.* 63.   [4] *Ibid.* 189.

The *Historia novorum* has nothing to say explicitly which throws light on the claim over Ireland. But it had quite a deal to say implicitly. It is not for nothing that this work is the 'principal narrative source for visits of episcopal nominees from Ireland to obtain consecration at Canterbury and for other relations between that see and Ireland'.[1] For this champion of the claims of Canterbury was naturally interested in this practical demonstration of primatial activity. Lanfranc in 1072 had only the historical record to argue from. Eadmer was recording present usage. Though far from amounting to a convincing case, it was a rather more plausible story than the misrepresentation of Bede.

[1] Kenney, *Sources* 763.

Appendix 2

THE ARMAGH ELECTION DISPUTE, 1202-7

The facts about the beginnings of the controversy over the election of a new archbishop of Armagh after the death of Tomaltach O Conchobair in 1201 are known from a letter of Innocent III[1] replying to his legate in Ireland, Cardinal John of Salerno, on whom fell the responsibility for settling the case. The Legate had found the affair so difficult that he did not wish to take any action until he had got advice from the Pope. He had given Innocent a detailed account of what had happened and this the Pope repeated in a lengthy summary, following the normal practice of the papal chancery, before giving the answers to questions raised.

It was the justiciar[2] who had begun proceedings by giving the electors permission to go ahead with the election. Through the archdeacon of Armagh he instructed them to meet at Drogheda. This was not the canonically required location. But the Armagh cathedral was *inter Hibernicos* and Drogheda was a strongpoint of the colony. The archdeacon issued the electoral summonses in proper canonical form, but on the appointed day the only electors to join him were two suffragans and the abbot of Mellifont who came armed with a privilege which he alleged gave him 'first voice' in an Armagh election.[3] These four proceeded to deliberate and announced a selection of three candidates: Simon Rochfort, bishop of Meath for the last ten years and one of the suffragans present; Ralph Petit, member of a family now well settled in Meath and archdeacon of that diocese for many years;[4] Humphrey of Tickhill, an Oxford

---

1 *Pont. hib.* I. 52. The events related here are drawn from this letter except where other sources are explicitly mentioned.

2 Probably Meiler fitzHenry, Richardson and Sayles, *Administration of Ireland* 75.

3 The abbot was an Irishman, Gregory (*c.* 1194-*c.* 1206) who was expelled by his community, very probably, as Fr Conway suggests, because his support of the foreigner did not commend itself to his brethren, *Story of Mellifont* 54, 231, 264-7. At first encounter, such a privilege sounds spurious. There is no other reference to it in Armagh history, so far as is known. But institutions were in a transitional stage in the second half of the twelfth century and it is not beyond belief that Mellifont, Malachy's foundation, had been accorded this especial and unusual privilege.

4 And bishop of Meath, 1227-30.

graduate and king's clerk, whom the King thought of as a potential future justiciar.[1] The other bishop there whose name remains unknown was to say subsequently that though present he kept silent and did not give his assent to what was done. The others, however, were to say that they believed he agreed since he was present and said nothing by way of contradiction.

Some time later—precision is impossible—the archdeacon of Armagh issued a second summons to the electors, bidding them attend, this time at Armagh itself. All those summoned presented themselves save only the bishop of Meath and the abbot of Mellifont who would on no account go there for fear of the Irish. In due course there was elected Eugenius, the abbot of the Augustinian house so closely connected with St Malachy, of Bangor. He was consecrated on the Sunday next after the election, as was Armagh custom. In the course of the ceremony he performed his first episcopal act in admitting an acolyte to his order, and that at a point in the ceremony not permitted by canon law. The Legate was to reprimand him severely for this but he replied that this was Armagh custom of long standing.

With this election very great strife arose between Irish and English, with the latter especially vociferous about their refusal to suffer an Irish archbishop. Certain churchmen of both nationalities came to the Legate and said that the election of an Englishman would be profitable for Armagh and for the peace of the whole realm.

The Legate suspended Eugenius. One of the suffragans then made complaint against him that he had stolen a silver ornamented panel from Armagh cathedral. The accused finally admitted that he had received the panel from the Armagh clergy and laity and had sold it for 20 marks. He promised restitution.

King John appealed to the Legate concerning the Drogheda nomination[2]—which the Legate, as Innocent III was to point out, persisted in wrongly calling an election. John's plea was that he had the right to assent to an elect, had done so for Drogheda but had not been consulted about the Armagh candidate.

Innocent III found that there were six objections to the legality of the Armagh election which needed to be made and answered. Three concerned the validity of the electoral procedure and three were about the defects of the elect himself.

---

[1] *Curriculum vitae* in Emden, *Biographical Register, Oxford* 3. 2222. The evidence that John thought him qualified for high political office is *Cal. Docs. Irel.* 160.

[2] Cf. also *Cal. Docs. Irel.* 168 (15 August 1202); *Rot. Litt. Pat.* 1. 16b. The King named the bishops of Clogher, Clonmacnois, Kells (*sic*), Ardagh and the archdeacon of Armagh as those hostile to him.

It could be argued that if, as the Legate kept saying, the Drogheda meeting was an election, nothing further should have been done unless it had been annulled. But, it was replied, since only four electors were involved it was not an election but a nomination. Those nominated acquired no legal right. Nothing therefore had happened at Drogheda to prevent an election taking place later, particularly if it was in the cathedral church of the diocese which was, according to canon law, the proper place for it to be held.

Secondly, it might be argued that since an appeal had been lodged (by King John), there should be no further electoral proceedings until that had been dealt with. But, Innocent ruled, there had not in fact been any impediment to the Armagh meeting. The King had no grounds for appeal since nothing had been done to his prejudice. For his right to assent is to an elect, one *elected* in an election, not to assent to a mere nominee, one of three *nominated*.

Thirdly, if the bishop of Meath and the abbot of Mellifont were not properly summoned, the election was invalid. This was a matter of fact for the Legate to investigate more closely, along with the degree of danger to which they would in fact have been exposed by going to Armagh. But even if not properly summoned, they could be allowed for the sake of peace and the disruption consequent on the annulling of the election to give their consent after the election had taken place.

There were then the arguments against the legality of the election based on what Eugenius himself had done.

He had performed an act of ecclesiastical jurisdiction (the imposition of minor orders) before his confirmation by the pope and reception from him of the *pallium*. The election and the consecration, however, had taken place before the Legate arrived in Ireland and it could therefore be argued that the pope, in the person of his legate, had been deliberately ignored. It was the practice of the curia, Innocent said, to permit administration before reception of the *pallium* for the archbishops of England, France, Germany and other distant parts, since where restitution of temporalities waited on canonical confirmation harm could result to churches where the securing of the *pallium* was inevitably protracted because of the distances involved.

Only the pope might confer orders on the day of his consecration. Hence Eugenius had acted uncanonically in this regard. But Innocent III allowed that a severe reprimand was adequate punishment. If, however, it proved that it had been done in following an established local custom, it was to be overlooked, 'propter simplicitatem et ruditatem gentis' if assurances were given that henceforth the custom of the universal Church be observed. The electors and Eugenius did ask pardon of this fault and

Innocent accepted that they had acted in good faith according to ancient custom.

Finally, concerning Eugenius' alleged theft, Innocent thought that he had acted at the will of the Armagh clergy and people and accepted that promise of restitution removed this objection to his confirmation as archbishop of Armagh.

There was no definitive judgment from Innocent III. That he was content to leave to his Legate. He made it clear that on the facts presented to him there was no insuperable obstacle to the acceptance of Eugenius as archbishop. But he did not himself confirm him. This he was to do at a later stage, when Eugenius had gone to Rome. Meanwhile he instructed the Legate that should he find that justice demanded a new election, he should try for a candidate who was neither English nor Irish.

Whilst Innocent III had been shaping a papal solution to the problem, King John had been pressing his. He sought to buy off Eugenius with a promise of a pension of 20 marks annually and of his assent should he be canonically elected to the bishopric of 'Louth' (Clogher) when it became vacant, if he would retire from the contest.[1] Apparently under the impression that Eugenius had agreed to this bargain, on 4 May 1203, the King announced that Humphrey of Tickhill was his man for the archbishopric.[2]

Eugenius, however, betook himself to Rome. John ordered the Armagh suffragans to support his candidate and to refuse Eugenius as their archbishop.[3]

The Legate left Ireland in 1203. His reaction to Innocent III's instructions cannot be known. He was to play no further significant part.

Humphrey of Tickhill died. King John announced in February, 1204 that Ralph Petit was now his candidate.[4] Nevertheless when almost exactly a year later fresh information becomes available, Eugenius as archbishop of Armagh and primate of Ireland was present at an assembly of bishops, abbots and priors, Irish and English, held in the heart of the Petit territory at Mullingar, and attended also by the other surviving nominee of the Drogheda meeting, Bishop Simon Rochfort of Meath.[5] It is obvious that by this date he had been accepted as the canonically appointed primate by the English of the Armagh province.

King John, however, seems to have needed longer to reconcile himself to the papal decision. The *Annals of Loch Cé* record under the year 1206 that

1 *Cal. Docs. Irel.* 176 (11 April 1203).
2 *Ibid.* 177 (4 May 1203); *Rot. Litt. Pat.* I. 29a.
3 *Cal. Docs. Irel.* 178 (22 May 1203); *Rot. Litt. Pat.* I. 29b.
4 *Cal. Docs. Irel.* 200 (10 February 1204).
5 *Reg. St. Thomas Dublin RS* 348-9 (February 1205).

the archbishop of Armagh went to the court of the king of England on behalf of the churches of Ireland and to lay complaint against the foreigners.[1] Nothing has survived to tell us what, if anything, transpired from this mission. But there is correspondence of August 1206 between the King and the justiciar concerning Armagh.[2] Two Cistercians of Mellifont had come to the King on behalf of the Archbishop offering money for restitution of the temporalities of Armagh as they had been defined by judicial enquiry before Hamo of Valognes when he was justiciar. It seems reasonable to suppose that John finally conceded defeat and the temporalities—for a price.

There is a postscript in a small piece of information that gives the story of the Armagh election a quite unexpected twist. In July 1207, John wrote to the keepers of the vacant see of Exeter telling them he was sending Archbishop Eugenius of Armagh to execute the episcopal office in that diocese.[3] Perhaps after all Eugenius had not managed to obtain secure possession of the see for which he had struggled so tenaciously. And perhaps, ironically, he found refuge with him who had done most to oppose him.

[1] I. 236–7.
[2] *Cal. Docs. Irel.* 301, 335; *Rot. Litt. Pat.* I. 67a.
[3] *Cal. Docs. Irel.* 291; *Rot. Litt. Pat.* I. 88a.

BIBLIOGRAPHY

MANUSCRIPT SOURCES

British Museum
Cotton Augustus II no. 104.
Cotton Cleopatra E.I.
Cambridge University Library
Ff. 1. 27.
Public Record Office, Dublin
Ferguson Collection (Transcripts).
Public Record Office, London
Q.R.Ir.Excheq. E.101/234/9.
Trinity College, Dublin
Reeves Transcripts (Armagh Registers).
Vatican
Barberini Latini no. 2126.
Instrumenta Miscellanea 516.

PRINTED SOURCES

Ancient Charters in the Liber Albus Ossoriensis ed. H. F. Berry *PRIA* 37 C (1908) 115–25.
Annales de Monte Fernandi ed. A. Smith in *Tracts Relating to Ireland* 2 (Dublin, Irish Archaeological Society 1843).
Annales Monastici 5 vols. ed. H. R. Luard *RS* (1864–9).
Annals of Clonmacnoise ed. D. Murphy (1896).
Annals of Connacht ed. A. M. Freeman (1944).
Annals of Inisfallen ed. S. Mac Airt (1951).
Annals of Ireland by Friar John Clyn ed. R. Butler (Irish Archaeological Society 1849).
Annals of the Kingdom of Ireland by the Four Masters ed. J. O'Donovan 7 vols. (Dublin 1848–51).
Annals of Loch Cé ed. W. A. Hennessy 2 vols. *RS* (1871).
Annals of St. Mary's Dublin. See under *Chartularies*.
'The Annals of Tigernach' ed. W. Stokes, *Revue celtique* 16–18 (1895–7).
Annals of Ulster ed. W. M. Hennessy and B. MacCarthy 4 vols. (Dublin 1887–1901).
Anselmi Opera Omnia 4 ed. F. S. Schmitt (Edinburgh 1949); 5 (1951).
Archives of the See of Dublin ed. J. T. Gilbert Hist. MSS Comm. 10 Rep. (1885) 204–19.
Archives of the See of Ossory ed. J. T. Gilbert Hist. MSS Comm. 10 Rep. (1885) 219–65.
Bateson, M. *Borough Customs* 2 vols. (Selden Society 1904–6).

Bibliography

Beati Lanfranci Opera ed. J. A. Giles (Oxford 1844).

Bede, *Opera Historica* (Loeb Classical Library 1930).

Bernard of Clairvaux *Vita Malachiae PL* 182; *Sermones de Sanctis PL* 183.

Black Book of Limerick ed. J. McCaffrey (Dublin 1907).

Bracton de legibus et consuetudinibus Angliae ed. G. E. Woodbine 4 vols. (New Haven 1915–42.)

Caithréim Thoirdhealbhaigh ed. S. H. O'Grady 2 vols. (Irish Texts Soc. 26, 27 London 1929).

Calendar of Archbishop Alen's Register c. 1172–1534 ed. C. McNeill (Dublin 1950).

Calendar of Close Rolls (1892–).

Calendar of Documents relating to Ireland (1172–1307) ed. H. S. Sweetman 5 vols. (1875–86). Cf. G. J. Hand, 'Material used in *Calendar of Documents relating to Ireland*' *IHS* 12 (1960) 99–104.

Calendar of the Justiciary Rolls, Ireland vol. 1 (1295–1303), 2 (1305–7) ed. J. Mills (Dublin 1905, 1914); 3 (1308–14) ed. M. C. Griffith (Dublin 1956).

Calendar of the Liber Ruber of the Diocese of Ossory ed. H. J. Lawlor *PRIA* 27 C (1908) 159–208.

Calendar of Ormond Deeds ed. E. Curtis 6 vols. (1932–43).

Calendar of the Register of Archbishop Fleming ed. H. J. Lawlor *PRIA* 30 C (1912) 94–190.

Calendar of the Register of Archbishop Sweteman ed. H. J. Lawlor *PRIA* 29 C (1911) 213–310.

Calendar of Papal Letters (1893–).

Calendar of Papal Registers. Petitions 1, 1343–1419 (1896).

Calendar of Patent Rolls (1891–).

Catalogue of Irish Pipe Rolls, Public Record Office of Ireland, Reports of Deputy Keeper 35–47, 53–4.

Chartae, Privilegia et Immunitates ... (Ir. Record Comm. 1889).

'Charters of the Cistercian Abbey of Duiske' ed. C. M. Butler and J. H. Bernard *PRIA* 35 C (1918) 1–188.

Chartularies of St. Mary's Abbey, Dublin; with the Register of its house at Dunbrody, and annals of Ireland ed. J. T. Gilbert 2 vols. *RS* (1884).

Cheney, C. R. and Semple, W. H. *Selected Letters of Pope Innocent III concerning England* (London 1953).

Chronica pontificum ecclesiae Eboracensis ed. J. A. Raine, *The Historians of the Church of York and its Archbishops* 2 *RS* (1886).

Chronicon Scotorum ed. W. M. Hennessy *RS* (1866).

Concilia Magnae Britanniae et Hiberniae ed. D. Wilkins 4 vols. (London 1737).

Corpus Iuris Canonici ed. E. Friedberg 2 vols. (Leipzig 1879).

Crede mihi: the most ancient register book of the archbishops of Dublin before the Reformation ed. J. T. Gilbert (Dublin 1897).

Davies, Sir John, 'A discoverie of the True Causes why Ireland was never entirely subdued' in *Ireland under Elizabeth and James I* ed. H. Morley (1890) 213–342.

Decretales. See under *Corpus Iuris Canonici.*

Diceto. See under *Radulfi de Diceto.*

'*Dignitas Decani*' of St. Patrick's Cathedral Dublin ed. N. B. White (Ir. MSS Comm. 1957).

Documents illustrative of English History in the Thirteenth and Fourteenth Centuries ed. H. Cole (1844).

Bibliography

Dugdale, W. *Monasticon Anglicanum* ... 6 vols. ed. J. Caley, H. Ellis, B. Bandinel (1817–30).

Duiske Charters. See under *Charters.*

Dunning, P. J. 'The Letters of Innocent III to Ireland' *Traditio* 18 (1962) 229–53.

Eadmeri Historia Novorum in Anglia ed. M. Rule *RS* (1884).

Ehrle, F. 'Ein Bruchstück der Acten des Konzils von Vienne' *Archiv für Literatur und Kirchengeschichte* 4 (1888) 361–470.

Extents of Irish Monastic Possessions 1540–1541 ed. N. B. White (Ir. MSS Comm. 1943).

Fratris Thomae vulgo dicti de Eccleston Tractatus de adventu fratrum minorum in Angliam (ed. A. G. Little Manchester 1951).

Foedera, Conventiones et Litterae ... ed. T. Rymer (London 1704–17).

Fordun, John, *Scotichronicon* ed. T. Hearne 5 vols. (Oxford 1722); ed. W. Goodall 2 vols. (Edinburgh 1759).

Franciscan materials, See under *Materials.*

Furness, Jocelin of *Vita S. Patricii* in *Acta Sanctorum* (March t. 2) 537–77.

Gesta regis Henrici secundi Benedicti Abbatis ed. W. Stubbs 2 vols. *RS* (1867). Cf. D. M. Stenton, 'Roger of Howden and "Benedict" ' *EHR* 68 (1953) 574–82.

Gilbert, J. T. See under *Historic and Municipal Documents.*

Giles, J. A. See under *Beati Lanfranci Opera.*

Giraldi Cambrensis Opera 1 ed. J. S. Brewer *RS* (1861); 5 ed. J. F. Dimock *RS* (1867); 8 ed. G. F. Warner *RS* (1891).

Hardiman, J. ed. *A Statute of the Fortieth Year of King Edward III enacted in a Parliament held in Kilkenny, A.D. 1367 before Lionel Duke of Clarence Lord Lieutenant of Ireland* in *Tracts Relating to Ireland* 2 (Dublin: Irish Archaeological Society 1843).

Harris: *Collectanea de Rebus Hibernicis* ed. C. McNeill *Anal. hib.* 6 (1934) 248–450.

Hexham, John of *Symeonis Historia Regum Continuatio* in *Symeonis Monachi Opera Omnia* 2 ed. T. Arnold *RS* (1885).

Hill, R. M. T. *The Rolls and Register of Bishop Oliver Sutton 1280–99 (Lincoln Record Society* 48. 1954).

Historic and Municipal Documents of Ireland ed. J. T. Gilbert *RS* (1870).

Howden, Roger of *Chronica* ed. W. Stubbs *RS* (1868–71). See also under *Gesta regis Henrici Secundi.*

Hugh the Chantor, *The History of the Church of York, 1066–1127* ed. and transl. C. Johnson (1961).

Irish Cartularies of Llanthony Prima and Secunda ed. E. St. J. Brooks (Ir. MSS Comm. 1963).

Irish Monastic and Episcopal Deeds ed. N. B. White (Ir. MSS Comm. 1936).

'Irish Pipe Roll of 14 John, 1211–12' ed. O. Davies and D. B. Quinn. Supplement, *Ulster Journal of Archaeology* 4 (1941).

Jean XXII (1316–34). Lettres communes analysées d'après les registres dits d'Avignon et du Vatican ed. G. Mollat 16 vols. (Paris 1904–46).

Keating, G. *The History of Ireland* ed. D. Comyn and P. S. Dineen 4 vols. (Irish Texts Soc. 4, 8, 9, 15 London 1902–14).

Lanfranci Opera. See under *Beati.*

Lawlor, J. H. 'Fragments of a lost Register of the Diocese of Clogher' *Co. Louth Archaeological Journal* 4 (1916–20) 226–57.

Lawlor, H. J. 'A fresh authority for the synod of Kells, 1152' *PRIA* 36 C (1922) 16–22.

Bibliography

Limerick, Gilbert of *De usu ecclesiastico; De statu ecclesiastico PL* 159. 995–1004.

Literae Cantuarienses 3 ed. J. B. Sheppard *RS* (1889).

Mac Niocaill, G. (ed.) *Na Buirgéisí XII–XIV aois* 2 vols. (Dublin 1964).

Malmesbury, William of *Gesta pontificum Anglorum* ed. N. E. S. A. Hamilton *RS* (1870).

Map of Monastic Ireland compiled by R. Neville Hadcock (Ordnance Survey 2 ed. Dublin 1964).

Materials for the History of the Franciscan Province of Ireland ed. E. B. Fitzmaurice and A. G. Little (Brit. Soc. Franciscan Studies 9: Manchester 1920).

Memoranda de Parliamento ed. F. W. Maitland *RS* (1893).

Morley, H. See under Davies.

Mynors, R. A. B. *Durham Cathedral Manuscripts to the end of the Twelfth Century* (Oxford 1939).

O'Grady, S. H. See under *Caithréim.*

Newburgh, William of (Continuator) *Chron. reigns Stephen, Henry II and Richard I* ed. R. Howlett *RS* (1889).

Parliaments and Councils of Medieval Ireland ed. H. G. Richardson and G. O. Sayles (Ir. MSS Comm. 1947).

Plummer, C. 'Vie et miracles de S. Laurent archevêque de Dublin' *Analecta Bollandiana* 33 (1914) 121–86.

Pontificia Hibernica: Medieval Papal Chancery Documents concerning Ireland ed. M. P. Sheehy 2 vols. (Dublin 1962–5).

Prynne, W. *Exact Chronological Vindication of our King's Supreme Jurisdiction* (1665–68).

Radulfi de Diceto … Opera Historica 2 vols. ed. W. Stubbs *RS* (1876).

Reeves, W. ed. *Acts of Archbishop Colton in his metropolitan visitation of the diocese of Derry A.D. MCCCXCVII with a rental of the see estates at that time* (Dublin 1850).

Register of the Abbey of St. Thomas, Dublin ed. J. T. Gilbert *RS* (1889).

The Register of John Swayne ed. D. A. Chart (Belfast 1935).

Registrum Epistolarum Stephani de Lexington ed. B. Griesser, *Analecta Sacri Ordinis Cisterciensis* (1946) 1–118.

Rotuli Chartarum, 1199–1216 ed. T. D. Hardy (Rec. Comm. 1835).

Rotuli Litterarum Clausarum, 1204–27 ed. T. D. Hardy (Rec. Comm. 1835).

Rotuli Litterarum Patentium, 1201–1216 ed. T. D. Hardy (Rec. Comm. 1835).

Rotuli Parliamentorum Anglie Hactenus Inediti ed. H. G. Richardson and G. O. Sayles (Camden 3rd ser. 51, 1935).

Rotulorum Patentium et Clausorum Cancellarie Hibernie Calendarium ed. E. Tresham (Ir. Rec. Comm. 1828).

Royal Letters, Henry III ed. W. W. Shirley 2 vols, *RS* (1862–6).

Salisbury, John of *Historia pontificalis* ed. M. Chibnall (1956).

Metalogicon ed. C. C. J. Webb 4 vols. (1929).

Sheehy, M. P. 'English Law in Medieval Ireland. Two illustrative documents' *Arch. hib.* 23 (1960) 167–75.

Statuta Capitulorum Generalium Ordinis Cisterciensis ed. J. M. Canivez 3 vols. (Louvain 1933–5).

Statutes and ordinances and acts of the parliament of Ireland, King John to Henry V ed. H. F. Berry (Dublin 1907).

Stubbs, W. *Select Charters* (9 ed. 1913).

Torigny, Robert of *Chronicle* in *Chronicle of the Reigns of Stephen, Henry II and Richard I* vol. 4 ed. R. Howlett *RS* (1889).

Bibliography

Ussher. See under *Veterum Epistolarum*.
Vetera monumenta Hibernorum et Scotorum Historiam Illustrantia ed. A. Theiner (Rome 1864).
Veterum Epistolarum Hibernicarum Sylloge ed. J. Ussher (Dublin 1632); *Whole Works* 4 ed. C. R. Erlington (Dublin 1847).

MODERN WORKS

Armstrong, C. F. R. *Irish Seal-matrices and Seals* (Dublin 1913).
Barlow, F. *The Feudal Kingdom of England* (1955).
 The English Church 1000–1066. A Constitutional History (1963).
Barrow, G. W. S. *Robert Bruce* (1965).
Binchy, D. A. 'The Irish Benedictine Congregation in medieval Germany' *Studies* 18 (1929).
 'The linguistic and historical value of the Irish law tracts' *Proceedings of the British Academy* 29 (1943) 195–227.
Brooke, Z. N. *The English Church and the Papacy* (1931).
Brooks, E. St. J. 'Archbishop Henry of London and his Irish Connections' *RSAIJn.* 60 (1930) 1–22.
 'The Family of Marisco' *RSAIJn.* 61 (1931) 22–38, 89–112, 62 (1932) 50–74.
Bury, J. B. *The Life of St. Patrick and his place in history* (1905).
Carrigan, W. *The History and Antiquities of the Diocese of Ossory* 4 vols. (Dublin 1905).
Champneys, A. C. *Irish Ecclesiastical Architecture* (London 1910).
Cheney, C. R. 'The Punishment of Felonious Clerks' *EHR* 51 (1936) 215–36.
 'A Group of related Synodal Statutes of the Thirteenth Century' *Gwynn Studies* 114–32.
Clarke, M. V. *Fourteenth Century Studies* (Oxford 1937).
Conway, C. *The Story of Mellifont* (Dublin 1958).
 'Sources for the History of the Irish Cistercians' *Proceedings of the Irish Catholic Historical Committee* (1959) 16–23.
Cotton, H. *Fasti Ecclesiae Hibernicae* 5 vols. (Dublin 1845–60).
Curtis, E. *Medieval Ireland* 1 ed. Dublin 1923; 2 ed. London 1938.
Curtis, E. and McDowell, R. B. *Irish Historical Documents, 1172–1922* (1943).
de Paor, L. and M. *Early Christian Ireland* (1958).
Dictionary of National Biography Comyn, John; Darlington, John of; Ferings, Richard de; Hotham, William of; Sandford, Fulk de; Sandford, John de (all by T. F. Tout); Lexington, Stephen of (by W. Hunt); MacCarwell, David (by C. L. Kingsford).
Dunning, P. J. 'The Arroasian Order in Medieval Ireland' *IHS* 4 (1944–5) 297–315.
 'Pope Innocent III and the Irish Kings' *Journal of Ecclesiastical History* 8 (1957) 17–32.
 'The Letters of Innocent III as a Source for Irish History' *Proceedings of the Irish Catholic Historical Committee* (1958) 1–10.
 'Sidelights on the Bishops of Raphoe from the Register of Pope Innocent III' *Father John Colgan O.F.M.: Essays in Commemoration* ed. T. O'Donnell (Dublin 1959) 50–60.
 'Pope Innocent III and the Ross Election Controversy' *Irish Theological Quarterly* 26 (1959) 346–59.
 'Pope Innocent III and the Waterford–Lismore Controversy' *Irish Theological Quarterly* 28 (1961) 215–32.

Bibliography

'Irish Representatives and Irish Ecclesiastical Affairs at the Fourth Lateran Council' *Gwynn Studies* 90–113.

Ehler, S. Z. and Morrall, J. B. *Church and State through the Centuries* (London 1954).

Emden, A. B. *A Biographical Register of the University of Oxford to A.D. 1500* 3 vols. (Oxford 1957–9).

A Biographical Register of the University of Cambridge to 1500 (Cambridge 1963).

Ferguson, J. F. 'The "mere English" and "mere Irish" ' *Trans. Kilkenny Archaeol. Soc. (RSAIJn.)* 1 (1850–1) 508–12.

Flahiff, G. B. 'The Writ of Prohibition to Courts Christian in the Thirteenth Century' *Mediaeval Studies* 6 (1944) 261–313.

Flower, R. 'Manuscripts of Irish interest in the British Museum' *Anal. hib.* 2 (1931).

Foreville, R. *L'église et la royauté en Angleterre sous Henri II Plantagenet* (Paris 1942).

Gleeson, D. F. and Gwynn, A. *The History of the Diocese of Killaloe* (Dublin 1962).

Gougaud, L. *Christianity in Celtic Lands* (1932).

Graves, E. B. 'Circumspecte Agatis' *EHR* 43 (1928) 1–20.

Gwynn, A. 'Nicholas Mac Maol Íosa, Archbishop of Armagh, 1272–1303' *Féilsgríbhínn Éoin Mhic Néill* ed. J. Ryan (Dublin 1940) 394–405.

'The Origins of the See of Dublin' *IER* 57 (1941) 40–55; 97–112.

'Ireland and Rome in the Eleventh Century' *IER* 57 (1941) 213–32.

'Lanfranc and the Irish Church' *IER* 57 (1941) 481–500; 58 (1941) 1–15.

'Pope Gregory VII and the Irish Church' *IER* 58 (1941) 97–109.

'St. Anselm and the Irish Church' *IER* 59 (1942) 1–14.

'The Origins of the Diocese of Waterford' *IER* 59 (1942) 289–96.

'Bishop Samuel of Dublin' *IER* 60 (1942) 81–8.

'Papal Legates in Ireland during the Twelfth Century' *IER* 63 (1944) 361–70.

'Provincial and diocesan decrees of the diocese of Dublin during the Anglo-Norman period' *Arch. hib.* 11 (1944) 31–117.

'The First Synod of Cashel' *IER* 66 (1945) 81–92; 67 (1946) 109–22.

'The Diocese of Limerick in the Twelfth Century' *North Munster Antiquarian Journal* 5 (1946) 35–48.

'Documents relating to the medieval province of Armagh' *Arch. hib.* 13 (1947) 1–29.

'Gregory VII and the Irish Church' *Studi Gregoriani* 3 (1948) 105–28.

'St. Malachy of Armagh' *IER* 70 (1948) 961–78; 71 (1949) 134–48, 317–31.

'The Origins of St. Mary's Abbey, Dublin' *RSAIJn.* 19 (1949) 11–25.

'Henry of London, Archbishop of Dublin: a Study in Anglo-Norman Statecraft' *Studies* 38 (1949) 295–306, 389–402.

'St. Lawrence O'Toole as Legate in Ireland, 1179–1180' *Analecta Bollandiana* 68 (1950) 223–40.

'The Bishops of Cork in the Twelfth Century' *IER* 74 (1950) 17–29, 97–109.

'The Centenary of the Synod of Kells' *IER* 77 (1952) 161–76, 250–64.

'The continuity of the Irish tradition at Würzburg' *Herbipolis jubilans* (Würzburg 1952) 57–81.

'Ireland and the Continent in the eleventh century' *IHS* 8 (1953) 192–216.

'The early history of St. Thomas' Abbey, Dublin' *RSAIJn.* 84 (1954) 1–35.

'Armagh and Louth in the Twelfth Century' *Seanchas Ardmhacha* 1 (1954–55) 1–11, 17–37.

The Writings of Bishop Patrick, 1074–84. Scriptores Latini Hiberniae 1 (Dublin 1955).

'The First Bishops of Dublin' *Reportorium novum* 1 (1955) 1–26.

Bibliography

'Archbishop John Cumin' *Reportorium novum* 1 (1956) 285–310.
'Raphoe and Derry in the Twelfth and Thirteenth Centuries' *Donegal Annual* 4 (1959) 84–100.
'Edward I and the proposed purchase of English law for the Irish c. 1279–80' *TRHS* 10 (1960) 111–27.
Gwynn, A. and Hadcock, R. N. *Medieval Religious Houses, Ireland* (1970).
Hand, G. J. 'The Dating of the early fourteenth-century ecclesiastical valuations of Ireland' *Irish Theological Quarterly* 24 (1957) 271–4.
'The Church and English Law in medieval Ireland' *Proceedings of the Irish Catholic Historical Committee* (1959) 10–18.
'The Medieval Chapter of St. Mary's Cathedral, Limerick' *Gwynn Studies* 74–89.
'The rivalry of the cathedral chapters in medieval Dublin' *RSAIJn.* 92 (1962) 193–206.
'The Medieval Chapter of St. Patrick's Cathedral, Dublin' *Reportorium novum* 5 (1964) 229–48.
'The Status of the Native Irish in the Lordship of Ireland, 1272–1331' *Irish Jurist* 1 n.s. (1966) 93–115.
'The Forgotten Statutes of Kilkenny: a Brief Survey' *Irish Jurist* 1 n.s. (1966) 299–312.
English Law in Ireland 1290–1324 (Cambridge 1967).
Handbook of British Chronology 2 ed., ed. F. M. Powicke and E. B. Fryde (1961).
Hughes, Kathleen *The Church in early Irish society* (1966).
Hore, P. H. *History of the Town and County of Wexford* 6 vols. (London 1900–11).
Jones, W. R. 'Bishops, politics and the Two Laws: the *gravamina* of the English clergy 1237–1399' *Speculum* 41 (1966) 209–45.
Kenney, J. F. *The Sources for the early history of Ireland: an Introduction and Guide. I. Ecclesiastical* (New York 1929); 2 ed. revised by L. Bieler (1969).
King, R. *Primer of the Church History of Ireland* 3 vols. 3 ed. (Dublin 1845–51).
Knowles, M. D. *The Monastic Order in England* (Cambridge 1940).
The Religious Orders in England vol. 1 (Cambridge 1948).
Lawlor, H. J. 'The Reformation of the Irish Church in the Twelfth Century' *Irish Church Quarterly* 4 (1911) 216–28.
'A Charter of Cristin, Bishop of Louth' *PRIA* 32 C (1913) 28–40.
'The Genesis of the Diocese of Clogher' *Louth Archaeological Society Journal* 4 (1917) 126–57.
'Notes on St. Bernard's Life of Malachy' *PRIA* 36 C (1919) 230–64.
St. Bernard of Clairvaux's Life of St. Malachy of Armagh (London 1920).
Lawlor, H. J. and Best, R. I. 'The ancient list of the Coarbs of Patrick' *PRIA* 35 C (1919) 316–62.
Lawrence, C. H. 'Stephen of Lexington and Cistercian University Studies in the Thirteenth Century' *Journal of Ecclesiastical History* 11 (1960) 164–78.
Leask, H. G. 'Irish Cistercian Monasteries: a pedigree and distribution map' *RSAIJn.* 78 (1948) 63–4.
Legris, A. *Saint Laurent O'Toole (Saint Laurent d'Eu) archevêque de Dublin (1128–1180)* (Rouen-Eu 1914).
Logan, F. D. *Excommunication and the Secular Arm in Medieval England* (Toronto 1968).
Lydon, J. F. 'The Bruce Invasion of Ireland' *Historical Studies* 4 (1963) 111–25.
Lynch, J. *De praesulibus Hiberniae* ed. J. F. O'Doherty 2 vols. (Ir. MSS Comm. 1944).

Bibliography

MacDonald, A. J. 'Eadmer and the Canterbury Privileges' *Journal of Theological Studies* 32 (1931) 39–55.

MacErlean, J. 'Synod of Rath Breasail. Boundaries of the dioceses of Ireland' *Arch. hib.* 3 (1914) 1–33.

MacInerny, M. H. *A History of the Irish Dominicans* (Dublin 1916).

McNeill, C. 'The secular jurisdiction of the early archbishops of Dublin' *RSAIJn.* 45 (1915) 81–108.

MacNeill, E. *Phases of Irish History* (Dublin 1920).

Early Irish Laws and Institutions (1935).

Mac Niocaill, G. *Na Manaigh Liatha in Éirinn 1142–c. 1600* (Dublin 1959). With French summaries.

Maitland, F. W. 'The Introduction of English Law into Ireland' *EHR* 4 (1889) 516–17 and *Collected Papers* ed. H. A. L. Fisher 2 (Cambridge 1911) 81–3.

See also Pollock, F. and Maitland, F. W.

Manuscript Sources for the History of Irish Civilization ed. R. J. Hayes 11 vols. (Boston 1965).

Martin, F. X. 'The Augustinian Friaries in pre-Reformation Ireland' *Augustiniana* 6 (1956) 346–84.

Mason, W. M. *History and Antiquities of the Cathedral Church of St. Patrick near Dublin* (Dublin 1820).

Mooney, C. *Racialism in the Franciscan Order in Ireland, 1224–1770* (Licentiate Thesis, Louvain 1951).

Moran, P. F. 'Bull of Adrian IV' *IER* 9 (1872) 49–64.

Norgate, K. 'The bull *Laudabiliter*' *EHR* 8 (1893) 18–52.

O'Doherty, J. F. *Laurentius von Dublin und das irische Normannentum* (Diss. Munich 1933).

'Rome and the Anglo-Norman Invasion of Ireland' *IER* 42 (1933) 131–45.

'St. Laurence O'Toole and the Anglo-Norman Invasion' *IER* 50 (1937) 449–77, 600–25; 51 (1938) 131–46.

O'Dwyer, B. W. 'The Problem of Reform in the Irish Cistercian Monasteries and the attempted solution of Stephen of Lexington in 1228' *Journal of Ecclesiastical History* 15 (1964) 186–91.

'Gaelic Monasticism and the Irish Cistercians, c. 1228' *Proceedings of the Irish Catholic Historical Committee* (1967) 12–28.

'The Impact of the Native Irish on the Cistercians in the Thirteenth Century' *Journal of Religious Studies* (1968) 287–301.

Orpen, G. H. 'Motes and Norman Castles in Ireland' *EHR* 22 (1907) 228–54; 440–67.

Ireland under the Normans 4 vols. (Oxford 1911–20).

'The Reform Movement' and 'Anglo-Norman Influence' in *History of the Church of Ireland from the earliest times to the present day* ed. W. A. Phillips vol. 2 (Oxford 1934) 32–77.

Otway-Ruthven, Jocelyn 'Anglo-Irish Shire Government in the Thirteenth Century' *IHS* 5 (1946) 1–28.

'The Request of the Irish for English Law, 1277–80' *IHS* 6 (1949) 261–9.

'The Native Irish and English Law in Medieval Ireland' *IHS* 7 (1950) 1–16.

'Knight Service in Ireland' *RSAIJn.* 89 (1959) 1–15.

'The Medieval Church Lands of County Dublin' *Gwynn Studies* 54–73.

'Parochial Development in the Rural Deanery of Skreen' *RSAIJn.* 94 (1964) 111–22.

Bibliography

'The Character of Norman Settlement in Ireland' *Historical Studies* 5 (1965) 75–84.
A History of Medieval Ireland (1967).
Petrie, G. *The Ecclesiastical Architecture of Ireland anterior to the Norman Invasion* (Dublin 1845).
Pollock, F. and Maitland, F. W. *A History of English Law before the time of Edward I* (Cambridge 2nd ed. 1898).
Powicke, F. M. *The Thirteenth Century, 1206–1307* (Oxford 1953).
Reeves, W. *Ecclesiastical Antiquities of Down, Connor and Dromore* (Dublin 1847).
Richardson, H. G. 'English Institutions in medieval Ireland' *IHS* 1 (1938–9) 382–92.
'Norman Ireland in 1212' *IHS* 3 (1942–3) 144–58.
'Some Norman Monastic Foundations in Ireland' *Gwynn Studies* 29–43.
Richardson, H. G. and Sayles, G. O. 'The Clergy in the Easter Parliament, 1285' *EHR* 52 (1937) 220–34.
The Irish Parliament in the Middle Ages (Philadelphia 1952).
The Administration of Medieval Ireland (Dublin 1963).
Parliament in Medieval Ireland (Dublin Historical Association: Dundalk 1964).
Richey, A. G. *Lectures on the history of Ireland down to 1534* (Dublin 1869).
Short History of the Irish People ed. R. R. Kane (Dublin 1887).
Robinson, J. A. 'Early Somerset Archdeacons', Appendix C. 'The early career of John Cumin, archbishop of Dublin', *Somerset Historical Essays* (London 1921) 90–9.
Ronan, M. V. 'St. Laurentius, archbishop of Dublin: original testimonies for canonization' *IER* 27 (1926) 347 ff.; 28 (1926) 247 ff.; 467 ff.
Ronan, M. V. 'The Union of the Dioceses of Glendaloch and Dublin in 1216' *RSAIJn.* 60 (1930) 56–62.
Ryan, J. *Ireland from 800 to 1600* (Dublin n.d.).
Irish Monasticism, origins and early development (1931).
Sayles, G. O. 'Ecclesiastical Process and the Parsonage of Stabannon in 1351' *PRIA* 55 C (1952) 3–23.
'The Rebellious First Earl of Desmond' *Gwynn Studies* 203–29.
Seymour, St. J. D. 'The Medieval Church' in *History of the Church of Ireland from the earliest times to the present day* ed. W. A. Phillips vol. 2 (Oxford 1934) 78–143.
Sheehy, M. P. 'The bull *Laudabiliter*: a problem in medieval *diplomatique* and history' *Journal of the Galway Archaeological and Historical Society* 29 (1961) 45–70.
Southern, R. W. 'The Canterbury Forgeries' *EHR* 73 (1958) 193–226.
Szoverffy, J. 'The Anglo-Norman Conquest of Ireland and St. Patrick' *Reportorium novum* 2 (1958) 6–16.
Talbot, Peter and W. E. Kenny, *Primatus Dublinensis. The Primacy of the see of Dublin and a compendium of the arguments on which the see of Dublin relies, for the enjoyment and prosecution of its own right of the primacy of Ireland* (Dublin 1947).
Ullmann, W. 'On the Influence of Geoffrey of Monmouth in English History' *Speculum Historiale: Geschichte im Spiegel von Geschichtsschreibung und Geschichtsdeutung* ed. C. Bauer et alii (Freiburg-München 1966) 257–76.
'A decision of the Rota Romana on the benefit of clergy in England' *Studia Gratiana* 13 (1967) 455–90.
Vacandard, E. *Vie de S. Bernard* 2 vols. (Paris 1920).
Ware, J. *The Whole Works of Sir James Ware concerning Ireland* ed. W. Harris 2 vols. (Dublin 1739–45). Vol. 1, a translation of Ware's *De praesulibus Hiberniae*, is important.

Bibliography

Watt, J. A. 'Negotiations between Edward II and John XXII concerning Ireland' *IHS* 10 (1956) 1–20.

'*Laudabiliter* in medieval diplomacy and propaganda' *IER* 87 (1957) 420–32.

'English Law and the Irish Church: the Reign of Edward I' *Gwynn Studies* 133–67.

'The Papacy and Episcopal Appointments in Thirteenth Century Ireland' *Proceedings of the Irish Catholic Historical Committee* (1960) 1–9.

Weckman, L. *Las bulas alejandrinas de 1493 y la teoría política del papado medieval. Estudio de la supremacía papal sobre islas, 1091–1493* (Mexico City 1949).

Wilmart, A. 'La Trinité des Scots à Rome et les notes du Vat. Lat. 368' *Revue Bénédictine* 41 (1929) 218–30.

Wood, H. 'The Templars in Ireland' *PRIA* 26 C (1907) 327–77.

'Letter from Domnall O'Neill to Fineen MacCarthy, 1317' *PRIA* 37 C (1926) 141–8.

INDEX

The spelling of the proper names of medieval Ireland often presents considerable difficulties. I have throughout tried to follow usages already in existence, opting for an anglicized form where there is a choice.

Index

Brackley, Walter of, 76
Bracton, Henry of, ix, 120 n. 1
Breathnach, David, bp Waterford (1204–9), 63
Brehon law, 11–12, 20 n. 6
breithemain, see Brehon law
Brétigny, treaty of, 198
Bristol, Ralph of, bp Kildare (1223–32), 74 n. 5
Bruce, Edward, invasion of Ireland by 182–6, 193, 199
Bruce, Robert, 186, 189
burgasia, 125
Burgh, Hubert de, bp Limerick (1224–50), 74, 76, 79 n. 1, 98
Burnell, Robert, chancellor of England, 170 n. 2

Cambridge, graduates of, 210
Canons Regular, 25–7
Canterbury, connexion with Ireland, 6–10, 16, 18–19, 22 n. 2, 36, 217–25
Carmelites in Ireland, 177
Cashel
    archbishops of, 44, 57 n. 1, 62, 68 n. 2, 68 n. 6, 73, 74, 75, 80 n. 1, 81, 122, 130, 156 n. 4, 158–60, 170, 173–5, 183 n. 2, 186, 201–2, 210; see also Donnchad; Fitzjohn; MacCarwill; O Briain; O'Brogan; O'Kelly; Ua h-Énne
    archiepiscopal borough of, 158
    Benedictine monastery of, 24
    chapter of diocese of, 56–7, 74, 81
    Cistercian monastery of, 159
    elections to diocese of, 56, 57–8, 75, 76–7, 184–5
    metropolitan status of, 11, 15–16, 31
    suffragans of province of, 31 n. 2, 44, 56–7, 81
    see also councils; primacy of Ireland
Casta Silva (Kilcreevanty, co. Galway), abbess of, 171
Cellach (Celsus), abp Armagh (1105–29), 5, 15–16, 18, 21–2, 109
Cesena, Michael of, Franciscan minister-general, 185
Chantor, Hugh the, 220, 224
Chartres, Yvo of, 13

chorepiscopi, 62
Christian (O Conairche), O. Cist., bp Lismore (1151–79), 25, 39
Christopher, Griffin, bp Lismore (1223–46), 74
Circumspecte agatis, 134, 139, 143
Cistercians, 24–5, 85–107, 159–60, 174–6, 188–9, 215
    as bishops in Ireland, 25, 54–5, 56, 63, 75, 94, 104 n. 2, 159, 160 n. 1; see also Froidmont; Lexington; Mellifont
Clare, Richard de, 42, 54
    Nicholas de, 166
clergy as royal officials, 49–50, 55, 66–7, 151, 156–7, 169–70, 186 n. 1, 190, 192, 210
clergy in royal courts, 136–43
clerical marriage, 67, 151–2
clerical privilege, 12, 122, 124–6, 131, 133–5, 136–9, 144–5, 168
clerical taxation, 117–18, 171, 201–2, 212
Clericis laicos, 167, 170, 186
Clifford, William de, bp Emly (1286–1306), 156
Clogher, diocese of, 59–60, 68 n. 6, 78, 154, 166 n. 3, 167, 168 n. 4, 194, 229; see also Armagh; Donatus; MacCathasaigh; Nehemias; Tigernach
Clonard, monastery and diocese of, 60
Clonenagh, lost chronicle (annals) of, 28, 108
Clonfert, diocese of, 25, 149, 150 n. 1, 156, 195
Clonmacnois, diocese of, 52, 140 n. 3, 194, 227 n. 2
Cloyne, diocese of, 74 n. 3, 75, 78, 140, 194–6, 210; see also Swaffham
Clyn, John, 184
coarbs, 3, 5, 27, 108
Colton, John, abp Armagh (1381–1404), 115 n. 2
Columbanus, St, rule of, 3, 23, 27
Comgall, abbot of Inislounaght, 19
Conchobhar, bp Killaloe (1201–16), 57, 68 n. 6
Connacht, 16, 32 n. 2, 43, 52, 67, 103–4

242

Index

Connor, diocese of, 22, 44–5, 54, 78, 140 n. 5, 152 n. 2, 191, 194; *see also* Eustace; Malachy, St; O'Kearney; Reginald

Constitutions of Clarendon, 46, 70, 142

Cork
  bishops of, 75, 160 n. 1, 173–4, 192–4, 195; *see also* MacCarwill (John); MacDonnchada; O Briain; Slane
  elections to see of, 56, 67, 77
  kingdom of, 67
  union with diocese of Cloyne, 194–6

Corpus Iuris Canonici, 57, 83, 120 n. 1, 163 n. 1

councils, diocesan and provincial,
  Cashel I (1101), 5, 9, 11, 12
  Rathbreasail (1111), 5, 10, 13, 15, 16, 18, 28, 29, 31, 60, 62, 108
  Kells–Mellifont (1152), 6, 15, 16, 19, 28–34, 59, 61, 108
  Cashel II (1171), 38–41, 50–1, 85, 131–2
  Dublin (1177) 43; (1186) 50; (1192) 68 n. 2; (c. 1320) 209 n. 1
  Clonfert (1179), 32 n. 2
  Mullingar (1205–6), 68 n. 2, 228
  Meath (1216), 21 n. 2, 61
  Drogheda (1262), 115
  Trim (1291), 118, 160
  London (1342), 203 n. 2
  Kilkenny (1366), 203–6

councils, general
  Lateran III, 48
  Lateran IV, 61, 65
  Vienne, 122, 143–6, 185

Counter-Remonstrance of Irish Council, 196–7, 199

counties, medieval, 116

Courcy, John de, 45, 54, 110–11

Cowley, Robert, Master of the Rolls in Ireland, 200

Cradock, Roger, o.f.m., bp Waterford (1350–1355), 196

crocea (crosslands), 134

Cromwell, Thomas, 200 n. 5

Cumin, John, abp Dublin (1181–1212), 42–3, 45, 49–50, 55, 62, 66, 68 n. 1, 69, 109, 111–12

Curtis, E., 66–7, 69, 183, 199

Cusack family, 151
  Nicholas, o.f.m., bp Kildare (1279–99), 117, 156, 175, 182

Darlington, John of, o.p., abp Dublin (1279–84), 155

Davies, Sir John, 130, 198

Dean, William, justiciar, 125

Decretales, see *Corpus Iuris Canonici*

Derry, diocese of, 151, 154, 166, 194
  monastery of, 27

De statu ecclesiae, 13–14

diocesan boundaries, 15–18, 27–31, 59–65, 81–2, 193–6

diocesan unions
  projected, in provinces of Armagh, Cashel, Tuam, 194–6
  Tuam and Achonry, 195–6
  Cork and Cloyne, 194–6
  see also Annaghdown, Waterford

Dominicans, Irish, 142, 171, 176, 178, 180

Donation of Constantine, 35, 37

Donatus (O Fidhabra) bp Clogher (c. 1218–27), abp Armagh (1227–37), 60

Donnchad (O'Longargain I), abp Cashel (c. 1208–16), 68 n. 6, 73, 74

Donnchad (O'Longargain II, O. Cist.), abp Cashel (1216–23), 81

Donngus, bp Dublin (1085–95), 7, 8, 217

Down
  bishops of, 22, 24, 54, 111, 175; *see also* Malachy, St; Ralph
  diocese of, 26, 52, 78, 139 n. 6, 175
  dispute between Bangor and St Patrick's over electoral right in see of, 81

Downpatrick, 54

Dromore, diocese of, 52, 78, 154, 165–6, 194

Dublin
  archbishops of, 42–50, 54–5, 62, 66, 68 n. 1, 68 n. 6, 69, 72, 74 n. 4, 109, 111–12, 122, 124–7, 143, 155–7, 203–6, 208–10; *see also* Bicknor; Cumin; Darlington; Ferings; Hotham; Lech; London; Luke; Minot; O'Toole

Index

Index

Index

O'Brogan, Stephen, abp Cashel (1290–1302), 170
Ochies, Walter of, abbot of Citeaux, 89 n. 1
O Conaing, Peter, abbot of Holycross, 130
O Conchobair, Tomaltach, abp Armagh (1180–1201), 57, 111, 226
O'Connellan, Abraham, abp Armagh (1257–60), 113–14
O'Connor, Rory, king of Connacht, 43, 48
O'Cormacain, Thomas, bp Killaloe (1317–22), 210, 211 n. 3
Octavian, cardinal, 42–3
O Cusby, David, O. Cist., bp Emly (1275–81), 130
O'Doherty, J. F., 32 n. 1
O'Dwyer, B. W., 105 n. 3
O'Grady family, 211
  John, abp Tuam (1364–71), 211
  Nicholas, canonist, 211 n. 3
O Hogain family, 151, 211 n. 3
  Matthew, bp Killaloe (1268–81), 130, 211 n. 3
  Maurice, bp Killaloe (1281–98), 211 n. 3
Oirghialla, kingdom and diocese of, 60
O'Kearney, James, bp Annaghdown (1323–4), Connor (1324–51), 191
O'Kelly, David O.P., abp Cashel (1238–53), 57 n. 1
  Ralph, O. Carm., abp Cashel (1346–61), 201–2
O'Laidig, Sean, O.P., bp Killala (1253–80), 123
O'Neill, Domnall, king of Tir Eoghain, 167, 186–7, 196, 197
O'Quinn, 180
Oriel, king of, 100, 167
Orpen, G. H., 110
O'Ruadhaín, Felix, abp Tuam (1202–33), 61, 68 n. 1, 69
O'Scannell, Patrick, O.P., abp Armagh (1261–70), 114–15, 122, 127–9
Ossory, bishops of, 54–5, 139 n. 2, 150 n. 3, 152 n. 2, 157, 183 n. 2, 191; see also Exeter; Fitzjohn; Ledred; Rufus; Tourville

diocese of, 73 n. 1, 140 n. 3
O'Toole, Adam Duff, burnt for heresy, 197
O'Toole, St Laurence, abp Dublin (1162–80), 43–9, 109, 158
Otto, cardinal, 113
Ottobuono, cardinal, 126
Otway-Ruthven, J., 40 n. 2, 52
Oxford, graduates of, 72, 81, 91, 107, 155, 157, 210, 211, 227

Pandulf, 72, 82
papacy
  admonished Edward II, 188
  approved English lordship of Ireland, 2, 34, 35–6, 39–40, 42–3, 51
  complaints to, concerning violation of ecclesiastical liberty, 123–5
  and composition of chapters, 80–1
  condemned discrimination, 73, 150
  and diocesan structure, 27–8, 60–1, 63–5, 81–2, 108, 193–6, 209
  and episcopal appointments, 70–1, 73, 76, 79, 82–3, 153, 155–6, 162, 226–30
  Ireland fief of, 84
  petitioned by Irish princes, 186–8
  rôle of, in Anglo-Irish relations, 212–13
  strengthened ties with Ireland in the twelfth century, 1, 10–11, 33–4
  supported Edward II, 184–6
  see also Clericis laicos; councils, general; Laudabiliter; papal judges-delegate; papal legates; popes
papal judges-delegate, 63–5, 123, 125, 126, 186, 190
papal legates, 10–11, 13, 15, 27, 28, 32 n. 2, 33, 39, 42–3, 46, 58, 60–4, 68 n. 2, 72, 73, 74, 82, 108, 114, 186, 226–9
Paparo, cardinal John, 28 n. 2, n. 4, 31, 59, 61, 108 n. 3
parliament in Ireland, 115–16, 119, 162, 174, 199
  individual parliaments: (Dublin 1291), 117; (Kilkenny 1310), 183, 186 n. 1, 187–8; (Dublin 1324), 191
  see also great council

248

Index

Patrick, bp Dublin (1074–84), 6–7, 217, 222

Patrick, bp Limerick (1140–8), 218

'Patrick, churches of', 113

'Patrick's land', 113

Patrick, St, 3, 4, 108, 110, 111

patronage, lay, 83 n. 1, 123, 145

Perpignan, Franciscan general chapter at, 192

Peter, O. Cist., bp Clonfert (c. 1152–71), 25

Petit, Ralph, bp Meath (1227–30), 226

Piro, William, bp Glendalough (1192–1212), 62

plenitudo potestatis, 83, 89 n. 3, 91, 156 n. 4, 165

popes
  Adrian IV, 2, 34, 35, 36–7, 40, 123, 124, 187, 197
  Alexander II, 220–1
  Alexander III, 2, 38–40, 42, 48
  Alexander IV, 113–14, 121, 122–3, 124, 125
  Boniface VIII, 155, 167
  Boniface IX, 61 n. 1
  Calixtus II, 222
  Celestine III, 62
  Celestine [IV?], 115
  Clement III, 21
  Clement V, 184
  Clement VI, 196
  Eugenius III, 28
  Gregory I, 16, 221–2
  Gregory VII, 1, 5, 33
  Gregory IX, 60, 82, 89, 93 n. 2, 97, 106, 107
  Honorius III, 46, 57, 61, 63, 71, 72, 73, 74, 75, 82, 111, 112
  Honorius IV, 165
  Innocent II, 23, 27, 34 n. 1
  Innocent III, 32 n. 2, 40, 58, 61, 63–5, 67, 69 n. 1, 70, 82, 83, 84, 111, 227–9
  Innocent IV, 81, 112, 150, 152 n. 2, 162
  Innocent VI, 196
  John XXII, 184–6, 188–9, 190, 192–7
  Lucius III, 42, 46, 50, 109–11
  Martin V, 196

Nicholas III, 181

Urban III, 42, 43

Urban IV, 115, 122

Urban V, 82, 196

primacy of Ireland
  claimed by Canterbury, 7–9, 36, 217–25
  claimed by Dublin, 112
  traditional seniority of Armagh, 108–9, 115
  primas Hiberniae; *primas totius Hiberniae*, 108, 112, 114, 209
  relations of Armagh and Cashel, 112–13
  relations of Armagh, Cashel and Dublin, 109–12, 115–16, 208–9
  relations of Armagh, Cashel and Tuam, 112–14

prohibition, writs of, 123, 124, 125–6, 134, 204

Quantok, Thomas, bp Emly (1306–9) and chancellor, 117, 170

quo warranto proceedings, 126, 139 n. 6, 163, 166

Ralph, O. Cist., bp Down (c. 1202–?24), 54

Raphoe, diocese of, 154, 164, 166 n. 2, 194

ratione peccati, see ecclesiastical courts, cognizance of sin

Red Book of the Exchequer of Ireland, 132

Reeve, Thomas, bp Waterford and Lismore (1363–94), 210

Reginald, bp Connor (c. 1178–1225), 44–5, 54

Reginald, o.p., abp Armagh (1247–56), 163 n. 1

Remonstrance of the Irish princes, 36 n. 1, 186–9, 196–7, 199

rex Hiberniae, 42–3

Rich, Edmund, abp Canterbury, 91

Richard II, king of England, 61 n. 1

Richardson, H. G. and Sayles, G. O., x–xi, 174 n. 1

Robert, bp Waterford (1200–4), 54, 63

Robert, bp Waterford (1210–23), 64–5, 81–2